Springs of Participation

Springs of Participation: Creating and Evolving Methods for Participatory Development

Edited by
Karen Brock and Jethro Pettit

PRACTICAL ACTION
Publishing

Published by Intermediate Technology Publications Ltd
trading as Practical Action Publishing
Schumacher Centre for Technology and Development
Bourton on Dunsmore, Rugby
Warwickshire CV23 9QZ, UK
www.practicalactionpublishing.org

ISBN 978-1-853396-47-2

Since 1974, Practical Action Publishing has published and disseminated
books and information in support of international development work
throughout the world. Practical Action Publishing (formerly ITDG
Publishing) is a trading name of Intermediate Technology Publications Ltd
(Company Reg. No. 1159018), the wholly owned publishing company of
Intermediate Technology Development Group Ltd (working name Practical
Action). Practical Action Publishing trades only in support of its parent
charity objectives and any profits are covenanted back to Practical Action
(Charity Reg. No. 247257, Group VAT Registration No. 880 9924 76).

Typeset by S.J.I. Services
Index preparation: Indexing Specialists (UK) Ltd
Printed by Replika Press

Contents

About the authors

David Archer is Head of Education at ActionAid International. In the 1980s he worked on literacy programmes across Latin America inspired by Paulo Freire (*Literacy and Power: the Latin American battleground* (Earthscan). In the 1990s he was involved in developing the *Reflect* approach to adult learning, co-authoring 'The *Reflect* Mother Manual' and 'Communication and Power'. He now supports coalitions and campaigns on the right to education across Africa, Asia and Latin America. Recent work focuses on IMF policies and education, and on HIV and education.

Carlos Barahona is a Senior Statistician at the Statistical Services Centre (SSC), University of Reading (UK), where his main duties involve consultancy and training. He has a BSc in agriculture and an MSc in biometry. His work has taken him to Malawi, Zambia, Kenya, Uganda, Ethiopia, Jamaica, Bolivia, Honduras and Guatemala. His interests include the use of statistics in agriculture, planning and supporting optimal research processes in developing countries, and the integration of statistical and participatory methodologies.

Karen Brock is a social scientist, editor and development consultant, and was formerly a researcher in the Participation Group at IDS, University of Sussex. She specializes in issues of natural resources management, social science research methodologies, policy processes and agropastoral livelihoods in Africa. She is the co-editor of *Knowing Poverty: Critical reflections on participatory research and policy* (Earthscan) and *Unpacking Policy: Knowledge, actors and spaces in poverty reduction in Uganda and Nigeria* (Fountain Press).

Robert Chambers is a Research Associate at the Institute of Development Studies, Sussex. His current interests include knowledge in development, perceptions of poverty, institutional, professional and personal learning and change, and participatory methodologies. Recent activities include facilitating participatory workshops and writing. His latest books are *Participatory Workshops* (2002) and *Ideas for Development* (2005), both published by Earthscan, London.

Dee Jupp is a social development consultant who has lived and worked for extensive periods in Bangladesh and Jamaica, helping governments, NGOs and community-based organizations to adopt participatory approaches. She has trained facilitators and led participatory research and workshops in Tanzania, Kenya, China, the Caribbean and Bangladesh on diverse issues including road and market design, health and education services, agricultural extension, community development, human rights, access to credit and banking services, crime and violence, peace-building and poverty assessments.

Sarah Levy is a macroeconomist. In 1998, she set up Calibre Consultants, which provides support for the design and management of research programmes in developing countries. From 1999 to 2004, she worked on monitoring and evaluation for a large-scale food security programme in Malawi, contributing to the development of an approach which generates national statistics using participatory methods. Recently, she edited the book *Starter Packs: A Strategy to Fight Hunger in Developing Countries? Lessons from the Malawi experience, 1998–2003* (CABI).

Linda Mayoux is an international consultant working on issues of empowerment, gender analysis, poverty and participatory impact assessment and research, in diverse areas, including micro-finance and ethical/fair trade in South Asia, Africa and Central America. Linda also has extensive academic research experience on gender and poverty issues based at Cambridge, the Open University and Glasgow University in UK. Her main current focus is the development of Participatory Action Learning Systems (PALS) and empowerment strategies, with partner organizations in Africa and Asia.

Sundaram Nagasundari has training in NGO Management and Development Education. She has worked since 2001 for the New Entity for Social Action (NESA), a network that works to secure life with dignity for marginalized communities. It has 40 partners who are engaged with 6.5 million people in 7,200 villages of southern India. She joined NESA to implement a project on participatory impact assessment and community planning through pictorial diaries, the Internal Learning System (ILS). Subsequently she has been involved in developing impact assessment indicators for NESA's programme work on rights, natural resources management and HIV/AIDS.

Maria Goreth Nandago is a teacher by profession with extensive experience in adult education, literacy and participatory development approaches. She works with the network of *Reflect* practitioners in Africa (PAMOJA) where she facilitates learning, sharing and the further evolvement of the approach, ensuring its continued relevancy in the rapidly changing context of Africa. She has contributed to several publications related to participation and adult education, including issues of *Participatory Learning and Action* and *Education Action*, among others.

D. Narendranath did his Baccalaureate in Mechanical Engineering from Kerala and then studied Rural Management at the Institute of Rural Management, Gujarat. He has worked with the NGO PRADAN (Professional Assistance for Development Action) since 1989, organizing poor women's self-help groups

(SHGs) and promoting microfinance and livelihoods. He helped to initiate the SHG concept, designing training, developing systems, and establishing credit linkages for a programme now involving 6,000 SHGs with nearly 90,000 members. Narendranath also directs the Research and Resource Centre in PRADAN, converting best practices into knowledge and documentation useful to other practitioners.

Kate Newman has worked with participatory approaches and in support of *Reflect* practitioners around the world, most recently as leader of ActionAid's Reflect Team. She played a key role in developing numeracy in *Reflect*, and exploring how *Reflect* can support a rights-based approach to development. She is interested in how participatory approaches can strengthen local governance and transform power relations. Building on *Reflect* experience, she initiated a process to deepen organizational understanding and practice on the role of participation across all ActionAid's work.

Helzi Noponen is a visiting associate professor at the Hubert H. Humphrey Institute of Public Affairs at the University of Minnesota, USA. Her teaching and research interests are in economic and sustainable development; microfinance; the informal economy; gender and development; NGOs in developing countries; and development in South Asia, where she has worked extensively over the past 25 years. She has been a key innovator of the Internal Learning System (ILS), a participatory approach to learning and self-assessment that has been piloted with self-help groups in India.

Jethro Pettit is a member of the Participation, Power and Social Change team at the Institute of Development Studies, University of Sussex. He works on the design and facilitation of learning for reflective practice and change in both organizational and educational contexts. He has worked in the past with international NGOs, including World Neighbors, Oxfam America and UUSC in Asia, Africa and Latin America, and with social justice, environment and peace movements in the US and UK.

Joe Remenyi is a professor of development studies at Deakin University, Geelong, Australia. He is an economist by training but has spent the greater part of his professional life working in agricultural and rural contexts. He has specialized in rural finance and poverty analysis, using participatory methods in action-research-based frameworks. He has worked on poverty projects in China since 1990, contributing to the development of China's Participatory Poverty Index (PPI). He is widely published and known for his work on microfinance, with the publication of four books in this area.

Alice Welbourn is an independent adviser on gender, HIV and communication. She recently served as Chair of the International Community of Women living with HIV/AIDS. Alice has been HIV-positive for 15 years and all her work focuses on promoting awareness and understanding of human rights issues around HIV, including treatment access, rights to participation, gender equity, sexual and reproductive rights, and respect for people with HIV. She wrote *Stepping Stones* as her coping strategy in response to her diagnosis in 1993–5.

Glossary of participatory methods and tools discussed in this book

Method/tool	Description	Chapter
Appreciative Inquiry (AI)	A process of reflection focused on facilitated conversations highlighting the positive	8
Community mapping with cards	A mapping and ranking exercise that can be used to generate numerical data, and can be combined with statistical sampling	10
Force field analysis	A visual technique to examine the constraining and enabling factors which affect the achievement of a desired objective	8
Internal Learning System (ILS)	A participatory impact assessment and planning system, implemented through the medium of diaries or multi-year workbooks in which programme participants keep individual or group records of change over time	4, 5, 6, 12
Mind maps	A concise way of displaying notes and information and their associations. A drawing that starts in the centre of the page with an issue or problem and works outwards in all directions like a tree to produce an organized list. Can be used by individuals and groups.	8
Participatory Action Learning System (PALS)	A repertoire of diagram tools and participatory princples tailored to specific issues and contexts with the aim of enabling people, including very poor non-literate women, men and children, to collect and analyse the information which they themselves need on an ongoing basis to improve their lives in ways they decide	7

Method/tool	Description	Chapter
Participatory Learning and Action (PLA)	A term used, sometimes together with PRA, to describe a range of facilitation approaches, methods and tools, as well as facilitator attitudes and behaviours, used to enable and empower people to express, share, analyse and enhance their knowledge of life and conditions, and to plan, act, monitor, evaluate, reflect and scale up community action (based on definition given by International HIV/AIDS Alliance, 2006)	3, 10
Participatory Poverty Index (PPI)	A method, developed in China, for calculating a community-level index of poverty based on community members' perceptions of poverty	11
Participatory Poverty Mapping (PPM)	A structured interaction between researchers and communities designed to gain a systematic understanding of local people's perceptions of poverty	11
Participatory Rural Appraisal (PRA)	An approach to group or community facilitation using visual and tangible methods and tools, enabling people to express their own knowledge and do their own analysis, assessment and action planning. Maps and diagrams are often made, usually on the ground using local materials, as well as matrix scoring and ranking exercises. Careful attention is given to the behaviour and attitudes of the facilitator in being sensitive to power differences.	13
Picture stories	Easily interpreted pictures showing different scenarios which are used in participatory group work to stimulate discussion about the situations they portray	4, 5, 6, 8
Protipholan	A group self-reflection process using simple icons, allowing groups to analyse their own activities and progress, which can also be used for external reporting	12
Rapid Rural Appraisal (RRA)	A coalescence of methods from sources including agroecosystem analysis, devised and used to be faster and better for practical purposes than large questionnaire surveys or in-depth social anthropology. Methods include semi-structured interviews, transect walks with	

Method/tool	Description	Chapter
	observation, and mapping and diagramming, all done by outside professionals.	13
Reflect	An approach to facilitated group learning and action planning, combining visual methods and Freirian adult literacy methods. Groups of adult learners, convened to learn literacy, develop maps, calendars and matrices analysing different aspects of their own lives. These become the basis for a process of learning new words, gaining awareness of the causes underlying problems, and identifying and taking forward action points.	1, 2, 3
Stepping Stones	A training and facilitation approach for raising awareness and action in relation to gender, sexual health and rights, and HIV/AIDS, and for developing communication and relationship skills using a wide range of participatory tools and methods.	2, 9

List of acronyms

AAI	ActionAid International
ALPS	accountability, learning and planning system
CBO	community-based organization
CIRAC	Circle for International Reflect Action and Communication
DFID	Department for International Development, UK
IDS	Institute of Development Studies, Sussex
IIED	International Institute for Environment and Development
INGO	international non-governmental organization
IRT	International Reflect Team
MFI	microfinance institution
NESA	New Entity for Social Action
NGO	non-governmental organization
ODA	Overseas Development Agency
PM	participatory methodology
PRADAN	Professional Assistance for Development Action
PVA	Participatory Vulnerability Analysis
SDC	Swiss Agency for Development Cooperation
SHG	self-help group
Sida	Swedish International Development Agency
STAR	Stepping Stones and *Reflect*
UNDP	United Nations Development Programme
WHO	World Health Organization

List of figures, tables and boxes

Introduction

Karen Brock and Jethro Pettit

What is this book about?

In recent decades there has been a veritable explosion in the use of participatory methodologies in international development work. A great variety of approaches has emerged, inspired by diverse traditions and experiences worldwide. While taking multiple forms, these participatory approaches spring from a shared appreciation of the need to learn from and respect the knowledge of poor and marginalized people. Development failures have too often been rooted in an absence of listening and learning. At the heart of these methods is the need to find ways of reversing hierarchies of knowledge and power, and allowing silenced voices to be heard in the making of decisions. With this basic intent in common, a great many practitioners have adapted and experimented with methods and techniques that allow people to reflect upon their realities, take action to improve their lives and influence higher levels of policy and governance. Yet what is this process of creating participatory methodologies really about? How and why do different approaches evolve and spread, and what are the tensions, pitfalls and risks encountered along the way?

This book brings together the experiences and reflections of a group of practitioners of participatory methodologies working in diverse situations and countries. They met in June 2005 to discuss their experiences of creating and adapting the methods they use in their work. This book, formed of their reflections and analyses, is one small part of a much wider picture that involves many thousands of development professionals in the constant creation and adaptation of participatory approaches to social change in different contexts. The experiences discussed here are not universal: the authors are all part of an English-language development tradition, and are embedded in the particular networks of learning and exchange facilitated by the UK-based research institute that convened the 2005 workshop.[1] There are doubtless many other methodologies, experiences and practitioners that tell different stories that would be equally instructive, but to cover the entire universe of participatory methodologies in one volume would not have been possible.

What then can be learned from these particular experiences of invention and innovation? Attention to the creative processes involved in the evolution of these kinds of methods has been limited. On the one hand, evaluating how particular participatory methods have evolved over time, and across continents, can help us understand the challenges of effective and sustainable methodological spread. On the other, there is much to be learned about the enabling and disabling conditions for developing new methods, and the tensions and risks that may be encountered.

This book discusses a rich range of participatory methods, as shown in the Glossary on page xiii. In the first part of the book, Chapters 1–6 focus on just two of these methods, *Reflect* and the Internal Learning System (ILS). *Reflect* began as a tool for group work to develop literacy and critical reflection, combining principles of adult education and awareness-raising with the power of visual participatory methods. ILS was designed to provide information for programme evaluation at the same time as supporting community members to reflect on and change their lives, using visual images in the form of personal and group diaries. Both methodologies have evolved considerably over a number of years. The chapter authors were involved at different stages of creating, evolving and spreading *Reflect* and ILS, which in some ways followed a similar trajectory. Each involved an initial creative process with one individual at its centre, followed quickly by the engagement of a range of other participants and institutions. Subsequently, the methodologies were adapted and have spread in quite different ways.

David Archer and Helzi Noponen, the original innovators of *Reflect* and ILS respectively, analyse what enabled them to innovate and the challenges presented by the spread of each methodology (Chapters 1 and 4). The story of *Reflect* is developed from different perspectives by Maria Nandago (Chapter 2), who discusses lessons about training drawn from her experience of implementing *Reflect* in East Africa, and Kate Newman (Chapter 3), who reports on how the *Reflect* team in ActionAid International (AAI) approached the challenge of internal learning and change. Subsequent chapters continue the story of ILS with D. Narendranath (Chapter 5) discussing the process through which Professional Assistance for Development Action (PRADAN), an Indian non-governmental organization (NGO), became partners in piloting the methodology, using it in their work building the capabilities and resources of self-help groups to generate sustainable livelihoods. Sundaram Nagasundari (Chapter 6) reflects on the dynamics of the transformation of ILS as it was taken up by a network of southern Indian NGOs working for the rights of marginalized groups to secure life with dignity.

The *Reflect* and ILS experiences show us that each stage of the process of methodological innovation and adaptation raises different issues: what is the role of the 'inventor' of a methodology beyond the initial stage? Do adaptations divert the methodology away from its original intent? What are the prime moments of realization that spark adaptation? What are the key stages of the process that ensure the preservation of its participatory qualities? Which actors are important in shaping outcomes?

Several of these themes are picked up in the second part of the book. In Chapters 7–13 the authors reflect on what enables and constrains creativity, adaptation and innovation, using examples of many different methodologies to illustrate their discussions. Their reflections come from two broad perspectives. The authors of Chapters 7–9 are all innovators who have worked principally as independent development consultants and advisers. The authors of Chapters 10–12 are researchers. These two common positions in the world of development and aid give rise to different challenges in creating and using participatory methodologies.

Linda Mayoux (Chapter 7) discusses the challenges of designing methods that facilitate the empowerment of participants as she charts the journey of developing the Participatory Action and Learning System (PALS), an eclectic mix of tools that she has developed and applied in a range of situations. Chapter 8 centres on Dee Jupp's reflections about what keeps processes of creativity alive and stimulates new innovations, based on her work in constantly evolving tailor-made participatory methodologies to use in different contexts. In Chapter 9, Alice Welbourn asks whether participatory methodologies can stem the tide of HIV/AIDS, analysing the evolution of the Stepping Stones methodology to highlight some of the challenges this implies.

The next three chapters all draw on experiences of using participatory methodologies for research. Sarah Levy, in Chapter 10, discusses the tensions of using participatory research to produce information that can be included in national statistics, using several examples from research with farmers and rural people in Malawi. In Chapter 11, Joe Remenyi reports on the political and institutional challenges of introducing participatory approaches to poverty reduction into government bureaucracies through his discussion of the development and spread of the Participatory Poverty Index (PPI) in China. In Chapter 12, Carlos Barahona discusses the trade-offs in using participatory methodologies for research, and in doing so crystallizes many of the dilemmas faced by participatory practitioners, whatever their approach or the aim of their work.

In the final chapter Robert Chambers brings together lessons both from his own experiences with Rapid Rural Appraisal (RRA) and Participatory Rural Appraisal (PRA), and from the other chapters, to draw some conclusions for donors and funders about how they might support the continued evolution of participatory methodologies in different arenas.

In their analyses of creating and evolving methodologies, all the authors draw our attention on the one hand to the enabling factors that supported their innovations, and on the other to the tensions and trade-offs involved in the practice of participatory methodologies, many of them context-specific. But the experiences reported in this book are also part of a far larger pattern. In the remainder of this introduction, we introduce the key themes of the book in the light of other streams of discussion about development and participatory methodologies. The broad contours of the development landscape are an important key to why the springs of participation we discuss in this book have evolved and spread in the ways that they have.

Mapping the landscape: opportunities and pitfalls

What has shaped the creation and evolution of the participatory methods discussed in this book? The immediate backdrops to the experiences discussed here are development aid organizations, and the world of development planning and management in African and Asian countries. Although these backdrops overlap, each gives rise to different factors that shape the possibilities for creating and evolving participatory approaches. It is important to note that not all traditions of participation have arisen in this context of official aid. Latin America, for example, has a long history of adult education and social mobilization that has had little to do with international development funding. Political approaches to participation in decentralized governance and democratic citizenship have arisen in many parts of the world and have little or nothing to do with the processes of development and aid. Yet the aid system has fuelled much of the recent expansion of participatory methodologies, even as this then evolves in unexpected directions, and it is this system that is the context for the experiences we discuss in this book.

Many of the authors in this volume, not surprisingly, are located in NGOs, both national and international; others are researchers carrying out donor-funded enquiries into development issues; and some are consultants and advisers, often carrying out donor-funded work. Systems of aid delivery, funding mechanisms for research and development work, the strategic perspectives of differently located development actors and their narratives of the best way to do development: all are important factors in shaping the spaces in which methods emerge and grow, and determining which actors animate processes of evolution. Authors provide numerous examples of how the rules, norms and power relationships of aid and development enable and constrain their practice. At the same time, there are examples of room for manoeuvre, in which communities and local organizations have developed and adapted methods in accordance with their own needs and priorities, sometimes in harmony and sometimes in tension with external forces and priorities.

What is participation used for in these landscapes, and what demands are practitioners meeting? In the institutional pathways of development, methods are needed to collect data for aid policy, to function in development programmes, to assist in the delivery of services and to monitor progress towards goals both global and local. Frequently, the use of participatory methods introduces the knowledges and voices of 'local' or 'poor' people into processes of development and aid management at different levels. Just as frequently, however, the methods are used to facilitate reflection and learning among local people, often in the spaces created by existing programmes, projects and group initiatives, with the objectives of transformation and empowerment. And it is not uncommon for innovators and practitioners of methods to attempt to fulfil a range of such purposes simultaneously.

The range of examples we discuss in this book has largely emerged in the context of donor and NGO demands and initiatives. As these methodologies have spread downwards towards communities and horizontally across different spaces at the lower levels of organizations and local governance, moving away from their point of origin, they have been transformed by the objectives of different actors, and have evolved in the light of available resources, existing participatory practice and other contextual realities. This trajectory raises two important points. First, the majority of the processes documented here has not automatically involved government actors, and has not been embedded in processes of local governance.[2] This has implications for the sustainability of methodological spread, and for potential learning and exchange with the ever-expanding world of citizen participation in local governance and participatory democracy.[3]

Second, the impetus for the creation of new participatory approaches discussed in this book tends to be located at a relatively high level of development management, among donors, international NGOs, development consultants and advisers, and the apex institutions of NGO networks. Evolution and spread tend to happen at lower levels, as a response to a new method, rather than emerging from the grassroots and being scaled up from there, even where local actors are able to negotiate their own terms of engagement, use and adaptation of the methods. As such, the springs of participation we discuss here are largely separate from the streams of experience that define participation in social movements or attempts to mainstream participation in state bureaucracies. Reflecting on this, Chambers argues that relationships with donors are critical in shaping the way that participatory approaches can evolve.

This top-down dynamic of much practice, and the types of tools and methods it introduces, have implications for southern NGOs (Adong, 2004). Narendranath and Nagasundari's accounts of using ILS in NGO development programmes highlight some of the challenges that emerge as partner organizations adapt externally originated tools to meet their own needs and priorities. However, as both Mayoux and Jupp discuss, these challenges can provide opportunities for creativity and originality, and for processes of institutional learning and change.

As the rich experience of the authors shows, the narratives, modalities and motivations of development aid can shape positive possibilities for the creation and evolution of participatory methodologies. Aid to governments increasingly comes through budget support and sector-wide approaches. To balance this focus on governments, aid to NGOs is frequently framed as stimulating the demand side of accountable governance and policy-making, providing opportunities for using participatory methodologies in working towards advocacy, empowerment and representation among marginalized groups. Examples of this kind of work include Jupp's account of working with commercial sex workers in Bangladesh, Mayoux's experience with area networking events (*melas*) for women's empowerment in India, Welbourn's account of using Stepping Stones to break global taboos about sex and death to fight AIDS, and Nagasundari's work using ILS with disempowered *dalit* communities in southern India.

Equally importantly, however, NGOs continue to be funded to run service delivery programmes in a world where state service delivery has often been either decentralized or privatized or both. In this domain, there are fruitful opportunities for using participatory methods in programme management and evaluation, and in direct engagement with local participants of projects and programmes. ILS is a good example of this. Noponen discusses how she created ILS to enable local women participants to reflect on their circumstances and work towards changing them, at the same time as providing a learning system for programme evaluation processes. Participatory methods that effectively bridge this gap create new knowledge that allows different stakeholders in development processes to learn about themselves and each other, and in doing so creates more effective and accountable provision of services such as credit.

Beyond effective service provision and accountable local governance, a third important narrative in the aid system that creates spaces for innovation in participatory methods is the drive towards evidence-based policy. Methods familiar from social science research have been adapted and recreated in a participatory frame in many contexts, involving researchers from very different backgrounds in generating information to inform policy-makers. But policy processes are extremely complex, and research using participatory methods has a range of both objectives and outcomes in relation to policy. Contrasts are illustrated by Remenyi's reflection on developing a methodology to allow local people in China some say in how government poverty reduction funds should be spent, and in Levy's argument for locally owned information systems to increase the efficacy of national development policy, based on her work in Malawi. These experiences illustrate the very powerful influence of context in determining how participatory methodologies might shape policy or influence policy processes.

The trade-offs involved in choosing different approaches to research for policy influence are discussed by Barahona, a statistician who has worked extensively in integrating participatory and statistical research methods. His discussion of the dilemmas posed by traversing different domains of development processes is located at the intersection of research, practice and policy, and shows that there are difficult decisions to be made by practitioners in this area. Indeed, many of the chapters articulate a series of tensions and challenges which face practitioners. In the remainder of this introduction, we outline some of these tensions. Navigating them is an essential part of the creative process, and learning from the experiences of others who have encountered them is a rich source of critical reflection for future innovators and practitioners.

Key tensions and challenges

Evaluating what drives and enables the creation of new participatory approaches in the landscape we have outlined above involves reflecting on some issues and dilemmas that are familiar to participatory practitioners. Issues of quality, intent and ownership in the use of participatory methods have been the subject of heated debate as the approaches have been scaled up and mainstreamed by development agencies large and small. The chapters of this book show that these tensions remain important areas for practitioners to be aware of if the chances of useful creativity are to be maximized.

Common words, different meanings

The authors of this book work in a range of contexts and have very different experiences of participation. One outcome of this diversity is that our understanding and articulation of what constitutes participatory practice is far from uniform. Although we have a word in common, we give it very different meanings.

This diversity of meaning and blurring of definition – not just of participation, but of many other words – is common in development (Cornwall, 2001; Cornwall and Brock, 2005). But in the case of participation, blurred meaning is a double-edged sword. For some, constantly changing meanings are a healthy sign that participation is not a static entity, but one that is constantly renegotiated through use and practice, reflecting a fertile ground for innovation and creativity. For others, the lack of a bottom line or some form of quality control means that the word is rendered meaningless, leading to weak hybrid strains of methods that bear little relation to the participatory principles of the contexts and processes which gave rise to them.

In terms of this book, it may be enough to recognize and point out that the term 'participation' embraces a spectrum of meanings. This suggests the danger of assuming a shared understanding of participation. Often, as development practitioners, we hear a word and conclude that we know what it means, and what the speaker intended by using it. The diversity of ways that the word 'participation' is used in this book alone suggests that challenging this assumption and interrogating meaning may well be an important part of understanding the different ways in which methods emerge and spread.

Scaling up and replicability

Another commonly held assumption among practitioners of participatory approaches is that scaling up, a process by which a method is widely replicated and used in different contexts, is universally a good thing. Yet, as Welbourn notes, a huge range of factors can militate against the transfer of a package from one context to another (p. 129). Archer's account of the spread of *Reflect* illustrates that even with a method firmly based in a range of geographical contexts, spread has not been without challenges. Remenyi's Participatory Poverty Index shows how a method which relied on an intensive process to ensure its participatory quality at the design and piloting stage may lose that very quality as it is scaled up by institutions that have different resources available to them and different political priorities from the innovators. The lesson here may be that exact replication is rare; but that the very process of adaptation and evolution can result in a loss of certain elements of a methodology that the originators considered essential to ensure its participatory nature.

One pattern that emerges is that innovators are sometimes privileged in terms of their access to resources, both expertise and time, and that this allows them to engage in process-intensive work. Those who are charged with taking the process to scale do not have the same resources (particularly, as Nandago and Nagasundari both note, in terms of the wages and time of implementing staff) or the motivation to replicate intensive processes. The result can be a simplification or instrumentalization of the original approach, and a change of intent in its application, for better or for worse.

This raises important and challenging questions. What constitutes success in the evolution of a participatory approach, and is scaling up always necessary to it? The experience of the authors suggests that scaling up does not have to be a measure of success. As Jupp observes, the drive to invent new approaches for new situations and challenges, rather than scale up existing approaches, is one of the things that keeps creativity bubbling. This warns us against simply assuming that scaling up is good and right.

Second, does scaling up always imply a loss of participatory elements? Is the density of facilitation that Nandago describes as necessary to ensure the participatory functioning of *Reflect* circles an achievable goal? Does scaling up inevitably mean thinning out and diluting? The experiences of the authors suggest both positive and negative answers to these questions. But the key lesson is that the evolution of a new method involves successive moves away from the innovator, involving different actors and institutional pathways. The possibilities for ensuring that basic principles and original intentions inherent in the method transcend these shifts are by no means assured.

Standardization or adaptation?

Participatory development practitioners often assume that the standardization of methods and indicators for use with larger population groups or numbers of communities is somehow anti-participatory. They argue that methods should be flexible and adaptive, and the priorities and indicators should emerge within each context rather than being imposed or generalized. But Levy, Barahona, Noponen and Remenyi, who speak from a research or data-gathering standpoint, all see a degree of standardization as necessary. They show ways in which participatory methods can be used during pilot phases to generate indicators or menus, which can then be more or less fixed so that people can select, rank and evaluate them in subsequent phases. This allows data to be aggregated and compared, usually by outside investigators, to inform policy and practice.

How much does standardization interfere with the principle of 'us' learning from 'them'? What is the appropriate balance of taking pre-set indicators and menus to scale with the use of more flexible and context-sensitive processes? There are risks in standardization. Indicators, such as the set of eight used in Remenyi's PPI, may not be updated over time or adjusted to context. Organizations using the drawings and response sheets developed in the ILS processes may not take the trouble to test and modify these to fit their local context.

The question of standardization or adaptation puts into relief the distinction between participatory research or participatory action research, on the one hand,[4] and research which uses participatory methods, on the other. The first is focused primarily on generating knowledge and awareness to stimulate local action, while the second is concerned with producing a more accurate picture of reality, principally for outsiders. Both practices make valid contributions. Adaptation, however, is more a feature of the first tradition, tending to be driven by the information needs of people in communities or of local organizations. Standardization meanwhile tends to stem from the externally driven information requirements of the second tradition, whether to measure programme impact and effectiveness, or to inform policy or theory.

What concerns the authors of this book is whether standardization for external purposes undermines the possibility of local needs being met, a tension we explore further below. This question is particularly important, as explored by Levy, Barahona and Noponen, where local and external needs are bridged with a single methodology. The two approaches may become blurred as they are used to simultaneously generate knowledge for local action and aggregate data for outsiders.

Thus far we have explored the issue of standardization of data within a given methodology, in the interests of reliability and comparability. But there are also tensions related to the standardization of methodological process. When is a standardized methodology a good idea in order to ensure quality and consistency in the process of replication, and when does this hinder quality by stifling innovation? The *Reflect* methodology, documented early on in a 'Mother Manual' to assist its spread, was later destandardized and the manual was abandoned to encourage flexibility and adaptation; Archer explores how this lack of standardization contributed to *Reflect*'s spread. The PPI was both standardized and used on a large scale by the Chinese government; would a less universal methodology have spread in this context? ILS, by comparison, was meticulously standardized and has not yet been replicated either in the organic and lateral manner of *Reflect*, or to the same scale as the PPI.[5] Stepping Stones, like ILS, was developed as a systematic process. It has an intended sequence of activities, and as Welbourn notes, it 'was never intended as a manual into which people might dip and pick; therefore it works most effectively where the road map of progressive exercises has been closely followed' (p. 126). Quality has suffered where this sequence has been ignored and the more sensitive issues dropped by facilitators. Nonetheless, crucially, the entire process has been adapted to context as it has spread. Yet how can the costs and benefits of standardization be weighed in different contexts, and what is the difference between seeking a uniform replication of methods, and achieving a consistency of quality while adapting them to context?

These questions are crystallized in debates about the pros and cons of producing manuals, an issue explored in several chapters. When do manuals enable spread and innovation, and when do they instead slow down innovation and cause a methodology to become frozen? The act of creating a manual can itself be a useful way to systematize and learn from experience and there are even manuals on systematization (e.g. Selener et al., 1997). An important question to ask is whether the manual is created in this spirit of learning and sharing the values and principles that underpin the methods, or whether it sets out to over-specify and micro-manage. Many innovators are cautious about publishing their methods, fearing that a manual will be incomplete or used in ways not intended. It is rare to find a manual on participation that does not contain a strict warning of some kind about how not to use the book.

External or local needs?

As noted above, the drive to standardize or adapt is usually determined by another tension, that of responding to the knowledge requirements of different sets of people. In their origins, many participatory methods have aimed to generate knowledge for use in immediate and contextualized ways, whether by marginalized people themselves (as in participatory action research), or by the front-line extensionists and NGO or government staff working with them (as in the early RRA and PRA traditions), or in some cases both (as in hybrids such as *Reflect* and many applications of PRA).

As participatory methods have been scaled up and out since the 1990s, the purpose of many has shifted to that of generating data and knowledge for donor planning, monitoring and evaluation (M&E), and for research feeding into debates about wider funding and policy priorities. The logic of this is compelling: if participatory methods can give a more accurate picture of people's needs and realities, then why not use them to improve the ways development is financed? But this has created tensions around what are sometimes seen as over-extractive uses of methods, what Mayoux calls 'policing and measuring', which reduce participants to "little more than unpaid data collectors" (Mayoux, personal communication, and see p. 98).

While there have been numerous efforts to introduce more participatory approaches which can bridge local and external information needs (Estrella et al., 2000), contradictions remain. The local and external tensions arise throughout this volume. Many authors have looked for ways to work both sides of the equation. Levy summarizes a common ideal in discussing her work on policy, that 'while collecting information that allows policymakers to take evidence-based decisions, we could also enable communities to improve decision-making processes and to support development at the local level' (Levy, p. 137). Others ensure they work both sides by placing a moral imperative on respecting the information needs of participants, as in Jupp's example, where a grassroots land rights movement in Bangladesh decided that 'whatever the evaluation process, it was imperative that it had to be first and foremost for the use of and valued by members' (Jupp, cited in Barahona, p. 167).

The evidence in these chapters suggests that while many try to strike this balance, and there are successes, it is remarkably difficult to do. Local and external information needs are often quite different, and so require different enquiry processes. Barahona reminds us that this is because each is grounded in a different world view, each prioritizing different aspects of knowledge. A more quantitative and inductive approach to knowledge, for example, will have different rules about quality and validity than one that is more qualitative and deductive (Barahona, p. 165; see also Kanbur, 2002).

This tension is compounded by the varied understandings of what is meant by local and external. For most participatory methods used in development work, the local constituency is nearly always created by an external agency. For example, *Reflect* circles and Stepping Stone participants are brought together by NGOs such as ActionAid, and the self-help groups using ILS were already set up by PRADAN and the New Entity for Social Action (NESA) for purposes of livelihood or microcredit activities. How do these external definitions of community or group shape the meaning of the term 'local'? In what ways do local groups shape and define themselves to make the most of external opportunities? In some cases the local constituency is entirely ephemeral, for example people at a community meeting who are gathered to rank different aspects of poverty for the PPI in China.

Expectations have risen that participatory methods can help people identify and use their local knowledge to improve governance and accountability, to articulate their rights and to have a voice in policy. Yet the role of information and knowledge generated by participatory methods is only one part of the complex challenges of realizing rights, citizenship and democratic governance. To what extent have these methods evolved beyond the project environment to play an effective role in strengthening citizen action? Jupp and Mayoux both give examples of participatory methods used successfully to stimulate people to express themselves on sensitive topics, including human rights, domestic violence, corruption and conflict. *Reflect*, similarly, was 'ideally positioned as ideas like "people centred advocacy" took root', giving people confidence and skills to speak for themselves (Archer, p. 23).

A key challenge for innovators seeking to move in this direction is to look beyond the information or learning role of participatory methods, and to examine whether other dimensions of change are present: effective civil society organizations, networks, alliances, strategies for influencing, state capacities and political openings. As the objectives of methods change, there is also an increasing need to analyse the dynamics of how policy gets made and the role of information in policy processes. Mayoux points to the various capacity gaps and power differentials that prevent marginalized people's voices from being heard, even where methods are used to encourage self-expression. We may also ask whether there has yet been sufficient exchange and learning between practices of participatory development and experiences of participatory governance, citizenship and rights.

Inevitably there will be trade-offs and compromises, as well as benefits, in seeking to bridge the local and the external. An important starting point for innovators and practitioners is to seek to make these tensions more explicit rather than assuming that all needs can easily be met at the same time, and using the same methods.

Information or learning?

Information, learning and knowledge are often used interchangeably, or with the assumption that one leads to another in a linear process, culminating in social change. Yet many authors have noted a tension in particular between using participatory methods to generate information and using them to facilitate learning. Several methods, such as Stepping Stones, *Reflect* and PALS, state the learning needs of participants as their primary and explicit purpose. These methods encourage people to reflect and to gain critical perspectives on their lives and realities, leading to shifts in awareness, self-confidence, behaviour and action. ILS and PALS also use participatory methods to stimulate organizational learning.

Challenges arise when the drive to produce information limits the time and resources available for facilitating learning. Information can clearly contribute to learning, but the former is a product and the latter a process. Learning occurs during the analysis of and reflection upon information, and taken together this might be seen as the creation of knowledge. So the act and locus of analysis will often be where the real learning takes place. Because of the demand for information from participatory methods, some authors are concerned that the learning-intensive aspects of methods, at whatever level, have tended to fall away, in part because they take time and resources which are in limited supply, and in part because learning is more difficult to measure in an evaluation-driven environment. Yet without learning, there is a risk that 'all that will result are some pretty pictures at the end of the training' (Mayoux, personal communication).

The evidence here suggests that investing in methodologies as a vehicle of learning does take time and resources, but that it has many positive benefits. Several authors show how participatory methods can be used to break the silence on sensitive issues such as sexual health, domestic violence and human rights, and motivate participants to take action. Welbourn points to the shift in approaches to HIV/AIDS that rely on mass communication and information-sharing, to strategies which encourage affected people to learn and reflect in ways that enable them to create and communicate their own messages (Welbourn, p. 123). Although formal research findings from participatory methods can also be effective in drawing attention to an issue, they are not likely to make an immediate difference to their informants in the absence of more intensive processes of learning and reflection among those most affected.

Pressures also work against the potential uses of participatory methods to facilitate learning and change at an organizational level. Not only do informational and reporting requirements tend to take priority over learning activities, there is often an assumption that methods should be used with communities, but not be applied internally, as several authors observe. With *Reflect*, Nandago finds huge challenges in training staff in non-participatory organizations, and believes that strong involvement of leaders and donor support for training are needed to internalize participatory practices. Staff at ActionAid, in a multi-country review of their uses of participatory methods, found that 'while we might be good at participation "out there" we do not necessarily practice what we preach within the organization' (Newman, p. 42). Issues of organizational power and hierarchy are the same as those faced when working with communities and addressing them would 'improve our understanding of participation, and the challenges involved in shifting power relations', in turn strengthening work at the community level (Newman, pp. 49–50). Welbourn found that Stepping Stones poses similar challenges to the organizations using it.

There may also be drawbacks in identifying participatory methods exclusively as methods for learning. *Reflect*'s close association with adult literacy was sometimes a hindrance, due to some participants' conventional ideas about what education is all about: 'most wanted a dominant teacher and wanted to be passive recipients' (Archer, p. 26). *Reflect* therefore shifted from identifying itself with adult literacy to adult learning and other entry points not even related to education.

Learning is sometimes understood in a narrow sense as being a process of analytical sense-making alone. While critical thinking is a vital part of learning, we know from educational research that other kinds of learning and knowledge are often at work. Participatory methods can be particularly good at stimulating learning that may be experiential, visual, artistic, emotional, practical or embodied in nature (Heron, 1999). One reason participatory methods are exciting and can be effective in generating local knowledge is precisely because they bring out alternative forms of expression through visual methods, role plays, storytelling and the like. Yet these dimensions of knowing tend to drop out of processes focused on aggregating or analysing more textual or numeric findings, and point again to the useful distinction between information, learning and knowledge.

When the purpose of a method is primarily to facilitate learning among individuals and groups, the authors in this book agree that flexibility and adaptation are vital. Because learning needs can vary enormously, they can be challenging to meet with a one-size-fits-all approach, and what is needed is not the spread of innovation so much as the spread of 'innovativeness' (Welbourn).

Conclusion: practitioners and participants

A final tension arising in this book is that between the practitioner and the participant. To what extent do innovators apply their methods to examine their own world views, biases and assumptions, and the effects these may have on the choices they are making? Many agree that it is important to be aware of your own positionality, identity and power if you hope to enable others to do the same. While all participatory methods are at some level about revealing hidden differences in knowledge and perspective, putting such reflexivity into practice appears in diverse ways and to different degrees, in the processes of innovation illustrated here.

Several authors feel a need to explain who they are and how their backgrounds, values and experiences have either inspired or hindered their work. Mayoux carefully examines the ways in which her life experience shaped her own world view and exposed her to the various participatory traditions which made their way into PALS. Welbourn traces a similar journey through her diagnosis as HIV-positive, and the impetus this gave her to develop Stepping Stones. Archer traces his roots in adult literacy movements in Latin America, and also looks at the ways in which his own ego and identity as a white, Northern man eventually affected his ability to innovate and lead within *Reflect*.

What role does this reflexivity by innovators and facilitators have on the evolution of the methods themselves, and the manner in which they are spread and adapted by others? There is growing interest in the role of first-person enquiry and reflective practice as important dimensions of participatory and action research (Marshall, 2001). When practitioners and facilitators can examine their own identity, positionality and world view as they work, their use of methodologies to address dominant norms of power and knowledge is strengthened. What then are the risks, if any, of ignoring the self and reflexivity when using participatory methods? There is a role for continued emphasis and innovation in bringing about the 'attitude and behaviour change' of facilitators often seen as a vital element of PRA, *Reflect* and other participatory methodologies (Chambers, 1997).

As the examples in this book have shown, creation and innovation in participatory methodologies is often in the hands of individuals. The paths they are able to take are shaped by the dynamic relationship between innovator and context. In introducing the chapters, we have largely focused on context. But we hope that through reflecting on the rest of the book, the reader will gain a sense of the importance of the energy and motivation of individual practitioners in moving the boundaries of participation forward. For while we may analyse the patterns of context for clues about how best we can support the emergence of new methods for meeting new problems, it is in the unique experiences of development practitioners, and the sense that they make of those experiences, that the catalysts of future innovations are to be found.

CHAPTER 1

Seeds of success are seeds for potential failure: learning from the evolution of *Reflect*

David Archer

In this chapter I attempt several things. First I tell the story of how a new participatory approach, called *Reflect*, was conceived and developed. Second, I outline how it has spread and evolved. Third, I look critically at the factors that contributed to its success and spread, exploring how these very factors were also potential seeds of its downfall and how this paradox was addressed in each case.

Origins of *Reflect*

Let me start with a very personal story outlining the conception and development of *Reflect* as I observed it. In the late 1980s I studied the impact of adult literacy programmes inspired by the Brazilian educator Paulo Freire on communities in eight Latin American countries (Archer and Costello, 1990). Freire's ideas had been routinized, co-opted or deliberately depoliticized. Even those who were committed to Freire's theoretical analysis often ended up in practice using traditional teaching methods, failing to stimulate real dialogue based on people's own issues. Yet enough inspirational examples existed to show that Freire's insights were of immense value.

In 1990–2 I was the Latin America desk officer at ActionAid. Through wider ActionAid links I came across Rapid Rural Appraisal (RRA) and Participatory Rural Appraisal (PRA), methods being used by exciting groups, especially in India and East Africa. I went to a couple of workshops, and enquired who was using these approaches in the field of adult literacy. No one could name anyone. This surprised me, as it seemed a self-evident idea.

The work we supported in Latin America was deemed somewhat too political for our major funders, and after a few too many conflicts I became an education policy analyst at ActionAid in November 1992. On Christmas Eve 1992 I woke up in the night with my head buzzing with ideas. It was obvious that Freire and PRA needed to be put together to develop a participatory approach to adult literacy. I wrote frantically for several hours. By January 1993 I had revisited my notes and added a few other bits from recent theory on literacy, from a gender perspective and from work on visual literacy and adult numeracy. I ended up writing a 10-page concept note on 'PRA, literacy and empowerment'. When I sent it to all ActionAid country programmes and asked if anyone was interested in starting a new adult literacy programme and testing these ideas out, seven responded enthusiastically.

I knew it would be impossible to test something new in so many countries and so chose the three most different contexts: one with former guerrillas in El Salvador, one in a remote part of Bangladesh with women's saving and credit groups, and one in Uganda in an area where three of the four major local languages had never been written. The UK's Overseas Development Agency (ODA) responded positively to a funding proposal for action research to pilot the approach, granting £125,000.

In August 1993 I went to Bundibugyo, Uganda for two months to work with a new team of ActionAid staff there. They had decided to build their programme based on this new participatory approach. We spent long days going to villages and talking to people and then long evenings with beer, rats and cockroaches working out how PRA and Freire could be put together in practice. There were huge gaps and major challenges, but the Ugandan team was brilliant. Within two months we had a local manual, which was the first document ever written in the area's two main local languages.

Emboldened by the experience in Uganda, I went to Bangladesh for six weeks and went through a similar process with another team of ActionAid staff. All sorts of changes had to be made, and it started to become clear what the fundamentals of the new approach were, and what needed to be adapted for different contexts. People in Bangladesh had some familiarity with PRA and so needed little introduction to the tools. The challenge was to transform these into an internal community process.

In early 1994 I repeated the same process in El Salvador with two NGOs, one of which had recently hosted a visit by Freire. Again the approach evolved radically. It became much more explicitly political: a means for an organization led by former guerrillas, accustomed to vertical command structures, to find new ways of communicating with the wider population, to transform lives through peaceful means rather than the armed struggle. Here it was the use of these particular visual participatory tools that was completely new.

In November 1994 we brought two people from each of the pilot countries together in Bangladesh. We spent a week visiting literacy groups and then had a national workshop to share the approach. Everyone agreed we needed a name. An evening brainstorm session came up with the name REFLECT: 'Regenerated Freirean Literacy through Empowering Community Techniques'. Personally I still cringe at the name, which sounds very awkward. After four years we started to abolish the full name and now we just talk about *Reflect*.

We had two other workshops to exchange experiences between pilot countries, also attended by many other organizations. Even in the first workshop in Bangladesh we had delegations from Nepal and South Africa and India, including inspirational people who would go on to play a key role in *Reflect*. In

1996 we completed the project, published a report for the Overseas Development Agency (ODA) and compiled the three practical experiences in a Mother Manual to help others who wanted to use the approach. Within a year or so this was translated into Spanish, French and Portuguese and distributed widely.

The *Reflect* approach has now spread through the work of at least 350 different organizations (including NGOs, community-based organizations (CBOs), governments and social movements) in more than 60 countries. In 2003 the Circle for International Reflect Action and Communication (CIRAC)[6] –was awarded the UN International Literacy Prize for the way in which *Reflect* has revolutionized the field of literacy in the past 10 years (Archer, 2004).

What is *Reflect* and how has it evolved?

At first *Reflect* was very focused on linking adult literacy to empowerment. Groups of adult learners, convened to learn literacy, would develop maps, calendars and matrices analysing different aspects of their own lives. These would be translated to flipchart paper using simple pictures drawn by the non-literate participants, and words would then be added to the visual images, serving as the basis for practice. The facilitator would write up key conclusions from discussions to use as texts for further study. Participants would identify action points and literacy would then be put to practical use in taking forward such actions. Each participant would end up writing their own book based on the language and issues discussed. Over a year or so the group would collectively produce their own local development plan, including their analysis of critical issues which development agencies should respond to. This was an inversion of traditional power dynamics in development, giving the poorest and most excluded time to do their own analysis and come up with their own solutions. *Reflect* has evolved rapidly, based largely on the variety of organizations that started to use the approach and adapt it to their own needs and contexts. There have also been many diverse developments with *Reflect*, taking it in wholly new directions beyond its origins in literacy, including the following.

- *Linking Reflect with the Stepping Stones methodology* in order to create a systematic approach for working in a world where HIV/AIDS affects almost every aspect of people's lives.
- *Linking Reflect to governance and accountability* by positioning it as an approach to 'creating spaces' in contrast to participating in 'invited spaces'.
- *Critiquing the evaluation of empowerment* by revealing the complexity of power dynamics around evaluation.
- *Linking Reflect and information communication technologies* through action research with poor and excluded people in Uganda, India and Burundi.
- *Adapting Reflect to work in schools* by using the citizenship curriculum as an entry point.
- *Using Reflect in institutions* by adapting it to organizational change processes.
- *Applying Reflect to ourselves* by focusing on personal behaviour and ensuring consistency between work and home life.

- *Using Reflect in coalition building and campaigning* by bringing together diverse actors into broad-based platforms to place education higher up the political agenda.

Despite the immense diversity of *Reflect* practice there are common threads to all of this work, united through national and regional networks and CIRAC. This means that some core principles and elements that underline all *Reflect* practice have been drawn out (see Introduction).

Seeds of success, seeds of failure

I have identified 13 critical factors in the success and spread of *Reflect*. Below I outline these and give the reasons why they were so important. I then look at how these same factors were potential seeds of failure or contradiction. Finally I outline what we did about this.

Reflect was innovative

People love something that is new. There is a disturbing but very real phenomenon of fashion in the development business. So when *Reflect* appeared, people leapt on it with excitement.

But you cannot be new for ever. People will always look for something newer. You cannot retain the label of innovative 10 years after it was first applied to you.

So CIRAC has supported the continual evolution of *Reflect*. There have been many innovations, and the key has been to keep in touch with diverse practitioners, encourage their creativity and avoid presenting a monolithic or static image of *Reflect*. Those things that are new are shared most vigorously. One of the problems with this is that organizations that are still using *Reflect* in the field of adult literacy are somehow looked down on as out of date, no longer fashionable. This can be very wrong. There are important insights about the field of literacy that have been accumulated through *Reflect* practice and distinctive opportunities presented by adult literacy as an entry point.

A strong identity

Having a name became incredibly important. It was not just a combination of PRA, literacy and empowerment, but a thing in itself – something larger than the sum of its parts. The name gathered a sort of mystique and identity that attracted people.

This was then multiplied when we came up with a simple and powerful logo for the front cover of the *Reflect* Mother Manual.[7] It captures something of the essence of *Reflect*: a circle of people, including women and children, each one distinctive, each engaged, gesticulating, communicating. The figure at the top, representing the facilitator, potentially the most powerful, is the most passive,

Figure 1.1 The *Reflect* logo.

with no arm movements. In itself, it is a visual image to represent a process with a strong focus on visualization and decoding of reality.

The logo certainly helped to create a sense of unity and identity for *Reflect* practitioners across languages and countries, uniting them behind something that was larger than all of them, and helping to detach *Reflect* from ActionAid's sole ownership.

But having a strong name and identity is not all good news. Some who were already doing excellent participatory and empowering work on adult literacy felt excluded. Even as it united people across countries and organizations, it created new gulfs between people who should have been working together. Sometimes those who were inside actively excluded others, and those outside rejected those inside. In a few rare contexts people claimed that they alone held the secret to this thing called *Reflect*.

Another related problem was that some looked at *Reflect* and saw it as just packaging, as simply a brand that was being marketed. For example, Rosa Maria Torres, a prominent popular educator from Ecuador, said that *Reflect* was grown from the diverse 'maize' of popular education grown in Latin America and that it was then repackaged outside the continent and sold back to Latin America as 'cornflakes'. The branding of *Reflect* may have obscured those elements that were new in *Reflect*. For instance, the visualization tools of PRA were not being used in Latin American popular education beforehand.

So we tried to defuse the dominance of the *Reflect* name. From 1999 we actively advocated for people to name their own process at local and national levels. A survey in 2002 found a diversity of names for *Reflect* in 50 different languages. The name *Reflect* was retained only as a shorthand for exchange between practitioners across countries. But some people do still refer to *Reflect* at a local level and still use it to cultivate the mystique and to perpetuate the power of some practitioners. Once something has been created with a strong identity this will be perpetuated on its own, and this will both attract some people and repel others.

A simple manual

One of the critical factors behind the rapid spread of *Reflect* was almost certainly the *Reflect* Mother Manual, discussed above. There had been much deliberation about whether to produce a manual, because we wanted people to adapt *Reflect* to their own context. The idea behind the Mother Manual was to make a resource that would help people to produce their own local manual.

The Mother Manual included a concise theoretical background, followed by suggestions of a process that people could follow to get started and to produce a local manual. Sample units demonstrated how to sequence a process, and simple illustrations showed what the visual tools might look like. We emphasized that people should not follow this manual but develop their own, adapting the hundreds of possible tools and innovating their own according to their context.

But the Mother Manual was too seductive and simple. Some practitioners would look at the sample units and, saying that these same issues affected their local community, would start to use them directly. Others made only cursory adaptations. The visual images were so clear and simple to follow that many people just used these rather than read all the long text on theory or process.

In other cases people would read it all but then feel that every word should be followed. In Bangladesh, for example, the manual initially became an absolute guide to everything, a sacred, all-powerful text. If something was not in the manual it was banned. This became a problem because new insights were being generated by new experiences, and progressive *Reflect* practice quickly moved beyond the manual, which became a conservative force, holding people back and restricting innovation and creativity.

Accumulating practice showed that stratification and power dynamics in communities and in *Reflect* circles themselves were critically important and needed to be the focus of active work. This highlighted the rather romanticized view of communities as harmonious places that prevailed in the Mother Manual. Other gaping holes emerged, and by 1998 we had decided that a new version was needed.

But by this time there was a strong movement to abolish the Mother Manual altogether. This was led by practitioners in Nepal who had avoided translating the manual into Nepali and who had embarked on a collective cross-institutional journey of reflection, action, training and networking that would adapt *Reflect* to the Nepali context. They exposed the inherent contradiction between the essence of the *Reflect* process and the idea of one set of instructions that embody a manual (Gautam, 1998).

So we never updated the *Reflect* Mother Manual, deciding instead to focus on building networks of practitioners: facilitator forums, trainers' networks, national umbrella groups and regional networks. These spaces for exchange and learning were used as a direct alternative to publications, to ensure that *Reflect* would remain as a living and evolving process.

However the pressure never really went away to compile some core resources for *Reflect* practitioners. As one way to address this, we created a trilingual website (http://www.reflect-action.org) containing a huge amount of material from different countries. But the idea of a single publication kept coming back. How could we produce something that would not end up as a static text, but which could concisely pull together core insights for practitioners? How could we ensure that editorial control was not limited to a few people?

Our solution was to work with practitioners from over 100 organizations in 2001–3, to compile 'Communication and power'. It was laid out in an open clip folder as a set of individual resource pages giving insights from practice around the world about how to work on power issues around the written word, spoken word, images and numbers. There was no sequence that people could follow and not enough information on any one thing for people to instantly copy. We committed ourselves to producing new resource pages, that could be written by anyone, every six months to keep it as a living document. But it has been difficult to sustain this momentum and to make sure everyone has access to the new pages. It is particularly difficult to create space for practitioners to write new pages themselves in appropriate formats, so the writing tends to be done by a small group of people who thus retain power and control. There is no easy solution to creating a living text.

Rooted in the work of Paulo Freire

Freire is an immensely influential figure globally. *Pedagogy of the Oppressed* (Freire, 1970) galvanized a generation and continues to inspire people today. In 1993 Freire came to London, just after I had returned from the first visit to Uganda to start up what would become *Reflect*. I showed him the local manual we had produced, and outlined how this new approach would work. He was incredibly enthusiastic, seeing how the new elements fitted together. Effectively he gave us his blessing, later also approving the use of his name in the *Reflect* acronym. I corresponded with him from that time, and he remained abreast of developments in *Reflect* practice until his death in May 1997.

This proximity to Freire in *Reflect* undoubtedly contributed to the rapid spread of success. People loved his work but everyone seemed to be grappling with how to translate the ideas into practice. What I had seen in Latin America in the 1980s was being replicated in Africa and Asia: a commitment to his theories, but often lamentable practice, with very little dialogue. When *Reflect* came along with the clear adherence to Freirean ideas, a coherent critique and a set of practical methods, people leapt on it. Though we did not push the idea of Freire's endorsement, this did come through in the confidence with which we spoke about him.

But the link to Freire was not all good news. While the association with Freire opened many doors, it also excluded us from access to some groups. Parts of the feminist movement were highly critical of Freire and this limited the interest of women's organizations in *Reflect*. This was a thorny issue. To some extent Freire's most prominent work was defined by the time it was written and there was too much talk of man and mankind and too much focus on struggles for public space and a class-based analysis of power, rather than acknowledging the importance of struggles in the private sphere and power differences rooted in gender or racial discrimination. Freire did make some links with the feminist movement later in his life but never fully overcame these critiques.

So an international workshop was convened in 1998 on 'Gender and *Reflect*', facilitated by Grupo Venancia, a women's organization in Nicaragua. Some core insights from this were compiled into a paper on gender and *Reflect* (ActionAid, 1998) which outlined the feminist critiques of Freire and gave practical suggestions about how to deepen the analysis of gender and women's rights in *Reflect*. However, despite fairly wide circulation to practitioners this paper was never published for a wider audience.

Part of the participation movement

Reflect had the immense benefit of being part of a wider participation movement. The 1990s was the heyday of PRA and everyone from NGOs to governments was starting to assume this new discourse. Even the World Bank was starting to co-opt it. There was widespread training in participatory tools going on, which meant that often *Reflect* workshops could build on existing knowledge and skills that people had picked up in other places.

But people had a tendency to focus on the tools and techniques. These were the most prominent features of the new movement – easy to pick up, tangible and concrete – and everyone wanted to learn the new tricks. The focus of training was often very reductive.

So we moved fairly early on to emphasize processes rather than tools. For example, in 1996–7, training workshops were often designed with a view to ensuring that everyone had learnt at least to use a certain set of tools, whether map, matrix or calendar. By 1998–9 this had changed and the focus became very much on ensuring that trainers or facilitators were themselves taken through a transformative process in the workshop, addressing their own issues, reflecting and acting on their lives. If they picked up tools in the process that was fine, but the process, attitudes and behaviours became the central focus.

Roots in three continents

When we started with three pilots in three continents I do not think that we were fully aware of how important this was to the future spread. It gave us a broad base of trained people and organizations from the start, and a strong sense of ownership in each continent. This ownership is hugely significant, partly as a result of persistent and deep-rooted racism. It is not easy to get organizations in Asia to learn from Africa. Latin Americans are suspicious of anything that is not home-grown. We have certainly tried to challenge this racism, for example by taking African practitioners to Asia and Latin America to co-facilitate workshops.

But there have been some continuing tensions between regions. The Latin Americans pushed beyond literacy very early on and then had a tendency to look down on practice in other continents that was still rooted in literacy. They built their own Latin American network based on democratic and humanist principles and challenged the legitimacy of practitioners in other regions who were not clearly elected representatives. In response, it is the African practitioners who have in fact built a more sustained, democratic network.

So although there are still some cross-regional tensions, we have a forum where these are addressed. CIRAC meets about once a year, bringing together representatives from different regions to analyse developments and plan strategic work. The important thing seems to be to celebrate the diversity, as evidence that *Reflect* has adapted and evolved in different contexts. If everyone were doing the same there would be no benefit from bringing people together. It is the diversity of participants and the power dynamics between them that make such workshops a valuable space for reflection and analysis.

A grassroots identity

At a time when many NGOs were starting to invest ever more in policy, advocacy, lobbying and campaigning, *Reflect* was something clearly rooted with poor and excluded people, a reassertion of the base. Over time, *Reflect* processes came to serve as a valuable mechanism that could bridge the discourse from local to national levels, and were ideally positioned as a place where ideas such as people-centred advocacy took root. If poor and excluded people are to speak for themselves they need space and time to do their own analysis and to develop their own communication skills.

But the celebration of the grassroots in *Reflect* has sometimes gone to extremes. For example, the fact that *Reflect* abolishes primers and textbooks has led some practitioners to declare that no texts, no external printed material should be allowed into the group. This becomes part of romanticization of the local, a belief that traditional or local knowledge is somehow inherently good when this is patently not the case. In some places this identity as a grassroots approach was a limit, cutting people off from contextualizing their local situation within a wider analysis.

So we have placed more emphasis on linking the micro and macro. We have also been encouraging people involved in policy or campaigning work to get out of their offices and to talk to people in *Reflect* circles at the grassroots, making bridges both ways.

ActionAid supported spread

There is no doubt that ActionAid, as an international NGO, had the capacity to help the spread of *Reflect* through our own programmes and partners. It is a relatively well-off international organization, funding organizations in over 30 countries. Without this infrastructure and support – and the wider credibility of ActionAid – this would have been hard.

But the irony is that *Reflect* spread first through other organizations, other NGOs that heard about it by word of mouth, received publications or went on training courses. Often local or national NGOs would approach an ActionAid country office asking for training and the office would know nothing. There was no moment at which ActionAid programmes were told to support *Reflect* and no means to do so. Usually country offices only started to support *Reflect* when they received demands from others.

When they did start, the truth is that ActionAid was responsible for much of the worst practice of *Reflect*. In the mid-1990s ActionAid mostly funded integrated development programmes, employing a range of professionals and spending quite a lot of money in a relatively small geographical development area. They often ran adult literacy programmes, and so when they did decide to take on *Reflect* they simply asked their literacy experts to do it. This was a recipe for disaster because *Reflect* circles would proceed to do an analysis of all local issues but would find that the ActionAid health adviser ignored their analysis and the agronomist paid no attention. The professionals employed saw no value in linking up with the circles. As an employee of ActionAid it was difficult for a time when it became clear that ActionAid was responsible for some of the worst *Reflect* practice.

So our response to this dilemma was to constantly use ActionAid publications like the magazine *Education Action* to highlight non-ActionAid experiences of *Reflect*. We celebrated the work of others and were discreetly quiet about our own work in public while trying to challenge it behind the scenes. We were hugely helped by the accelerated pace of change within ActionAid as an organization, such that by the late 1990s there was a commitment to a rights-based approach and a move away from traditional service delivery. *Reflect* was much more consonant with a rights-based approach.

External validation by ODA/DFID[8]

The fact that ODA published our first action research report gave a remarkable boost to *Reflect*. It validated the approach and brought it to the attention of many bilaterals and multilaterals as well as academics, other NGOs and governments. It gave *Reflect* a credibility that no amount of material published by ActionAid would have done. Indeed, the report became a bestseller for ODA/DFID, and a special print run delivered copies to the World Education Forum in Dakar in 2000.

But one of the downsides of this link was that people started asking for money to do *Reflect*. They saw a big donor had endorsed the approach and so would approach either ODA/DFID or ActionAid for money to run *Reflect* programmes.

So we made an early decision to refuse to pay anyone to run a *Reflect* programme. We did not want people to do it only to get funding. Instead we insisted that organizations access their own funding or use existing funding from other donors. This way they had to make *Reflect* into an active choice, to show commitment. When we had funds available we invested in training and then networking rather than running programmes.

Support from big players

One of the most surprising things that happened after the initial success of the *Reflect* pilots and the publication of the action research report by ODA/DFID was a visit from World Bank officials. They were very excited by *Reflect* and, after meetings said that they wanted to support us and asked us to 'write a two page concept note for how you would like to scale up'. We did, expecting this to be the first stage of a long and tortuous application process. Instead they gave us $200,000 a year for the next four years without any detailed budget or plan.

One way of looking at this is that the World Bank wanted to buy into success. Another is that it really wanted to learn how this would work on a large scale. Another is that it wanted to keep an eye on or co-opt *Reflect*. We used the money to support networking and exchanges and to support documentation and learning, and the funds certainly helped us to maintain relationships with organizations around the world that facilitated the spread of *Reflect*. However, we never widely publicized the World Bank's support, as we felt a little embarrassed by it.

But then in 2000 ActionAid's CEO went to Washington with ActionAid's patron, Prince Charles, to meet the president of the World Bank, who was very complimentary about ActionAid's education work and said if we ever needed money – any amount – we should just ask. The CEO returned and said we should ask them for millions of dollars. After two days of meetings of the *Reflect* and education teams we concluded that it would compromise us too much; that if we took the money, especially from such a level, we would be co-opted. We took a decision never to take money from the World Bank again and we wrote to ActionAid directors and trustees urging that this become an organization-wide position.

So, it was not easy saying no to a blank cheque, but we did not regret it. We entered into extensive correspondence on why we would not do this work. But the bottom line for us was that we had decided that we did not want the World Bank's endorsement. We could see by then that much of the exciting work with *Reflect* was developing it with people's organizations and social movements. The support of the World Bank would discredit *Reflect*. So we pulled back from the brink of being co-opted.

Adult literacy: a powerful entry point

There are adult literacy programmes run by many governments and NGOs, and in the 1990s there was a clearly established concept of adults convening in groups on a regular basis in order to learn to read and write. This gave two advantages for *Reflect*. First, people coming together for something with a headline of adult literacy were willing to dedicate significant time to the process. Second, there was a wide network of people doing this, albeit poorly resourced. Once established with credibility, *Reflect* could spread across the sector fairly quickly.

But there were serious constraints. The use of adult literacy as the entry point distorted the sort of process we were looking for. Learners who came together for something called literacy came with a complex set of expectations. Most wanted a dominant teacher and wanted to be passive recipients of a formal process. The motivation to join the class was often linked to the social status that could be gained, to join the educated elite whose status came from years of schooling.

This may be a slight exaggeration but long-term research in Uganda and Bangladesh helped to bring such issues out (Fiedrich and Jellema, 2003). We wanted a democratic, transformative learning process with a facilitator sensitive to power dynamics, but as soon as the label of literacy was put on it, there was a fight against assumptions and expectations. The great convening power of literacy was always tempting, but it came with costs. Strong facilitators can turn expectations around, changing the parameters of the space from the start and retaining the advantages without suffering the constraints. It is not easy, but it can be done, and is one reason we have highlighted the critical role of facilitator training and support.

So we had to start asking fundamental questions about the construction of literacy. Where did the concept come from that adults, when convened to learn, should have reading and writing as the dominant focus? Fiedrich and Jellema's powerful historical critiques helped us move away from using the term 'literacy' with its loaded baggage of empire and colonialism, towards the more expansive term 'adult learning'. We have also used other entry points, working with pre-existing community-based organizations of different types, so that people are gathered with different expectations and logics. But often these bring their own constraints, and few existing spaces offer the potential for the intensity of contact that education does.

Reflect was not controlled

We made no attempt to control the use of *Reflect*. There was no patent or copyright. There were people who urged us to restrict distribution of core resources to those who could be trusted, but we just sent things to anyone who asked.

But this lack of control led to some dubious effects. Some people have probably done terrible things in the name of *Reflect*. I know that evangelizing Christians have used it for ends that make me feel very uncomfortable.

So the only response that we could have was to give the oxygen of publicity to people doing good work and to ignore those who are not. There may be some cases where we are critical of people who have distorted the approach, but mostly we just ignore it. We have focused efforts on bringing together people who are doing effective work.

However, the 'we' remains problematic here: who are 'we' to pass any judgement on who is doing well or not?

A vocal champion

By 1996 the success of the approach aroused the interest of other funders and this meant that we could recruit a small team. I became the Head of International Education and we started to engage on a wider education agenda, including schools and non-formal education. This work grew into an education campaign from 1998 onwards, focused on building civil-society coalitions on education in different countries across Africa, Asia and Latin America and then helping to form the Global Campaign for Education. In all this work I was very conscious of how we were applying learning from the *Reflect* experiences. And of course I remained closely involved with the evolution of *Reflect*. I made sure that I visited *Reflect* programmes in each continent at least once a year. I documented experiences that I observed and shared these widely with other practitioners, and focused on building CIRAC from 2000.

There were of course many other people involved in this work and I certainly do not claim credit for it all. But I was a constant presence and a recognized voice. I shared details of *Reflect* all around the world, with UN agencies, the World Bank and at academic conferences. When people challenged *Reflect* I was quick to respond, exposing the flaws in their arguments and challenging them.

But this intense personal involvement was not without problems. First, I was often very defensive. While in *Reflect* circles we had created a strong culture of self-criticism – and believed in this passionately – we were not so ready to accept the criticisms of others. We felt that at least our self-criticism and debate was well informed and ahead of the people who were criticizing us. But I think it came across very differently at times.

But the second reason took longer to understand. At various points people would call me the architect, founder or guru of *Reflect*. When I travelled, people would elevate me into a position that I did not have, introducing me as 'professor' or 'doctor'. Furthermore, I was seen to embody *Reflect*. My own contributions carried a weight with them that was disproportionate to their value. Another participant might say something brilliant, but it was not given the same significance as me saying something.

This problem became ever clearer as *Reflect* came to focus on issues of communication and power, and when workshops were designed to focus on the internal power dynamics of the group as a resource for reflection and analysis. There were some people who were systematic in addressing this, raising the contradiction of my own inherent power and status in the group.

So I was at first a little resistant but rapidly came to revel in these challenges to my power. It became clear to me that if we are going to talk about empowerment and transforming power for others, we have to be able to talk about our own power. Subsequent to that, in the International Education Unit in ActionAid, we started to create our own process to put power on the table for reflection. My colleagues maintained pressure on me to reflect on my own practice of power. It was this that helped lead to the Participatory Methodologies Forum in 2001 in Bangladesh, where 40 senior management people from across ActionAid gathered supposedly to discuss participatory methods. The meeting ended up as a reflection on our own individual and institutional power, recognizing that rather than denying our own power, we need to work to positively transform how we use that power. One-off workshops do not usually change things, and we were not able to sustain that process of transformation. But, nonetheless, it was an important moment for many individuals and contributed to the continuing dramatic process of change within ActionAid.

But the issues about my own ego and power in relation to *Reflect* did not go away. We continued a process in the team that kept this on the agenda, forcing me to confront my power in its various manifestations – as a white, Northern, educated man in a position of institutional power. Progressively some of the formal power I had was shared or handed over. But this did nothing to change the informal power that I had of being the perceived founder. For me that came sharply into focus when, in September 2003, we won the UN International Literacy Prize for *Reflect*, something that meant a lot to me as I had always seen this prize as one of the great achievements of the literacy crusade of the Nicaraguan revolution in 1980. At the same time I became aware that I had been working on *Reflect* for 10 years. I recalled the organizational development literature about the challenges posed when founders hang on too long.

Things were brought to a head in 2004 when in consultation with the team and many others we decided to separate the *Reflect* team from the International Education Unit. *Reflect* had moved beyond literacy and education and so needed to be repositioned, and education needed a clearly focused team. This forced me to make a choice. Recognizing that my own power would increasingly become part of the problem in *Reflect,* I chose education and have taken a big step back from *Reflect.* The coordination of CIRAC is now moving to PAMOJA in Uganda, completing this process of making the coordination of *Reflect* fully independent.

I am aware that some of these last reflections seem a little self-indulgent, focusing on my own role and perhaps aggrandizing it. But it does seem to me crucially important for us to be able to place ourselves in our work and to reflect on our own power. Egos so often become a big part of the problem. We talk about the importance of attitudes and behaviour and yet are not always consistent ourselves. The transformation of power relations cannot start with other people.

CHAPTER 2

Training and facilitation: the propellers of participatory methodologies

Maria Nandago

Introduction

Training and facilitation are the key enablers of the spread and success of participatory methodologies (PMs) all over the world. Experience has shown that without proper internalization of a PM through training, very little gets translated into best practice. Training, or what is sometimes broadly referred to as capacity-building, is a commonly used avenue for transferring and disseminating PMs. In many cases it has been believed that once a training of some sort happens, there will be an automatic internalization of that methodology, taking care of the skills and knowledge acquisition and change in attitudes, behaviours and values. Whether one can learn participation and change attitude through training to enable the facilitation of transformational learning, remains a big question that this chapter will attempt to examine. I draw on my experience as well as that of different practitioners of PMs, with particular reference to the *Reflect* methodology.

Context: who is training who?

Reflect is a PM that links literacy to empowerment. Initially developed by ActionAid International (AAI) (see Archer, this volume), it has now spread to more than 360 different organizations across the world. Facilitators are central to the methodology, in which *Reflect* circles of local people meet regularly with a facilitator. They are facilitated to critically analyse their environment, identify issues and problems affecting them, and work out practical solutions for sustainable development training.

Reflect practitioners have categorized training into two: training of trainers (TOT) and training of facilitators (TOF). Graduates of the TOT train facilitators, and these facilitators in turn transfer the knowledge and skills so acquired to the *Reflect* circles at the level of the community. This kind of training process is referred to in some circles as cascade training. This refers to a process whereby trainers train new trainers, who in turn train facilitators.

My experience working with the *Reflect* approach is based in different parts of Uganda and other countries in Africa. For some time, *Reflect* has been targeting two core categories: the trainers and facilitators. Trainers are a core team of people who have either been in at the initial stage of designing the approach in the adopting organization, or who have perfected the art out of their long experiences interacting with the methodology. The trainers are normally identified from the programme staff of the potential implementing organization, which may be grassroots, local or national.

Facilitators, on the other hand, are the closest persons to the communities for which the programmes are developed. The facilitator, who is selected by and from the community, takes full responsibility for steering the learning processes of a *Reflect* group or circle. S/he mobilizes and facilitates learning sessions with the participants, both in the specified learning centre and session as well as outside those confines. For example, s/he may make follow-up visits to participants to facilitate their learning from their homes, or from other areas the group chooses as part of its hands-on learning. The success of the *Reflect* process, as with any other participatory approach, depends very heavily on these facilitators; therefore it is critical that due attention is paid to their selection and competence development.

Challenges of training

Training entails the transfer of skills from one group of people to another group for a given purpose. Many of us subscribe to the notion that 'there are many ways to skin a goat'; there are many ways of transferring knowledge and skills in PMs. The issue that has always remained, even with the many ways of getting the goat skinned, is how one ensures that at the end of the day, one gets a clean slaughtered goat retaining all the valuable parts.

Training has been one of the main ways through which skills in participatory development methodologies can be transferred from the promoters – in the case of *Reflect*, the adopting organization – to the facilitators and then to the community. This brings into play different levels in the cadre of people accountable for the spread and use of the methodology.

It is true that there are people born with a special talent who can facilitate a learning process of any form. However, most of the facilitators I have worked with are made not born, and this has been mainly through training and other accompanying processes. Made or born, what is interesting to note is that any form of capacity-building goes a long way towards uplifting the standards, the morale and performance of a facilitator; hence any programme intending to employ participatory approaches should not downplay the significance of facilitator training.

But there are challenges in training, whether of trainers or facilitators. How can there be effective transfer of skills at all the different levels, but with minimal natural wastage, which affects quality at different levels? A group of trainers, commenting on the dangers of half-baked or improper training, remarked that once the trainers of any participatory process undergo a substandard training, it implies that they will only get a limited percentage of what they ought to get, and they will only be able to transfer an even smaller percentage of what they learn. What then can you expect at the next level? These trainees will get an even smaller percentage, and the ultimate effects will be reflected in the nature and quality of the programme being implemented on the ground.

Selecting trainers and facilitators

If a *Reflect* process is to be truly participatory, the selection of facilitators ought to involve all key stakeholders in the programme. This might include the prospective participants, members of the wider community, programme staff from the organization promoting *Reflect* and local community leaders. This involvement would help ensure better accountability, not only to the implementing agency but more importantly to the communities with whom the programme is being implemented and the circles that the facilitators will be charged with facilitating.

The selection of facilitators is not problematic as long as there are jointly agreed criteria and the full sensitization of communities about the role and entitlements of the facilitators once selected. Community sensitization here involves a dialogue with the community on the management and requirements of the programme, which helps define the kind of people best suited to facilitate the learning process.

However, more challenging is the selection of trainers. Coming across people who are committed and share a vision about participatory approaches is no simple task. I am always at a loss for words when asked how we identify the trainers. It is often the case that the implementing agency simply chooses the trainable ones among the programme staff. When an organization is approached to select staff to be trained as trainers who will in turn train facilitators, that organization will usually apply their own selection criteria. One often therefore finds a group of trainees with very varied backgrounds, ambitions and expectations. A number of them join with a motive only to enrich their CV, others are there because the line manager has demanded that they represent the organization on that training and some treat it simply as a break from their hectic regular routines. Among all of these, several may not have the attitudes and values that can enable them to appreciate and internalize participatory approaches. The result of the training is a group of certified trainers, only a handful of whom is able to propagate the approach beyond the confines of the training hall. What a waste of resources. There is a general lesson to be learned here. I think it is high time that promoters of participatory approaches institute a tight screening process for trainer recruitment. We could take a leaf out of Stepping Stones[9] where a form of contract is initiated between the prospective implementing organization and trainer. The agreement commits the trainee and the implementing organization to guarantee that whatever training is received is put into use.

On the positive side, however, trainers and facilitators have been pivotal in propelling the spread of the *Reflect* approach. Targeting programme staff in different institutions, a team of core trainers have been charged with the task of building the capacity of the organizational staff with the view that these will be able to equip the community-based facilitators with the skills and knowledge in *Reflect*, hence creating a multiplier effect. The beauty of this kind of arrangement, when it works well, is that training at each of the levels is designed to fully address the needs of the trainees in question. For instance, it is a requirement that the TOF is done in the local language to enable participants to better understand the concepts. At the same time it is comforting to note that in moving down the levels of training, the relationship between trainers and trainees gets closer. For instance, the trainer of facilitators and the facilitators themselves are normally from the same locality, and sometimes do speak the same language. Both of these contribute to more effective communication, support and hence a better internalization of the principles and practice of the participatory approaches.

Training methods and content

Reflect trainings are always designed to be very practical and based on participants' own experiences in order to achieve the aims of self-reflection and strengthening a participatory culture. To this end, training sessions are based on participatory methods, using group discussions, role-playing, individual presentations and audiovisual technology such as video recording. Over time the realization is growing that training should not end once the course is completed, but that follow-up and refresher training should be adopted to ensure that the knowledge, skills and attitudes have indeed been influenced and developed.

Opportunities for using the newly acquired skills and knowledge are another prerequisite for better grounding in participatory approaches. This is similar to the acquisition and perfection of language skills: once you learn a language but have no opportunity to either speak or write it, then in no time it evaporates like water vapour. This kind of scenario where there are no such opportunities for practice leaves no room for trainees in PMs to explore and enrich their knowledge and appreciation of the approach, which are key ingredients for transformational learning and attitude change.

Linked to content is the issue of timing. *Reflect* training requires resources (both human and material), sensitivity and commitment – crucially, time. It should not be rushed. Training should not be treated as a one-off event that happens for one or two weeks in a training hall; it demands more than that.

Every training has its own objectives, and it is very important that both the trainers and trainees are very clear about those objectives if there is to be a genuine sense of ownership of the process and the training outcomes. In practical terms this means that there is need for space through which the trainer and trainees can interact even before the training event, to enable them better understand their backgrounds and the context of the training.

What is the best way to train or build capacity in PMs? There is always the temptation to lecture on PMs. This is not appropriate: the danger is that trainees will always reflect or replicate the experience they go through in their own training, so if they are lectured they will go to the communities and lecture. During our first trainings in *Reflect* in many countries, we used simulations of participatory contexts, with the result that the facilitators in turn tended to simulate even when they were involved in real learning processes. Similarly, *Reflect* facilitators will frequently use only those tools that have been tried during their training, ending up, for example, using maps and trees for every discussion. Creativity beyond the visuals from the training is limited.

I recall in my very first training in Participatory Rural Appraisal (PRA), the trainer was a guru in the approach. This was true in that he had all the theory at his finger tips, and he managed to lecture us well on many of the tools and techniques. I learnt later on that he had focused on theory since a field trip was planned where participants were to try out all the tools and techniques. In the field, we tried out the tools one by one, but even picking out the appropriate tool from the tool basket was a big challenge. One should be able to learn, feel and live participatory approaches right in the training hall where the skills are being imparted. How can you talk about the principles of participation in theory, and not practise any of them during the process? That is the hard part, living the principles of participation. How many of us practitioners are able to do that?

From this discussion there are fundamental questions that arise when looking at training content and methods, as follows.

- How do you facilitate transformational learning that allows for a gradual transfer of skills, knowledge and change of attitude over a given period of time and for different kinds of people who intend to utilize the acquired skills in different ways?
- How do you facilitate change of behaviour and attitude?
- How do you deal with the power relations between trainers at different levels?
- How do you build capacity for creativity in the use of PMs?

I do not have any direct answers to these questions because these are the very issues that we have been grappling with in training over the years. However, experience is the best teacher, each training experience has presented us with different lessons on how to deal with the issues highlighted, and I do believe each of you out there have your own experience of each of the above issues.

Introduction and use of participatory methodologies in non-participatory organizations

While training is one way of ensuring the spread of PMs, the extent to which methods will be adopted is heavily influenced by the nature of institution or organization that takes it up. The commitment that the institution has to PMs and their way of working will determine how far you can go with the methodologies. Sometimes the uptake of a participatory approach depends entirely on an individual. If it is an institution where hierarchy or top-down management is the norm, a mere training of its staff in PMs may never yield any significant change. The culture of learning needs to be embedded within the organizations involved.

The question often asked is how you then promote and sustain PMs in organizations that are not participatory in nature. It has increasingly become important that the institutional leaders, or community leaders in the case of grassroots work, like *Reflect*, are brought on board if we are to see a sustained change in people's lives through the use of participatory approaches. This can be done through an orientation process that is most effectively done at the outset of the programme when the approach is being introduced to the community or the organization.

Where leaders are excluded, chances of success are limited. In the past, *Reflect* programmes were mainly targeting trainers and facilitators, but monitoring showed that often trainees had not moved a step towards putting what they had learned into practice. Often, behind this inability to act there was a leader who did not appreciate the approach, and would not give the space for it to be tried out. Nevertheless even where it is clear that an ingredient – in this case, leadership support – was missing, the blame would often still be put on the methodology itself.

Tailor-made trainings or orientation for managers or local leaders are a crucial step in the effective implementation of PMs. This does not only ensure support for the programme, it also limits the tendency of the approach to become a privilege of a few staff in the organization, which can cause many problems once these staff leave. In cases where the institutional capacity to document is weak, the departure of the few PM experts deprives the organization of all the institutional memory of participatory approaches.

Orientation processes for leaders should not stop at the conventional introduction of the approach to the leaders. Orientations should also emphasize the significance of the approach and its applicability. How it is going to add value to the work of those leaders other than directly benefiting the communities with which they work? In one of the tailor-made trainings we did for local leaders, when we introduced the importance of participatory tools, we used the resource map with them, and these leaders were able to see how this would help them identify the resource people they had in the village, which was the adult population eligible to pay taxes. That was enough to stimulate their interest in the programme which they then supported.

Ultimately the goal should be to develop a critical mass of people with a capacity to facilitate and sustain a quality learning cycle. This is easier said than done. It requires devotion to the ideals of the learning process and commitment from the donors, participants and all other key stakeholders. Experience has shown that while it might be easy to get the trainers to give their time to frequent and sometimes lengthy trainings, it is becoming more and more difficult to get donors and consequently managers to approve budgets that have significant allocations for training or capacity-building. This is self-defeating: how can we ever dream of sustainable human development if we do not invest in building the human resources? Tailor-made workshops for donors, managers and local leaders are needed if they are to appreciate the potential impacts of participatory processes, as well as the demands they make.

Power issues in training

The issue of power relations has to be approached with caution when facilitating PMs, for power relationship issues are not only limited to training but follow through to community implementation. *Reflect* circles, for example, are heterogeneous, often containing a cross-section of the social stratifications in a community. This presents an enormous challenge for the facilitator handling a group with such power diversity.

In a mixed group containing local leaders, if the facilitator is not prepared to deal with the power relations, s/he may find it hard to manage the dominating tendencies of those with positions of power. Similar problems exist within villages: if the facilitator is of a lower status in any way than the village leader, s/he will find it difficult to challenge the leader if necessary. Gender presents a particularly complex set of power relations, and we have found many facilitators are culprits, perpetuating patterns of gender relations through what they say and do.

Much as *Reflect* seeks to address power relationships and change the status quo, there is no one straightforward way of training facilitators or trainers in dealing with power issues. It relates very much to the attitudes and values of the people involved; and these are not very easy attributes to change.

We have, however, tried out a number of tools and techniques to help trainers and facilitators deal with power. We have found Venn diagrams, role plays and case studies particularly useful tools for power analysis. In the Venn diagram, circles of different sizes are used to analyse the power of a particular person in the group or community. The distance from one circle to another illustrates how close the relationship is between the categories of persons being analysed.

Case studies depict real situations from other contexts, which are used for the analysis of power relations; these can sometimes be developed during the training, based on what is actually happening. For example, in 2001 during a training of the leadership team of a CBO, my co-trainer and I found that after two days of training, participants were not opening up, and we were not able to deal with the real issues to facilitate an effective organizational development process for the community-based organization (CBO). Analysing the power dynamics, we saw that this women's group was led by a male chairperson, who was so powerful that he had condemned the entire executive, mostly women, into a culture of silence. They could not say anything in his presence; imagine that even in the training session, before they could say anything, they had to get his approval through eye contact. We developed learning material out of this situation, changing names and details. The following day we went to the session armed with our case story. In one of the sessions on leadership, we issued the story to each of the participants to read on their own. After reading on an individual basis, they were grouped in threes to analyse the story using a number of guiding questions. It was very interesting to see the group members – including the very powerful chairperson – tearing apart the character in the story, criticizing the chair's style and making many recommendations about what they would do in such a circumstance. After the analysis, we brought the discussion into plenary and asked one question: had they ever experienced such a scenario in their own group?. You can begin to imagine what happened; it was at this stage that the group started to realize that all that was represented in the case story was a version of what was going on in their own group. It ended up by them setting a date for re-electing their executive, which I later learnt took place after the training.

The quality of participatory processes: setting standards for training?

Who sets the agenda for participatory training? My case is that, in order to ensure the quality of our programmes, we should think of having minimum standards and a minimum of content that should be covered for trainees to appreciate the concept of participation and begin to practise with some of the key principles.

There has been lots of debate on setting standards for participatory processes. With long lists of dos and don'ts, we risk reducing PMs to mechanical processes with limited room for creativity. However, I also subscribe to the school of thought that minimum standards are needed if ever we are to see a reduction in incidences of bad practice or abuse of PMs. There is so much that goes into PM training which requires adequate time and the right kind of people in order to internalize, experience and learn. No practitioners can tell you precisely how many days it took them to internalize the PMs, for it is a long and winding journey; all put together, the period needed to gain confidence to adapt PMs is rather long. Numerous PM trainings take only two or three days. How possible is it for one to substantially handle the skills and knowledge acquisition, attitude and values change which are the basics of any training and are critical for PM adaptation in such a short time?

There is a need to establish minimum standards in terms of the number of days for training in PMs and the training content that will ensure that the acquisition of skills, knowledge, attitude and values for PMs is fully propagated. What I see as basic for the minimum package are the participatory tools and techniques, minimum knowledge of the concepts related to participation itself and the particular participatory approaches, power relations, gender relations, communication and any area of thematic concern, such as HIV/AIDS, environmental issues or education. Who should set the minimum standards? I would like to challenge all of us who are PMs practitioners and promoters to do that, set those standards and to go ahead to advocate for or enforce them.

Investing in the facilitator

Asked who are the most important persons in the development, spread and evolution of high-quality PMs, without hesitating I will respond that it is the facilitator. As argued above, trainee facilitators need more than just the defined training. Investing in those who have been trained to facilitate participatory processes is as important in ensuring quality as the establishment of minimum standards.

In the case of *Reflect*, after the training someone goes out to meet the newly trained facilitator to discuss the challenges to be faced and make plans. You cannot imagine the impact of such a visit. Visiting and monitoring the session facilitation and giving instant feedback go a long way in improving performance. Peer support for facilitators is another important element. This involves facilitators teaming up to support one another, say through co-facilitation, and mentoring one another, complemented by regular facilitators' meetings to review progress, identify challenges and map the way forward, working together to boost the morale and performance of the facilitator. I do fully appreciate the limitations, where inadequate funding features prominently, but there is no justification strong enough to sacrifice the quality of programmes. There is a need to refocus our priorities when it comes to programme design and implementation, illustrating the fact that proper investment is required for PMs. In addition to putting adequate resources into capacity-building; there should be mechanisms through which facilitators of social change are enabled to grow, develop and enrich their knowledge of experiential learning.

How else can we invest in facilitators? As part of capacity-building for PM practitioners, it helps to have trainers and facilitators closely linked through some sort of network. They need to have follow-up meetings to compare notes and share learning, putting together their experiences and building a common vision. In *Reflect*, there are different levels of networking. The facilitators are linked through a forum, as are the trainers, both at a national level. There is then a broader-based networking, which spreads more widely, taking care of all the other levels. This is the case for PAMOJA Africa *Reflect* Network, which links all *Reflect* practitioners in Africa. PAMOJA has country-level chapters, which are a composition of different agencies and communities involved in implementing *Reflect*. PAMOJA's basic business is to facilitate learning and sharing among *Reflect* practitioners and practitioners of other PMs. PAMOJA in turn is linked to the global *Reflect* Network, CIRAC.

As well as being linked upwards and outwards, there need to be more links between the facilitator and other processes taking place in the community. Facilitators need to be exposed to other happenings and debates so that they are seen to be using the skills they have acquired. Information is power; facilitators need to continually update their knowledge and gain access to the latest information, perhaps by taking on opportunities for further education. In the *Reflect* programme run by GOAL Sudan, for example, over 60 per cent of the facilitators have enrolled for further studies, some even for university education. Their work should expose them to more opportunities that will build them mentally, socially, economically and physically. That is the only way they can play the role model they are supposed to be.

The personal commitment of individual facilitators is key to high-quality participatory processes. Facilitating a *Reflect* circle does not only stop in the session where the people discuss, it goes beyond, and indeed it takes a lot of the facilitator's time. Unless the facilitator is really committed we do not see much happening. This commitment has to be recognized which means we need to consider the issue of motivation in a broader sense. In some places facilitators work as volunteers, which may be positive in terms of sustainability; but we have to recognize that even volunteering has limits. It is also a moral question: why do we expect facilitators to work as volunteers while the rest of the programme promoters may continue to earn big money?

The argument in favour of volunteering is that there are a number of embedded benefits that accrue to that facilitator during the course of service, and that the facilitator at times gets some other benefits in kind from the participants. We should be looking at the output. In Uganda, for example, I have observed a marked difference between the performances of facilitators who have a small allowance and those who are volunteers. Volunteer or not, there should be a comprehensive system of motivating the facilitators to enhance their development.

The origin of the facilitator also influences quality. Generally our programmes have emphasized the need to recruit local facilitators because of their local knowledge, but sometimes local facilitators find it difficult to handle certain issues, particularly the sensitive areas of sex, sexuality and death, which have become urgent with the spread of HIV/AIDS. There should be the flexibility to enable external facilitators to come in to handle some issues. This also acts as a booster to the learning process, for participants always look up to new people with the great hope of learning something new.

A challenge is how to deal with facilitators who do not perform well. There are many factors that may lead to underperformance, some of which are related to issues discussed above, like poor training and low motivation. But there are also cases where poor performance can be blamed entirely on the person, either because of the lack of initiative and creativity or because of lack of interest in the subject. This is the hard part to deal with, yet it is common with some of the facilitators. The question is whether anything can be done about people who are bad at facilitation. This is a delicate issue, especially if only identified by the promoting agency staff. The selection of facilitators and the definition of roles and duties together with clearly established lines of accountability is one solution. In this process, the measuring sticks for performance should be applied and the consequences clearly defined. That way, bad facilitation can be spotted early by all and the subsequent reprimand effected.

This is only part of the solution. There is also a major problem of bad practice: bad facilitators, weak methods or methods that are good but are used inappropriately or in the wrong situation. These are issues that have been discussed often, but no solution has been found and they are giving a bad name to participation. The outstanding questions remain.

- Should we take a clearer stand against bad practice?
- Should there be an attempt to regulate facilitators? How could this be done?

Whether you call it training or capacity-building, what is important to note is that training and facilitation processes propel the development, spread and sometimes the distortion of PMs. Ensuring positive, high-quality outcomes will depend on how much is invested in the capacity-building processes. Our attitude to training and facilitation will to a great extent determine the effectiveness of the participatory approaches that we promote.

CHAPTER 3

Can an international NGO practise what it preaches in participation? The case of ActionAid International

Kate Newman

Introduction

ActionAid International (AAI) has used participatory methodologies (PMs) in different ways across its 35+ country programmes for over 15 years. In fact, we often claim that this aspect of our approach to work makes us different from the many other international non-governmental organizations (INGOs); it is central to what we are.

In 2005, the new International Reflect Team (IRT) in AAI (see Chapter 1 for more details on *Reflect*) were asked to map what the organization's staff were doing in relation to participatory approaches, and ask them their vision for an international participatory resource which could support them in their work.

As a member of this team, I am writing this chapter immediately after having gone through an intensive internal process of mapping out and reviewing the different participatory approaches that we use. As I explain in detail below, the mapping has been positive, and two weeks ago nearly 30 staff from 16 country programmes, two regional and six international functions met to devise a strategy for strengthening our participatory practice. However, this is just the start of a long process. By the time this book actually goes to print what the reality is now will have changed; the recommendations from country programme staff (the grassroots of the organization) might or might not have been taken seriously by international directors (the power-holders?). The question now is whether we got our mapping process right. Is the mobilization and momentum sufficient to force (or at least encourage) a big INGO like AAI to really change? What makes an organization change? And should AAI be practising what it preaches anyway?

In this chapter I share the recent process we have been through and then look at the politics within this process. I follow this by sharing some of the current challenges we are facing before returning to the question of whether AAI can, and should, practise what it preaches in participation.

Context

AAI has been using PMs for some time. We first started experimenting with participatory approaches in the late 1980s with work with farming communities and in primary schools. As the participatory movement has evolved, ActionAid has continually contributed to debates, writing, analysis and critiques of the various methodologies. We have been involved in the evolution of *Reflect* and Stepping Stones (see Chapters 1, 2, 4 and 13, this volume); we regularly use PRA or PLA (Participatory Learning and Action) to inform our programme design and implementation; and more recently we have made innovations with participatory vulnerability analysis, social audit, citizens' juries, participatory budget analysis and so on. Moreover, our accountability, learning and planning system (ALPS)[10] is premised on a participatory process with downwards accountability at its core.

In 1998, following an external review of all our work called 'Taking Stock', ActionAid began 'Fighting Poverty Together', which was our strategy from 1999 to 2004. The strategy period reflected a move from largely being a service delivery agency to following a rights-based approach (or rights-based approaches, recognizing that different approaches are appropriate in different contexts). In 2004 we underwent 'Taking Stock 2', and in 2005 we entered a new strategy period with 'Rights to End Poverty' (R2EP).[11] R2EP not only reflects our new organizational structure (see below) but also signals a deeper understanding of rights issues and power. Moreover, unlike 'Fighting Poverty Together', this strategy period is accompanied by a change management plan and investment in building staff skills and capabilities. This reflects a recognition that the move to a rights-based approach has not been universally successful, and some country programmes are still grappling with this new way of working. It also signals the belief that if we are going to enhance the quality of our practice, and be able to implement the new strategy, we need to prioritize the capacity-building of our staff.

As indicated above, ActionAid has been involved in the development of different participatory approaches which have evolved in line with our changing understanding of poverty and development. While we initially used participatory methods as a way of consulting with people, to improve our programme design, we have gradually become more political in our understanding of participation and in our innovation with approaches. However, although we are an organization which dedicates considerable time and resources to participation, we have been weak on bringing these different methods together, at exploring what we really understand by participation in the context of our strategy and our rights-based approach. In addition, we are increasingly recognizing that while we might be good at participation out there we do not necessarily practise what we preach in the organization. Participatory principles do not necessarily inform how we develop our partnerships, decide our policy positions or do our advocacy work, or our attitudes and behaviour. For example, we might partner an organization that is smaller and less powerful than us, and expect them to agree to our values, terms and conditions. Or we might publicize the success of lobbying at an international meeting, while ignoring the small-scale participatory process which is happening in a community in Uganda.

There had been two previous attempts to draw together our participatory practice. The first was in Dhaka, Bangladesh in 2001, the 'Participatory Methodologies Forum'.[12] Although the initial aim had been to look at the diverse practice in ActionAid and share learning, the forum was dominated by discussions on power, and the importance of understanding power in relation to participation. This was an important point in AAI's history, as the organization was beginning to understand that we were not a neutral force in the development process. We have political bias, organizational power and a belief set that affects the focus and outcome of our work, and in the case of participatory methods, how we use them has an effect on their outcome. However, while the meeting was rich in analysis, there was limited practical discussion, and even less follow-up at the international level. Initially there were attempts to continue the Participatory Methodologies Forum as an ongoing email debate at international level, but there was no clear objective for this and it soon faded away. The analysis, however, did affect those involved in the meeting, and has had an impact on our programmes, and through sharing the workshop report the discussions have also been disseminated beyond the organization.

Two years later there was a meeting in Addis Ababa where participants examined the tools we were using from the perspective of our rights-based approach. This involved thinking through how specific tools and methods could and should be adapted to further our approach. Unlike the Dhaka meeting there were specific recommendations for ensuring continued reflection around participation and rights, and a series of suggestions about how to spread the learning throughout the organization.[13] But the main coordinator left ActionAid shortly after the event, and unfortunately outcomes were not followed up and little changed in relation to our global participatory practice.

The year 2005 was one of change for AAI. The organizations was going through the process of internationalization (with the move of our headquarters to South Africa and country programmes recruiting national boards, registering as national NGOs and becoming part of a federal structure); we had the new strategy (R2EP); and were restructuring to put six themes (women's rights; education; governance; HIV/AIDS; human security; and food and hunger) at the centre of our work. This new strategy deepens our understanding of rights, and highlights the importance of understanding power. Participatory practice is critical to securing rights and transforming power, so in the middle of all this change it was an appropriate time to re-examine our participatory work.

The process

In January 2005, *Reflect* left its home in the International Education Unit in order to embrace the diversity of *Reflect* practice which had moved beyond its roots in adult literacy and empowerment (see Chapter 1, this volume). Over the last few years the way *Reflect* is used has expanded dramatically. Following intense debate in 1998 when the original Mother Manual, along with the focus on literacy, was called into question, different organizations have experimented widely with the approach. It is now difficult to say precisely what *Reflect* is. In order to overcome this issue David Archer and I facilitated a process in 2003 of structuring the approach around a series of nine principles.[14] In 2004 the *Reflect* team initiated a discussion in AAI on whether these principles could actually serve to guide all our participatory practice. The mapping was an attempt to take this discussion further.

The first stage in the mapping process was to recruit a country programme staff member on secondment who could bring a different perspective to a mapping exercise. The IRT was a small unit made up of two people, based in London, and had an international, rather than practitioner, viewpoint. We also wanted to work with someone who did not come from a *Reflect* background, who could help us think beyond the approach we already knew considerable amounts about. Ravi SK from ActionAid India, whose work at national level focused on children's rights, joined us for six months. At the same time as recruiting Ravi, we also set up an international steering group made up of senior management and programme staff across the organization. The aim of this steering group was twofold. The first was to give us advice as we developed the mapping, ensuring that it was responsive to a wide range of perspectives. Second, it was the role of the steering group to champion the process: to encourage country programmes to take part in the mapping, and to ensure high-level buy-in to the process and its outputs.

Over the first two months we (Ravi SK and I) researched other mapping exercises that had taken place in AAI, looking at what happened and what worked. We spent time thinking through how a mapping exercise could both generate information that was valuable as a central resource, and build momentum and interest in a bigger project. We asked ourselves how we could be participatory, especially given our position at the old centre of the organization during a period of reorganization. We were also very aware of the need for concrete results, especially in the light of previous experiences that had produced interesting discussions but little action.

Ravi took the lead in developing a three-part mapping exercise, which was sent to 25 country programmes. A slightly different version was sent to the head of each of AAI's six strategic themes.[15] The exercise asked people to work in groups of between six and eight to carry out the mapping. This group would ideally include staff represented from programme and policy work, finance, HR and sponsorship/communications. This was to ensure that different perspectives were brought into the mapping, and to help us move beyond seeing participation as something that was done out there in communities, to something that could also be relevant in here, within ActionAid.

The first part of the mapping aimed to collect basic information on how and where people were using participatory approaches, and to explore how participation was understood. This was done in the form of tables listing the different participatory approaches and asking if they were used at community level, in the organization, in building partnerships or developing policy. We also asked questions to explore links between community-level participation and communication and advocacy functions. In this part people were expected to *reflect* on what they had learned while using participatory approaches, covering a range of issues concerning participation from community experiences, training and capacity-building, evaluation and documentation, networking, institutionalization, organizational behaviour and funding. Those involved in responding to the questionnaire thought through how they understood participation, considering, for example, what distinctions they made between participation *per se* and participatory approaches, and whether the *Reflect* principles could be used by AAI as a basis for all our participatory work. The final set of questions in this part focused on future directions for participatory practice. We asked if people thought it would be valuable to have some sort of international participatory resource: what they would hope to gain from it, and what they would contribute to it. At this stage we chose not to define what we meant by a resource, as we wanted to see how people would define it. We wanted to know if they thought it would be useful to have a participatory structure, a team of people working on participation, or a virtual resource, for example, a database of participatory practitioners, a library of materials or themed training events.

The second part of the mapping was a series of reflective exercises, using PRA tools and case studies to generate discussion and analysis to get people really thinking about participation. These exercises linked concepts of participation and organizational behaviour. Based on a series of tools we had used to discuss networking in *Reflect*, we asked people to think about the types of information and communication which were useful for them, and to explore issues of power relations, opportunities for and obstacles to accessing information and sharing experiences.[16] The third was a more focused questionnaire on *Reflect*. Completing all three parts of the mapping would take at least one day.

We sent out the questionnaire in June 2005, and gave respondents a month to return the completed versions. During this time we worried that no country office would take the exercise seriously, and that we would have a low return rate. Within ActionAid's structure there is no way to ensure participation in such exercises; it was not a mandatory requirement, and we were relying on local interest and our organizational power to keep this process moving. Despite our anxieties the response we had was amazing, with 22 country offices (out of 25 who had received the mapping) and five themes (out of six) returning the questionnaires. Unfortunately fewer returned documentation of the reflective exercises. This was due in part perhaps to the time needed to do these exercises, but also because actually documenting what happened was more complicated, and we probably did not give enough support for this to happen.[17]

From this we started a process of analysis, and based on the responses, invited country offices to send staff to an international meeting to develop a participatory approaches strategy. Twenty-six people attended the meeting from a good cross-section of themes and countries, including programme staff, impact assessment/shared learning advisers, country directors, function heads and an international director. There were people working at the local level, as well as the national, regional and international, and we worked to bring these diverse perspectives into the meeting.

Although people were speaking from a range of viewpoints at the meeting, there was a considerable amount of consensus as to what the issues were and how we should be tackling them. Over the four-day meeting we explored the challenges and potentials facing AAI, and developed these into four problem statements, as follows.

Why is there a proliferation of tools and approaches with no coordination, and a lack of learning or sharing between them (referring specifically to the lack of knowledge about how to link on, or mix and match the different approaches)?

Are our approaches and understanding up to the challenge of delivering R2EP?

Does R2EP create tensions and disincentives for participation?

Why doesn't ActionAid always practise what it preaches in relation to participation?

Groups discussed each problem, and came up with recommendations based on their analysis, and these recommendations were then worked into three strategic and two organizational goals for participation. The goals were unified under this vision:

ActionAid International would be an organization grounded in and run according to participatory principles, so that participatory practice empowers people to challenge unequal power relations and fight for, and secure, their rights.

A three-tier structure consisting of a coordinating group, an international team and communities of participatory practice, was suggested to support this vision. The meeting was timed to fit in our three-year planning process, and the challenge is now to turn this strategy into action.

The politics, or challenges to the process

By calling this section 'The politics', immediately a feeling of tension and conflict is created. It is a loaded word, and what follows here is just one perspective. I cannot pretend to be speaking on behalf of ActionAid, or indeed others involved in the process, but I hope that the comments I share here are thought-provoking and useful.

The first challenge came last year when we began discussing the idea of the IRT. As mentioned above, AAI was going through a period of change, with everything becoming structured along thematic lines. A participation team did not fit well within this structure. Moreover, we were unwilling to define our team's long-term aims or objectives as we wanted to follow a participatory process. We had seen too many initiatives die in AAI because they were decided at the centre with little thought for the realities of Development Areas (DAs) around which AAI structures its work. In a big international organization with so many people working in different places and spaces, it is difficult to design structures which respond to everyone's needs. All too often those playing international roles believe they know what people who work with a programme focus need and want, without having experienced their reality or perspective. In addition to these structural difficulties, we were a small, London-based team, led by women in an organization which had just admitted to being patriarchal,[18] but had had little time to think through how to challenge this. AAI had moved its headquarters to South Africa, and it was unclear how the international teams in the London office would relate in this new structure. We had little organizational power, and our objective was to start a process. How could we convince others to value and fund this process, especially if we could not be clear about what the outcome would be?

The second challenge was with the process itself. How could we design one which was true to our participatory principles? First, we wanted to involve people, but we had a limited time frame, and were aware that staff around the organization had hundreds of other calls on their time. In addition, AAI is an organization of 2,000 staff working in four continents in over 30 countries. It was not going to be possible to involve everyone, but how could we ensure that those who did speak were truly representative of the wide range of staff in the organization? We needed to devise a process which maximized involvement and influence over the final decision-making, while avoiding being onerous. We wanted to inspire people across the organization, and build momentum for change. Second, we knew that we had to have a concrete output. We needed information that we could compare and analyse, and we needed to have a clear strategy to take this work forward, otherwise it would collapse as the previous two initiatives had. We wanted to create a participatory process which was not extractive, that mobilized interest across AAI and kept people involved throughout. How could we do this and deliver concrete recommendations in six months?

Third, we had the challenge of the personalities and the brands. As is seen from other chapters in this book, personalities and brands help participatory methods evolve and spread. But they can also be problematic, leading to power struggles and curbing innovation and change. In AAI different staff members were aligned to different methods. It was part of their identity, who they were as workers, and allowed them to compete for resources and space in their country programme. These branded programmes made it easier to set up projects with a clear focus, to convince donors to give funding and to position oneself in the organization. In Emergencies there was PVA (Participatory Vulnerability Analysis), in HIV/AIDS, Stepping Stones (and more recently STAR, Stepping Stones and *Reflect*) and in Education, *Reflect*. Was it really an advantage to bring these methodologies together, to look holistically, or would it just undermine the clarity and sense of purpose of both the methodology and the staff members involved?

The fourth challenge was around the facilitators of the process. We devised the set of mapping exercises centrally, and although we had some input from an international advisory team, there was no time to pilot the materials or to train on them. We were dependent on local initiative to decide how to form the group, run the discussions at national level and determine the level of participation. The different styles (and quality) of facilitation can be seen clearly in the returned questionnaires. Some have considerable depth of reflection and analysis, others report more superficially. This is also likely to affect the interest and momentum built at country level, and is perhaps reflective of the way participatory approaches are being framed and implemented, and how power relations are understood. How much freedom and support should we give the national-level facilitators to implement our process? How can we ensure that good facilitators are chosen, given our lack of knowledge of (or control over) local power structures and hierarchies? And how could we say what would make a good local facilitator anyway? Is it appropriate to define this internationally, from the centre?

A fifth challenge could be described as understanding power and power relations. Each organization has its own culture and way of working. This culture is both formal, shaped by the structure of the organization, and informal, influenced by personal relationships, custom and practice. Culture inevitably affects how change can be made and the potential for participatory processes. AAI is largely decentralized, with a light international secretariat and regional offices, and the majority of decisions are taken at country level, based on the theory that strategic decisions are best taken by those with country context and knowledge. Although our structure has changed with the new strategy (elevating thematic heads above the country directors), this still means that what happens in a country programme is largely dependent on national-level decisions and the country director's style of leadership. The mapping was developed with the aim of building momentum from the grassroots upwards. This was based on the belief (or assumption?) that if ActionAid was to strengthen its participatory practice this would need to be led from below, to be built by staff across the organization who were already applying participatory principles in their work. However, it was also important to recognize that the final decision-making still resides among a few, who sit at the top of ActionAid's hierarchy. How could we build a process to mobilize people to challenge these power structures and gain their support to implement change? Would the mobilization of the grassroots be enough to change the way AAI makes decisions, to transform power and enable AAI to practise what we preach in participation?

Finally, how could we get people to say what was really happening, to share their reality, not what they thought we wanted to hear? Part of the mapping process was aimed at getting people to think about what they had been doing and why, to encourage them to question their own practice and reassess it. We stated clearly in the mapping that it was not meant to be judgemental, that we wanted to know what was really going on. We said it was not an evaluation, but an honest assessment of their current reality. But it came from the former head office, with a covering letter signed by an international director. While this definitely increased the likelihood of people following the process, it may also have given rise to a wish to impress, to second-guess the answers we were looking for, which ultimately could undermine the process. How could we design a process in which people feel they can be honest and participate for their own benefit rather than ours, when we are seen as the power holders? Who was creating the participatory space?

Reflections

The politics of the process as worded above could be translated to any participatory process. If we start to imagine AAI programme staff around the world as the community, as the grassroots, we can see how these issues we faced as the coordinating team are comparable with those facing any participatory practitioner working with community groups. So this leads me to return to the question: Should AA practise what it preaches in relation to participation?

We believe in participation because we believe that people should have a voice in decisions which affect them. However, we also target those people who are most poor and marginalized, with the belief that their voice is seldom heard. So a key issue to consider is whether the grassroots staff of AA lack voice, and whether the institutional system is structured to marginalize (and exploit?) them. The answer to this question is likely to depend on whom you are asking. And while many would say that grassroots staff lack a voice, it is unlikely that people would feel the ActionAid's structure is loaded against them in the same way as poor and oppressed people experience structural discrimination worldwide.

A key argument for AAI to practise what it preaches is that we believe that we should, and have devised structures to help us do so. ALPS requires us to be participatory in our attitudes and behaviour, to be downwardly accountable, and to share information openly and transparently. We ask our partner organizations to do this, and expect community members to do so also, as we think that this will strengthen poor people's ability to secure their rights and transform power relations. In many ways ALPS was designed to internalize our participatory approaches. And in many places this has worked well; it has enabled us to plan more flexibly, to focus on reflection and learning, and it has also encouraged transparency around our budgets with the people with whom we work. We need to build on the processes begun by ALPS and ensure that it is properly understood and used across the organization. This will contribute to our ability to practise what we preach.

However, there are also other reasons why we should endeavour to do this. The challenges presented above suggest that we would learn from practising what we preach. By experiencing our own participatory process we should improve our understanding of participation, and the challenges involved in shifting power relations. This in turn should sharpen our practice at community level and enhance our impact.

Another reason for practising participation is because we criticize other organizations for their lack of transparency and accountability, for their secret discussions and decision-making. By investing in our own participatory process we could move beyond criticism to providing alternatives. We would be able to speak from our own experience and present a concrete strategy for organizational transformation to challenge the present dominant power structures.

Conclusions: can AAI practise what it preaches?

The discussion above gives clear reasons why I believe AAI should practise what it preaches. However, as I arrive at my conclusions here I think it is important to acknowledge that there are arguments against this idea also. As someone with a strong belief in participation, and a long history in working with participatory approaches, I am clearly biased in my view, and I am choosing to use this space to support my view, rather than attempting to provide a balanced alternative. I will leave it to others to decide whether to agree with, or challenge me on this.

So, to revisit to my original question whether AAI can practise what it preaches, and what challenges we might face in trying to do this, there are five practical challenges which we face, and these relate directly back to the problems highlighted earlier.

First, we return to ideological issues: whether AAI really wants to practise what it preaches, and whether this is coherent with its new strategy, which, among other things, aims to increase our profile and influence. In order for this new strategy to be true to our values, we need to start looking at ways of raising our profile (and funding) through the way we are doing things, to focus on the process in addition to the output. This is never easy, especially given the speed with which decisions need to be made in order to engage with and influence international players (where media coverage is crucially important). In addition, we need to be aware of our funding relationship and supporter base, and ensure that we bring them along with us if any change is to be sustainable. However, if we are able to balance external pressures with well-structured efficient and transparent internal processes, we might be able to overcome this tension.

Second, we need to look at how we understand participation in respect to our strategy and rights-based approach. At the moment AAI is engaged in work which covers the spectrum from consultation, through planning and implementation, to learning, mobilization and change. We will regularly use participatory processes in a one-day consultation on a specific programme. And this is qualitatively different from an ongoing learning process such as *Reflect*, which aims to transform power and build community organizations. We need to ask whether we are happy working across the spectrum, and if so what this means for our internal process of practising what we preach. For example, if we accept all forms of participation are equally valid and useful, then practising what we preach could mean anything from publishing a document on the intranet (i.e. making it available to those looking for it), to a series of focused reflection and analysis days which build strategy from the bottom up. We are united by one strategy and therefore we can think through what we understand by participation in relation to our strategy. From this understanding we can generate a set of principles to guide our practice, and be held accountable to them, both internally and externally.

Third, we need to be realistic and practical. Stating that we are practising what we preach does not mean that every decision should be taken with the full involvement of every staff member in AAI. We need to develop pragmatic decision-making and communication procedures and be held accountable to them. We need to be open and transparent about when we are being participatory and when we are not, and explain how these different kinds of decisions are made. Perhaps publicity, like this chapter, will help us in this.

Fourth, we need to look at ourselves and question whether we have the systems, skills, capacity, aptitudes and behaviour to achieve this goal. It is not easy to share power, to value and include others, especially if you have been working differently. While it is easy to say we practise what we preach, it is harder to understand what this might mean in practice. This capacity needs to be built and valued, staff need to be supported through a change process and we need to recognize that this will not happen overnight.

Finally, we need to understand more about how organizations can change, and specifically how AAI can learn and change. The key to the success of this initiative is to tie any change plan to the current structures and cultures which exist. The mapping initiated a bottom-up process and without doubt caused interesting reflections and discussions to take place across the organization. This is likely to influence pockets of practice in different places. However, if we want to fundamentally shift the way AAI works in order to strengthen our coherence throughout our work, this bottom-up process needs to be complemented with a top-down decision, to create the space and value the efforts people are making to transform their practice.

So, can AAI practise what it preaches? Well, we are definitely trying, and if the political will is there, the potential is high. The mapping process has definitely built momentum at country-programme level around bringing together our participatory practice, systematizing our learning and tightening our understanding. Would it be correct to say that the grassroots has been mobilized? Maybe not across the whole organization, but if we focus on those representatives who participated in the mapping and attended the meeting, I think so.

There is a clear structure and strategy being recommended to take this participatory work forward. Moreover, representatives from nearly all ActionAid country programmes have endorsed this strategy. Participants in the meeting are currently facilitating report-back sessions and similar discussion at country level. But is grassroots mobilization enough to convince the power-holders that the strategy is sound and worth funding? The participatory process was supported by the power-holders, will it now be followed through when it comes to the decision-making? I hope so.

Afterword

Following the participatory process described in this chapter the recommendations from the mapping process were submitted to senior management, which decided to locate participatory support at the regional level across ActionAid International, rather than take on the three-tier model suggested. This was due to wider structural change, as part of the internationalization process. At the time of submitting this chapter the exact details of the new structure was undecided. (The AAI secretariat may be contacted for information on the final decisions.)

CHAPTER 4

It's not just about the pictures! It's also about principles, process and power: tensions in the development of the Internal Learning System

Helzi Noponen

Introduction

What is most striking and appealing about the Internal Learning System (ILS), pictorial workbooks in participant hands, is also what causes the most tension and misconception. Potential adapters of ILS are drawn to the pictorial aspects of the system, seeing simple picture scenes on a variety of development indicators that participants can understand and use. They do not always appreciate the underlying principles of participation that are aimed at reversing power relationships in the use of impact data so that poor, often illiterate participants are the first to benefit from learning, and make changes based on it.

They also do not see the research design process that underpins each version of the diary. Successful adaptation to a new context means involving all programme stakeholders, including the target group, in an interactive and participatory manner, to determine questions, types of analysis, indicators and measurement variables. They also do not see the process of field-testing the resulting design solution – not just pictorial representations, but research content and participant learning needs – or the facilitation and learning processes that are implicit in implementing ILS over time within an organization. What looks simple on the surface is in reality multi-faceted, requiring careful thought and commitment. ILS is therefore a challenge for organizations to adapt to, and to use to its full potential.

ILS was also quite challenging to create. Without a doubt, the pictures play a key role in the system, enabling illiterate participants to participate fully, and allowing comprehensive and telling facts about a poor participant's life to be reflected back to participants and outside stakeholders. This chapter reviews some of the key tensions and turning points in the evolution of ILS, with the objective of informing potential adaptors of the complexities and less visible but rich participatory principles, processes and power implications that are involved in ILS. It also gives insights on why the spread of ILS beyond the original creator and NGO partners has been more hesitant than other methods.

What is ILS?

ILS was conceived as a participatory impact assessment and planning system originally developed for microfinance and livelihoods programmes, but since adapted to other sectors such as environment, human rights and health. The medium for ILS is diaries or multi-year workbooks in which poor, often illiterate programme participants keep individual records of change over time by noting their responses to scenes representing development indicators. Women draw lines and simple tick-marks to denote quantities, yes/no responses, multiple-choice answers and satisfaction scale ratings. At the start of using the diaries, ideally when they first enter the programme, participants record their current conditions in red pencil or ink as a baseline record of their starting conditions. When a change occurs, it is noted in lead pencil. Fellow group members, in a mutual learning process, cross-check the accuracy of the data entries. The impact diaries are enhanced with a variety of pictorial learning elements and action tools for goal setting, prioritizing and planning that meet practical needs, achieve strategic interests and reinforce programme values. Poor participants, therefore, are the first to learn about programme impact and performance, and alter plans as a result. This is a reversal of normal power dynamics; typically, managers and researchers at the top extract information from participants, conduct the analyses and respond to the results. In ILS, participants are not only data gatherers, but they are also analysts, planners and advocates for change. Programme managers benefit when users share their impact assessments, lessons learned and revised strategies.

The diaries are simple to facilitate in a group setting, so it is feasible for all participants in a programme to use them for learning purposes. For formal programme impact assessment purposes, data from a smaller random sample of diary users are captured by research staff in periodic interviews. These impact data can be statistically analysed on a cross-sectional or longitudinal basis by research staff or programme managers, either by comparing the conditions of participants with a suitable comparison group, or by analysing changes that have occurred in the lives of a sample of participants. So, while participants are the first analysts, tracking and thinking about their conditions and planning changed priorities, programme managers can also demonstrate impact and examine different outcomes.

Other elements in the system include group diaries designed to improve village self-help group (SHG) functioning or track wider impact issues such as collective actions to improve area conditions or change negative social practices. Field staff diaries are designed to help organizers identify lagging and excelling performance among groups, reflect on possible underlying reasons for the performance and plan appropriate remedies.

Initiation

The original aim of the ILS was to create a participatory monitoring and impact assessment system that would be internally driven, responding to the ongoing needs of organizations and their participants, rather than external funders, to learn what is working, not working and why, so that changes could be made in a timely manner. Given this emphasis on the objectives of internal learning or improving rather than proving,[19] it is ironic that the project was actually initiated in 1993 by a funder, Jane Rosser, the livelihoods programme officer of the Ford Foundation in New Delhi, India. Ford, particularly the New Delhi office, has a rich history of sponsoring experimentation on innovative participatory methods. I believe that she was disappointed with the dependence on one-off, post-programme impact evaluations using standard methods that did not feed back usable and timely information to improve programme operations. There was often a total lack of impact evaluation for the mushrooming numbers of small and less sophisticated NGOs starting microfinance and livelihoods programmes in the early 1990s. I was asked to develop the system with three microfinance and livelihoods NGOs funded by Ford,[20] and later I worked on further developments with four other NGOs.[21] Initial and repeated funding and networking support from the Ford Foundation itself and other Ford-funded programme partners would play a crucial role in the development of ILS.

Inspiration for the medium of pictorial diaries

Because of the visual nature of the pictorial diaries some people assume that they are inspired by Participatory Rural Appraisal (PRA) diagrams and charts. The initial inspiration for the design, however, comes from a traditional quantitative method. During an earlier longitudinal study of microfinance, intra-household dynamics and women's empowerment, I had adapted the generic event history technique, typically used by demographers to collect life histories of individuals in specific areas such as life-cycle events, fertility behaviour and migration. I adapted this technique, focusing at the household level, to study the impact of microfinance interventions in the context of household dynamics such as crises and stress events, coping strategies, family labour supply decisions and intra-household resource allocation processes. I dubbed it a Family Labour Supply and Survival (FLSS) matrix. This focus on studying the key role that women play in sustaining poor families over time and the impact of interventions that explicitly target their earning role greatly inspired the form that ILS took.

For an ILS to be participatory, an extractive questionnaire format such as the FLSS matrix was not feasible. Yet in my longitudinal study I began to realize that respondents were starting to learn the matrix and were better prepared in subsequent interview rounds to answer questions. They had also begun to see and analyse gender dynamics, and were revealing ingenious coping strategies with respect to their husbands that I would never have imagined. Could women track these events and changes themselves over time in their own diary? Would there be value in women keeping this record themselves and reflecting on the changes, perhaps eventually taking steps to address the issues as a result? The design would have to be simple, inviting, and – because of female illiteracy and innumeracy – largely pictorial, using simple marks for responses.

The prototype ILS design was an impact diary containing pictures representing impact indicators with response cells to record simple tick-marks for yes/no responses, multiple-choice responses and quantities at baseline and one-, two-, and three-year intervals. The level of analysis was the individual woman who had been targeted for a microfinance intervention. There was also a strong gender focus to the analysis, especially the status and role that women play in the household and market economy. Women may take and repay multiple loans but gender inequities in the home, the workplace and the community may limit gains in socioeconomic welfare for them and their households. Knowing the importance of these factors may help women themselves, field officers and programme managers to devise strategies to improve the effectiveness of the savings, credit and livelihood interventions.

Three phases of ILS evolution: prototype design, field test and field trial

I received three rounds of Ford Foundation funding to develop ILS, each relating to distinct phases of development: prototype design, field test and field trial. The one-year prototype design phase focused on the innovation of the medium of pictorial learning diaries. This included experimenting with hand-drawn pictures to ensure that they could represent a wide range of development indicators to poor illiterate participants, devising symbols to record responses, testing the effectiveness of various diary formats and layouts, and most importantly, discovering whether women could correctly understand and respond. Is the design effective and efficient? Is it easily understood and does it function as planned? Is it user-friendly?

In the three-year field test, multiple adaptations of the prototype design were made for the three NGO partners to suit the needs of each organization's programme assessment or participant learning purposes and field-setting characteristics. These included production diaries for embroidery producers,[22] salt farmers, gum collectors, nursery producers, watershed users, balanced farming and handloom producers. Other diary adaptations also focused on SHG functioning, livelihoods planning and SHG group–bank linkage, targeting the ultra-poor below the threshold of microfinance, and tracking human rights for *dalits*, *adivassis* and people affected by HIV/AIDS.

This involved extensive participatory exercises with participants at all levels to learn about their stakes in the development programme and find appropriate indicators to measure their progress in achieving them over time. The adapted design was then tested on small but representative segments of the target users. Are the pictorial indicators and response options appropriate to the target group and research questions in the assessment exercise? Can the target group understand and use the adapted design? A field test often resulted in several changes being made to the content but also the design of different elements in the system, that had to be tested again. Because of these rapid changes, it was important that only a small number of participants were included in a field test. Revisions on a large scale would have been costly. A large number of changes would also have been confusing to participants.

A third phase of development was needed in ILS: a large-scale field trial in which the diaries were used by a larger number of participants over longer time periods. I was fortunate that a new Ford Foundation programme officer, Rekha Mehra, continued the ILS project funding for a three-year field trial with one NGO. The field trial provided important information on the feasibility of the ILS facilitation process in the adapting organization. Changes in the diary may be needed, not because individual picture cells fail, a fact that is usually caught in the field test, but because the data collection, analysis or sharing process is too complex or time-consuming. A field trial was needed to test and improve on the efficiency of these processes. What are the best facilitation methods? What are the gaps in information sharing and exchange? How do ILS activities mesh with other NGO programme activities? Are there conflicts? How can ILS operations be streamlined and integrated into routine programme activities in a seamless manner so that they do not appear as an added burden on programme staff?

A large field trial also provided feedback on the value added of using ILS among all participants to enhance programme outcomes. Are the learning benefits for those participants using ILS in the field trial – compared with participants not using ILS (but receiving the same level of other programme inputs) – substantial enough to justify going to scale with ILS among a census of users?

Innovations during the field-testing phase – finding and asserting the essence and core principles of ILS

As the prototype design began to work, with women maintaining their diaries over time, a concern lingered. Is this truly participatory? Even in a seemingly innovative pictorial system, am I merely shifting the burden of data collection on to poor women and still extracting information? The solution I devised was to engage women more fully for their own benefit and not take the data away from them for analysis solely by managers or researchers. I defined five ILS tasks that all levels in a programme would carry out, from poor participants to SHGs, field officers to managers. These tasks – collecting data, assessing change in data, troubleshooting outcomes, planning solutions and the documentation, sharing and reinforcement of programme values – were designed so that all participants, including illiterate women, could carry them out. In addition to the pictorial data collection formats already designed in the prototype.[23] I created pictorial problem-sorting, goal-setting and priority selection exercises for women participants.[24] I developed group diaries for SHGs and field officer diaries for sharing some data and learning upwards and engaging them in the same five activities appropriate to their level.

ILS is flexible in structure, content and processes. Each can be shaped to the needs, human-resource capacities and financial constraints of different organizations. The structure can be varied according to the programme levels using ILS diaries. Content is determined through a participatory stakeholder analysis that includes the inputs of all users. For field staff and managers, a participatory workshop of between one and three days is held using a variety of tools including small group discussions, card-storming exercises and ranking exercises. For poor participants, the process is a series of focus group discussions held in villages. A technique called the 'three faces' story is used, in which participants themselves tell the facilitator a story about what causes a difficult, fair or happy life for a woman, using pictures of a woman with sad, neutral and happy faces. This simultaneously elicits indicators from the women about what shapes life experiences and how changes might occur, while also introducing the idea of using a pictorial diary to keep a record of change over time.

ILS users can also opt to select among and enhance a set of ILS processes. Some NGOs use the system more intensively in a rich interactive process of learning between field staff and participants in which ILS modules fit together logically into a sort of pictorial rural development curriculum. Other NGOs, because of resource constraints and other priorities, have done only minimal facilitation and the participant community, on its own as individuals and in group actions, has made its own unique uses of the diary, while the NGO has used the information only selectively for advocacy efforts.

The principle of ILS, solidified in the five ILS tasks, is that participants are fully engaged in a rich learning and action process that enhances programme impact because they are analysing their situation, absorbing programme values and becoming empowered to make individual and collective development plans. If these important processes are ignored, then the participatory principles surrounding the five ILS tasks will be violated. Some observers fail to see beyond what is most visible – simple diaries in participant hands that contain pictorial development indicators – to the interactive and participatory investigation processes that yielded the indicators in the first place, and that are also essential to analysing and responding to the data results on an ongoing basis. Interested adapters who borrow an existing diary without background and training materials or without trying to understand the principles and reversed power relationships or the adaptation and testing processes involved are likely to end up with a flawed design for their programme needs that extracts information from participants while placing the burden of doing so on them.

Innovations during multi-year field trials – 'Ah-hah!' moments and mini-meltdowns

Enhancing the diaries with non-formal education learning elements

The experience of poor women participants and groups using ILS diaries in multi-year field trials led to further innovations. In one small NGO, the Handloom Weavers Development Society (HLWDS), the women began to call the ILS diary their sacred book. They successfully used it in place of a ration card or Below Poverty Line certificate, which show eligibility for subsidized grain rations, when engaging with government officials and to lobby for development services. They were inspired by the domestic violence indicator to talk about and then act upon this sensitive issue with striking results (Noponen, 2001). They asked that an indicator on sexual harassment in the workplace be added to the diary design. They saved five people from suicide due to violence or sexual abuse by using the diary in their collective action on these issues. Women also spoke of individual plans to improve children's education, to improve shelter conditions and to reduce social spending. Women told how they use the diary daily to reflect on their day and their life in general: 'like you women have your *Femina* [Indian women's magazine] we have this book' (Noponen, 2001: 51).

My fear was that this galvanizing effect of keeping a diary might get old fairly fast, so I began to enrich ILS diaries with learning elements from non-formal education to enhance the reflection and motivation functions. I added elements such as six panel stories and bad/good scenes,[25] dream scenes and panoramas, illustrated folk tales and cautionary cartoons. After initially being intrigued by the use of the diary to leverage government services, as an economic development planner I thought that improvement was possible. I developed a pictorial planning format[26] so that women could first act to solve their problems on their own before approaching development officials for grants and subsidies. My work with Professional Assistance for Development Action (PRADAN) to develop and field-test an adaptation of ILS to their SHG microfinance and livelihoods programme also helped to sensitize me to the fact that the ILS diary should also be a tool for building capacities for the independent functioning of women and groups, as well as a way to lobby for a fair share in resources, services and targeted grants. Women can now show development officials what steps they have taken on their own over time to solve their problems as they ask for assistance. Of course some needs are beyond the scope of individuals or village groups to fulfil on their own, such as safe water connections. In this case, women in Kerala successfully lobbied for water connections by organizing a procession during which they turned their ILS diaries to the page showing water conditions and held them aloft.

Towards a pictorial rural development curriculum

In the process of integrating learning elements in the existing diary layout, I realized that the content of the diary had been sequenced along the pattern of a questionnaire. Indicators were grouped by categories, with basic and non-sensitive information asked first, followed by more complex questions, and ending with sensitive questions or those requiring reflection or open-ended responses. I thought that if women were reading and reflecting on their diary entries and dreaming of a better life, then perhaps another layout sequence to enhance this motivating function could be devised. I regrouped the indicators into thematic modules and sequenced or linked them into a logical whole. The diary is named by participants ('Boat of Life', 'Reflecting Pool', 'Learning Friend', 'Community Eyes') and special scenes, pictorial ice-breakers and learning elements introduce each chapter or module.

In PRADAN's 'Boat of life' adaptation, for example, a woman first reflects on her living conditions and poverty status in a wellbeing module. She next investigates why she is at this level of material welfare by examining her financial situation in a finance module or the balance of income and expenditures, and resulting debt and savings positions. This sets the stage for improving a household's financial position and resulting standard of living through incremental improvements in the household's livelihood base. The livelihood module that follows systematically guides her through analysis of her total availabilities in forest, land, livestock and labour and enterprise activities and prompts her to make strategic use of credit and other scarce resources in improving them. The next module focuses on the enhancing effects of better gender relations and women's fuller participation in decision-making in the home and mobility in the public arena on livelihood and welfare improvement. In a concluding module the woman examines the quality of her own as well as the village group's and field officer's participation and behaviour in the development programme as enabling or hindering her progress. This linked set of modules, analysis and planning exercises, each building upon the lessons from the previous one, is akin to a pictorial rural livelihoods curriculum for very poor illiterate women and their households.

Influence of the Imp-Act programme – qualitative and quantitative tensions

The Ford Foundation programme officer, Rekha Mehra, again played a pivotal role in the evolution of ILS by connecting me with another Ford-funded project, Imp-Act. This global multi-year programme involving 29 NGO partners and technical experts at three UK universities aimed to improve the monitoring of social performance in microfinance. I attended a regional meeting of partners in India and was later invited by one of the partners to work with them to adapt ILS to their needs. Through this affiliation and sponsorship by Imp-Act I was able to attend other regional and global meetings. I received terrific feedback from interaction with Imp-Act technical advisers and NGO partners. I was influenced in two different directions. On the one hand, from those experienced in PRA, I was impressed with in-depth assessment aspects of PRA exercises, especially in analysing aspects of livelihoods, which were weak in the ILS prototype. I also learned of new PRA exercises for the household rather than at village level, such as income and expenditure trees, that fitted well with the ILS participant diary approach. On the other hand, from more quantitatively oriented technical advisers, I was challenged on questions of research design and data reliability, especially with a pictorial and participatory approach.

This pulled ILS innovations in two opposite directions: the need to incorporate more in-depth, flexible and interactive PRA-type assessment exercises going in one direction, and the need for more standardization of diary formats for data rigour and generalizable results on the other. I cast these tensions as balancing participant learning needs and programme impact assessment needs. They influenced the ILS design towards simpler and free-form designs enriched with more learning elements and good processes on the one hand, and more structured and complex formats for data clarity and generalizable results on the other.

Incorporating PRA elements

I did manage to incorporate PRA elements such as seasonal calendars, income and expenditure trees and five-scale satisfaction ratings into ILS, but in a distilled manner, using predesigned response icons and simple lines or tick-marks rather than text, numbers or symbols. The aim was to find simple ways that all participants, particularly illiterates, could carry out a PRA exercise in their own diary for learning purposes, reflect on it, use it as a basis for planning better outcomes and revisit it in order to track further changes over time.

At the same time, there was a desire to capture the results of the individual PRA exercises on a sample basis in a way that would be context-neutral, so that patterns across the population could be discerned. One of the most interesting and perhaps disturbing results of ILS data analysis was captured from the ILS version of the income and expenditure tree derived from the PRA tool kit. This showed that as women's participation in microfinance programmes increased, there were changes in the gender pattern of household income-earning. Men were withdrawing contributions to the household from their own earnings, while the expenditure burden on women increased. We were able to quantify this information easily because of the distilled set of response icons that ensured that all sampled respondents carried out the exercise in a similar and therefore comparable manner, rather than taking the more flexible approach often pursued in PRA exercises.

The trade-off in adapting PRA exercises to ILS was to accept the distillation of a rich process that in its original form was more in-depth, flexible, contextual and interactive. The hope was that facilitators would aim to use the distilled formats as the base for an enriched facilitation process with groups of participants, rather than simply focus on completing pictorial diary chapters.

Capturing reliable data

After trying to solve the data reliability problem through improved training of facilitators and research team members, I realized that a design solution was needed. The data detail that I added, however, began to complicate the diaries and threaten the participants' learning needs. I decided to separate the two functions of participant and impact learning. After all, participant learning activities were to take place on a census of participants, but impact data were needed only for a random sample of participants and an appropriate comparison group. Why complicate the learning needs of all for the data collection needs of a few? The solution I devised was for impact data from a random sample of diary users to be captured during a relaxed interview session. An investigator sits alongside a sampled respondent, reviews her diary entries and records the information in a similar page-per-page pictorial diary that is slightly more complex, and contains prompts for probing and cross checks, precise variable definitions and response codes. Because the same pictorial formats are used, however, the respondent is able to participate and understand how her information is being recorded. The interview event is not taking place across a clipboard but in a side-by side sharing of diary entries.[27]

The big meltdown – letting go of unneeded complexity

During the field trial of PRADAN's adaptation, field promoters complained that it took too much time for staff to explain to participants in which response cell under which time period to record their answers. Embedded tables in the response formats were time-consuming for participants to learn to navigate. But these same promoters, who are highly educated professional-degree graduates from premier rural management, forestry and agriculture schools, had added more detail to some of the livelihood indicators in the field-testing phase. For example, the land assets indicator was originally set at three variables, the number of plots of rainfed, irrigated and mortaged land. This increased in the field test to the number of plots of homestead, upland, midland and lowland (irrigated and rainfed) as well as plots of mortgaged-in and mortgaged-out land, encroached land and wasteland. This added complexity in format design and content and caused the diary to fail.

It failed not because poor women could not understand it or were unwilling to use it, but because field promoters could not sustain the facilitation activity over time along with their other programme tasks. They were left with a bitter taste from ILS as a result of trying to implement it in even a small number of groups (see Narendranath, this volume). Some promoters eventually admitted that although they might like to see this level of detail when contemplating livelihood options for a single household in the abstract, in everyday use promoting livelihoods among hundreds of households was too much. This underscores the danger of NGOs seeing existing diary examples and wanting to adapt them for their own use without considering the entire research process and learning needs of the programme and its participants.

Recovery – an organization's core values provide a second chance

It would be ironic for ILS to work in relatively unsophisticated NGOs with few participatory values, and fail in high-quality NGOs that value promoting the capacities of the poor over delivering services or giving subsidies. A complete overhaul of the PRADAN diary design was needed and PRADAN leaders at the top and even some field staff were willing to give it a second chance. Having separated the data capture function from the participant learning function, as described above, it was possible to once again make the diary format much simpler. In addition to paring down the number of indicators, I removed the recording spaces for the baseline time period and yearly time periods. Instead, participants record baseline data in red pencil and they mark changes over time as and when they occur in regular lead pencil. Progress achieved since the baseline period can be assessed at any point in time over a multi-year period by comparing lead-pencil markings with red baseline markings.

I also removed complex embedded tables and women can now simply draw connecting lines to note their selection from a multiple list or to connect production activities to seasonal icons. Other embedded tables were redesigned even when this meant losing pictorial bar charts and time lines. For example, in an exercise on problem-sorting, women were not interested in building bar charts by stacking icons under pictures of happy, neutral and sad faces. Instead they preferred a more free-form design where they drew lines from the scattered icons into cloth bundles with happy, neutral and sad faces pictured on them. It is the same information but without the analytical structure – tables, matrices, bar charts, time trend lines – that as an academic researcher I first envisioned.

Instead of ILS activities being an add-on task for field promoters, PRADAN has taken steps to fully integrate ILS activities into routine SHG promotion activities so that it makes them more efficient and less time-consuming. ILS learning elements and exercises are now contained in a SHG promotion manual and tool kit of over 150 tools in 20 categories (with most being participatory and pictorial) that I helped to create with PRADAN. ILS will only be implemented with newly formed groups rather than with existing groups. Existing groups experiencing problems can be selectively targeted with individual ILS modules on a need basis. If older groups desire to use ILS diaries, peer-to-peer women facilitators can assist them (see Narendranath, this volume).

Conclusions: the spread of ILS

ILS as a method has not spread much to other NGOs beyond my direct involvement either as a donor grantee, paid consultant or volunteer. Part of the explanation for this was a conscious decision on the part of the initial funder not to share information on ILS (nor allow me to do so) until it had been fully tested and many of the problems worked out. The funder was concerned that if prematurely disseminated with major flaws the method would not only get a bad reputation but also unnecessarily burden NGOs and even harm participants.[28]

Because of the pictorial aspect that seemed to promise an easy and accessible alternative to more complex standard impact assessment methods, there was intense interest in ILS right from the beginning. In reviewing the highlights of ILS's evolution, one can see that earlier versions were indeed flawed, either too simple or over-complex. At certain stages the diary design was boring, akin to administrative records involving participants mostly in data collection tasks. It is unlikely that these versions would have been sustainable over time. These mistakes were quickly fixed and other NGOs were potentially spared the headaches and expense of failure, redesign and retraining.

I am aware of one or two attempts at ILS adaptation by NGOs in South Asia arising from borrowing copies of early flawed diaries. Each has resulted in failure. In one case, the diaries, besides using poor picture technology, have excessive indicators and time periods, with a problematic recording system and complex embedded tables. Women had to be guided by field staff where to mark each time for each indicator, and there was a dearth of learning elements. I was later hired to revamp that diary adaptation. The women were still fond of the original diary no matter how flawed, which shows the power of putting pencils in their hands. In comparing the old with the new they remarked, 'We can mark our old diary, but this one we can mark but also read.' In another case, the NGO had successful pictures and recording system but no data analysis plan. The data that have been collected have not been analysed by managers in any meaningful way. Furthermore, participants themselves are not engaged fully in the five tasks and with the lack of other enriched learning elements one wonders what they gain by continuing to keep the diaries. Unfortunately, this same NGO is rapidly spreading their adaptation to other small NGOs.

I am particularly grateful not only to not be responsible for these and other potential failures, but also to have been able to fail and recover myself in the creation of ILS outside the glare and scrutiny of the development spotlight. In that sense my funder protected me, others and ILS itself. The other side of the argument, of course, is who knows what positive directions ILS might have taken by now had others been involved earlier? It is clear that the networking with Imp-Act technical experts and global partners had a positive effect in the development of ILS midway through its evolution. It would have been beneficial if this interaction could have been built into the development grant at an earlier stage through planned feedback sessions with participatory experts and quantitative researchers It is interesting to note that the initial partners for ILS were chosen by the funder and several were not very interested in the idea of impact assessment at the time and their involvement in the project was quite passive, devoting few institutional resources such as staff to the effort despite accepting funding to do so. This occurred while other, more enthusiastic NGOs were being kept at bay. A better approach might have been to ask for letters of intent and select partners that demonstrated a true commitment and willingness to devote resources and time to the effort.

Throughout the process of developing ILS there has been a conscious effort to assert the core values and principles of ILS. The idea of using picture scenes of development indicators came rather early in the ILS prototype design. ILS, however, is not just about the pictures. It took successive diary refinements to codify the principles of ILS in the five ILS tasks: that the system be really participatory, with participants engaged not only in supplying information or collecting data, but fully involved in the use of the data and their ownership. Poor participants truly are the first users of ILS data. They not only collect information on themselves or their groups but they have input into determining what is to be collected. They are the first to assess the direction of change over time, to reflect on the causes for the change and to feed back their learning. They are also the first to attempt to revise their strategies, as a result perhaps setting new goals or priorities or attempting new plan steps or different uses of programme resources. They hold the document or record in their own hands. It is a record of their changing situation as they participate in the development programme and a reflection back to them of a poor woman's life in a comprehensive view. Because it is also enriched with development messages and motivation and action tools it also shows them the possibilities for positive change. In the words of one participant, 'We see the paths in the diary and we have to make a choice – the good path.'

CHAPTER 5

Steering the boat of life with the Internal Learning System: the oar of learning

D. Narendranath

Paro, a fragile looking migrant labourer in her twenties, sits in the corner a little away from the other SHG[29] members and peers intently at the picture on the page opened out in front of her. The book is the ILS workbook, and the picture is that of a man beating his wife. She is determined today to mark the picture; she is not mindful of the presence of even her mother-in-law who is also a group member, sitting in the other corner. Paro, otherwise usually quiet and not given to extreme emotions, has a stern expression on her face today as she circles the picture. It is only when one observes that she has circled the picture not once, but five times, does one realize how serious a victim is she of this abuse, and yet never ever raised a voice about it till the ILS came along...

A Cluster[30] meeting in Chhattisgarh State, Central India: 54 representatives from 18 SHGs have assembled. The meeting is facilitated by an NGO staff member using an ILS workbook. The Cluster leaders assess their own individual SHGs using the ILS pictorial indicators. One of the issues they identify is that the SHG leadership is not rotating and so other members in the SHGs are not getting the opportunity to take up leadership roles. The discussion is animated. At the next monthly meeting, most of the SHGs have changed their Cluster representatives.

These two examples show how ILS workbooks are bringing about fundamental changes in the way rural poor women are learning about themselves, and are making shifts in the way they think, reflect and act. Issues that were swept aside or ignored before are now getting urgent attention. One woman whose group had used an ILS workbook said: 'Hamari zindagi ka sab kuchh is mein likha hai.' [This book has everything about our life.]

This chapter describes the efforts of Professional Assistance for Development Action (PRADAN), an Indian NGO, to adapt the ILS to its needs. ILS is a system aimed primarily at helping microfinance group members to reflect and learn about various aspects of their lives and livelihoods, and also helping NGOs managing microfinance programmes to measure and report social performance. The first section gives an overview of the organization, looking at PRADAN's philosophy and mission, and its approaches to livelihood promotion, which revolve around SHGs. The discussion moves on to PRADAN's discovery of ILS and its adaptation to its needs in terms of member and group learning and impact assessment. The second section describes the different workbooks used in ILS. The third section narrates the experiences of the field officers who worked with ILS, and whose feedback was the basis of adapting ILS. The final sections describe the plans that PRADAN has for scaling up ILS to the whole of the organization, and some issues and concerns connected with this.

PRADAN: a mission to promote livelihoods

PRADAN has been working towards the generation of sustainable livelihoods for the rural poor in India for the past 22 years. Its approach is to build on people's own resources and capabilities with a view to enabling them, rather than delivering services. PRADAN's livelihood projects therefore use participatory approaches extensively. Community ownership and working with women have been major guiding principles in all PRADAN's interventions.

PRADAN works in Bihar, Chhattisgarh, Jharkhand, Madhya Pradesh, Orissa, Rajasthan and West Bengal, some of the poorest regions in India, where the majority of the population lives below the national poverty line.[31] PRADAN works with about 90,000 rural poor families in the areas of microfinance, natural resource management, livestock rearing and micro-enterprises.

The promotion of women's SHGs is an important step in PRADAN's approach to enabling communities. Staff who facilitate group formation also provide training and other inputs as required to strengthen institutional values, norms and systems. Once a SHG has become mature and self-reliant, it is supported to link up with commercial banks to access mainstream finance. Simultaneously, inputs are also provided to help each individual member develop a vision for her own livelihood, and the resolve to realize the vision with group support. SHGs bring women together and reinforce the value of mutual help, and are a medium for PRADAN's goal, the empowerment of women.

There are equity and efficiency reasons for focusing on women. PRADAN's experience, like that of many others, shows that women are much better money managers and more conscientious about loan repayments than men. Women have shown more responsibility than men in utilizing loans and spending money equitably across family members, as well as influencing other group members to repay. Moreover, women's groups have displayed more discipline compared with men's groups in the same villages. They are regularly available in the village, so that it is possible to initiate institution-building processes around them that require steady and long-term commitment.

On equity grounds, targeting women is an affirmative action, favouring them as the more disadvantaged among an already disadvantaged group. They usually own no assets, are not part of any important decision-making processes either in the family or outside, and sometimes hold quite a poor view of their own capacity to achieve. They are often isolated in their homes, which limits their ability to access information and resources and to participate in social or political activities. Since it is difficult to reach them, welfare and development programmes run by government and even NGOs often exclude them.

PRADAN's approach is that women are as capable as men of being actors in the development process, but given their situation, special efforts need to be made to reach out to and include them. The SHGs are a platform to systematically reach women of a community: group membership allows them to be central in the planning and implementation of microfinance and livelihood programmes. As the SHGs mature, the women also start establishing linkages with a number of external institutions, which in turn help to widen their horizons. Using the strength of the collective, they are able to have an influence in a wider arena. The most important changes happen at a personal level when the women start to view themselves as respectable individuals and feel that they can be instrumental in bringing about changes in their own as well as others' lives.

Working with women in SHGs is not guaranteed to reach the poorest. Women belonging to very poor communities who are isolated or excluded on ground of race (tribal communities) or caste (*dalit* communities) are often understandably obsessed with the troubles and travails of the present, bordering on a state of hopelessness and resignation. This is caused and compounded by material deprivation and oppressive social customs, and means that women are unable to respond fully to development initiatives. Overcoming despair and beginning to see rays of hope has to happen before a process of change begins.

PRADAN's approach for doing this generally goes through the following stages.

- Organizing into a group where discussion time is used for helping the SHG member reflect about herself and her current situation.
- Helping her analyse her situation with respect to her peer group.
- Encouraging her to generate a vision for a better life and future for herself and her family.
- Helping her concretize the goal in terms of specific outputs, time frames, help needed.
- Encouraging the group to assure support to her, monitor her progress and keep up her motivation.

PRADAN field officers had already been experimenting with pictorial tools in the SHGs, as part of 'visioning exercises' used in a variety of training programmes. These exercises formed part of the steps above, and illustrate that PRADAN had already begun to develop its own participatory learning systems before it had the opportunity to take up and adapt ILS.

Discovering ILS: from impact assessment to learning for empowerment

Between 2001 and 2004, PRADAN participated in the Imp-Act[32] project, which provided a useful opportunity to search for and adapt participatory learning systems that were being practised in different organizations and contexts. Imp-Act aimed to enable microfinance organizations all over the world to develop appropriate social-performance monitoring systems. The relationship with Imp-Act triggered PRADAN's search for an appropriate participatory methodology (PM) to implement monitoring systems which would provide the information needed at the same time as build on existing systems for participant learning at the SHG level.

With the help of Linda Mayoux, experienced in the field of participatory learning systems, PRADAN scanned the environment for an appropriate system that could be adopted and adapted to its own needs. She brought different practitioners together in September 2000 in Delhi for a conference entitled 'Participatory learning systems for women's empowerment'. At this conference, practitioners of different tools and methodologies made presentations, and sought comments from the invited participants who ranged from practitioners to researchers to donors. Participants were facilitated to compare and contrast the methodologies from the point of view of women's empowerment.

This experience helped PRADAN tremendously in the search for an appropriate participatory learning system for impact assessment. The presentation on ILS was done by Helzi Noponen, the original developer of ILS, herself. For ILS, which PRADAN had used before, the seminar helped in getting an update on the system and comparing it with other methodologies before adopting it. ILS found acceptance with PRADAN because the concept of internal learning, which is its foundation and which is also at the core of PRADAN's enabling approach. Enabling happens when the clients assess their own situation, analyse causes for change or lack of change, and plan future actions by themselves, seeking help where required. ILS operated around these basic tasks, but needed adaptation to suit the specific needs of PRADAN. The visioning exercises that PRADAN already used could, for example, be built upon in order to use the pictorial formats of ILS.

The value of ILS for PRADAN was in its objective of initiating and sustaining a process of change deep within the mind of the SHG member; helping her to dream and take steps to attain her visions. Thus, even though ILS came to PRADAN in the context of impact assessment, the value was more in learning. Thus ILS would become an intervention in itself, and not only a methodology for impact assessment. ILS in that sense proved to be an adaptable methodology, from learning and empowerment, to group facilitation, livelihood planning and impact assessment.

The ILS workbooks: engaging at different levels

The essence of ILS is that it puts the learning process in the hands of the SHG member. The broader vision and goals for the future are first articulated by using exercises and dream scenes. Once the woman has articulated a vision, further modules on well-being, mobility, empowerment, livelihoods and so on help concretize the vision by building up the different components. At the end of each of the submodules there are specific output targets and time frames, and help is sought. The group also plays the role of monitoring and support on an ongoing basis. Each of the modules has dream scenes, good scene–bad scene combinations, stories, folk tales, modules to map the current situation and planning modules. Since all these modules are part of the same story, which is of her life, they interconnect for her.

Experience quickly showed that when using the pictorial mode in place of facilitated discussions, the women would become reflective and often lead the discussions. Use of pictures gave women the space and opportunity to legitimately speak about a whole range of issues they never spoke about in the normal course of things; there was no saying what the effect of any picture would be. The pictures sparked thought processes that would otherwise not have occurred.

ILS essentially consists of three workbooks with an assortment of indicators relevant to the respective levels: the member workbooks to be used by the individual members; the group workbooks to be used by the group as a unit; and the staff workbooks for the field officers. The following gives a brief narration of the different workbooks, the indicators and also the adaptations made in them to further the learning and empowerment agenda.

Individual member diaries

The ILS member workbooks have been designed around broad topics which help the member reflect on different aspects of her life with the assistance of pictures created around indicators crucial to her. While the set of broad topics have remained the same, the way that the modules are used has undergone considerable adaptation since the time they were introduced.

ILS as it was originally introduced to PRADAN was designed to require the individual member to make markings in her diary, which would be collated upwards at the group and staff levels, for impact assessment. This required the use of techniques such as tally-marks, counts and embedded tables that were quite complicated for women to comprehend easily. This meant that the staff members trying to introduce ILS in the groups needed to spend a lot of time in training the women to use it, even before the process of reflection and learning could be initiated, time that staff members often did not have. An impact assessment focus also led us to over-designing the indicators which resulted in complex tables.

During the field test these issues became more evident. The field officers as well as the women found the modules quite heavy to administer. The embedded tables and counts took an enormous amount of time, and made the whole exercise a burden rather than a constructive and creative exercise. The field officers wanted modules that were simpler and easier to train, learn and use, that would facilitate reflective learning in the groups. Data collection for impact assessment was not an important objective for them. Thus in the subsequent versions the modules were simplified to lessen the data entry load and facilitate more reflection. An example of the kind of changes made is illustrated below. The old version of the land utilization table is a complex embedded table. If filled up it

Land Utilization Table (only part of the table table shown)																									
Put a √ in the appropriate place																									
	Fallow				Grains				Pulses				Oil seeds				Vegetables				Fruits				
Annual	0	1	2	3	0	1	2	3	0	1	2	3	0	1	2	3	0	1	2	3	0	1	2	3	
 Winter — Nov																									
Winter — Dec																									
Winter — Jan																									
Winter — Feb																									
 Spring — Mar																									
Spring — Apr																									
 Summer — May																									
Summer — Jun																									
 Rains — Jul																									
Rains — Aug																									
Rains — Sept																									
Rains — Oct																									

Figure 5.1 Land utilization table.

could have given quite useful information about the land utilization pattern of the SHG member's family in the previous year.

The revised version does not give such accurate information, but is a more useful tool to enable the SHG members to think of the overall pattern of cultivation in the previous year.

The modules which had no complicated tables, and helped to reflect, found favour with both SHG members and field officers. The field officers also found

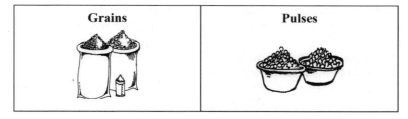

Figure 5.2 Revised land utilization tool – selected images.

that not only was it easier to work with such modules, but also more exciting, because these modules allowed open reflection rather than getting locked into specific numbers. Simplifications like these were eventually made in several areas, with less attention to complicated details and numbers.

The realization was that when dealing with clients who are not accustomed to thinking creatively about their resources, the effort should be to get them to revisit their attitudes towards themselves and their resources rather than get into technical details such as what seed will be used or how much area will be cultivated. Once the women were able to sort themselves out on the basics, the detailed planning for specific resources would be easier. It was more important to create in them a positive attitude towards life; detailed planning would be taken up subsequently.

This realization formed the basis of the amendments that we made to the individual member diaries. Many of the complex tables and complicated questions were replaced with modules of a reflective nature. We introduced components such as good scene–bad scene pairs, open-ended stories and dream scenes that would help to generate discussions in groups. The idea was also to enhance the learning value, reduce data collection and wherever possible make it fun.

The box below reproduces a picture from the ILS member diary called 'Gender benders'. This is an example of how an attempt was made to pass on a serious message in a light manner.

Box 5.1: Gender benders: a member diary page on gender relations

The picture tries to depict very non-traditional roles for male and female members of a family in South Asia. The details show male members serving food, cleaning, and doing *purdah*. The females are shown sitting as equal with men, climbing trees, riding

bicycles and, most important, ploughing. This is partly to generate laughter but at the same time it also tries to tell the women that there is nothing sacrosanct about these roles. This picture causes reactions ranging from staunch denial that this can happen to many members agreeing to the argument that gender roles need not necessarily be fixed.

The feedback from the changed version of the modules was positive and encouraging. The current set of individual member workbooks have the following revised modules.

- In the **well-being** module, a woman reflects on her current standard of living, in terms of living conditions, assets, poverty status and health.
- In the **finances** module, she examines how her living standards are affected by her household's pattern of income and expenditure, and its resulting savings and debt situations.
- The **livelihood** module guides a critical assessment of the member's livelihood system, in order to maximize the use of their total available forest, land, livestock, credit and labour resources.
- In the **empowerment** module, the woman examines her treatment and status in the home and wider community, either as a liberating or an inhibiting influence on her reproductive and productive roles.
- In the **programme participation** module, the woman reflects on the respective roles that she, her SHG and the PRADAN promoter play in helping her achieve her goals.

The livelihood module is particularly important in helping the SHG member with future planning, and is an adaptation of ILS unique to PRADAN. Having critically evaluated her resources, as outlined above, she then makes a plan for optimizing resources. She then shares this plan in the SHG, which helps her to sharpen it and mobilize financial resources to support the activities in the plan. The facilitation of the livelihood modules is done in the group, although the plan is made at the individual level. The purpose of this is for the member to draw support from the other members wherever required, in understanding issues, thinking through solutions, planning and implementation. The process allows the individual member to carry out quite a lot of thinking on her own before turning to the group or the facilitator, so the ideas in the plan are rooted in the individual, rather than imposed. The following incident is quite illustrative.

In one case, a PRADAN field officer was invited by an SHG to come and help them out in livelihood planning. He went prepared to plan a group dairy activity with the women, because after discussion with a few members he had the impression that they were all interested in taking up dairying. For a change he thought of using the ILS livelihood workbook, using the livestock module to initiate the discussion. After the livestock module was completed it became clear that only a couple of vocal members of the group actually wanted to do dairying, while the majority actually wanted to do goat-rearing, an activity that requires less capital investment and recurring expenses, and was more popular with poorer group members. In this case the ILS diaries helped the silent members of the group to articulate their priorities more clearly.

Group diaries

In the earlier versions of ILS, the group diary was conceived as a book to collate the numbers from the individual diaries. We found during trials that this is a process that takes a lot of time and also did not add much value for the members or the group. For the members it did not matter much what the total number of assets were with the members of the SHG, or the group's average number of children. These were numbers that mattered more to an external researcher. So we decided that if we were to collate these types of numbers, it would be done though a separate exercise, but not through the medium of the group diary.

We wanted the group diary to be a mechanism that would help the group as an entity, to build the collective spirit and reinforce group values, systems and norms. In PRADAN's scheme of things the group is a forum that provides support for the members to set their achievement goals and realize them, as well as being a morale and confidence booster for individual members in their pursuit of a better life. The fact that the group may also provide individuals with some of the financial resources to pursue their dreams amplifies its value.

Therefore in the group diary we incorporated modules that looked at the group's health at different stages of its growth and evolution. As the group diary has evolved it is a tool for the promoter to initiate the group, help set norms and systems and help the group monitor its progress over a period of time.

The group diary deals with the various parameters of interest to the group as a whole, and the members fill it in together during their meetings. The members assess whether they are functioning well together as a group, whether they are following the various norms, systems and disciplines, and whether they are adhering to the values of the group. The group also assesses its capacity as a financial intermediary and a vehicle to influence external agencies such as government departments.

An example from a village in Jharkhand shows how the group workbook can influence group function. In one particular group, there were a few members who were poorer than the rest, who were not being treated well by the rest of the group members. During the ILS group diary session, they talked about SHG values such as equality of opportunity and equal access to resources. This gave these members a voice to talk about the unequal treatment they were receiving in the SHG, and they decided to move out of the present SHG and form another one of their own, comprising women as poor as themselves, something they had not thought about doing in the two years they had been part of the first group.

Beyond examples like the group in Jharkhand, an important indicator of empowerment is when women start showing interest in issues that affect them outside their homes, in the village. The ILS group diaries have a set of indicators in which the SHG members assess the quality of public services that they receive, such as schooling for children, health care, the supply of other amenities and development programmes. They also make plans to address any issues that they may have with public service providers. The inclusion of these indicators in ILS is another way of catalysing the women to begin to think about wider issues, and gradually ensure their participation in arenas beyond the household.

How did ILS work in villages?

In the locations where ILS was field-tested, it received very exciting responses at the community level. The medium of the pictorial workbooks allowed teams to ensure the active participation of all the SHG members. It helped the members to be more reflective and internalize the inputs provided much more effectively, compared with the earlier mode of verbal interactions. The livelihood modules in the ILS workbooks gave the women a broad perspective on making livelihood choices. The other modules, such as those on health and gender empowerment, generated lively discussions in the SHGs.

The field officers also found the ILS modules very useful as a group facilitation tool. Group facilitation skills varied from person to person, but ILS helped to standardize facilitation processes considerably. Once the pictorials are introduced, the women are often inspired to talk, rich discussions are generated, and women often follow up discussions with concrete action. This is unlike earlier times, when the ownership of key issues stayed with PRADAN staff, and it was necessary to conduct follow-up to ensure some action was generated; now, the level of women's ownership of the issues and decisions is also much higher than previously.

Another important benefit brought about by ILS is that it was now possible to generate discussions of a wide variety of sensitive issues which officers had previously found difficult to raise. This applied most notably to gender, especially violent behaviour by a husband, and women's reproductive health and family planning.

An immediate effect of the experience of using the pictorial methodology is that the officers are branching out and devising their own pictorial modules to address specific needs. Two such examples already in practice are the modules prepared for streamlining paddy cultivation in West Bengal, and for improving dairy farming practices in Rajasthan. Drawing on these experiences, the plan is now to design ILS workbooks for individual livelihood activities. They would not only include improved practices, but would also provide space for each woman to take a critical look at the activity in the context of her resources, monitor the activity across a season, make concurrent changes and at the end of it, track the income generated from the activity and monitor the use of that income.

As noted above, because of difficulties with complicated tables and numbers, it was decided to delink data-gathering for impact assessment from group reflection and learning. During the time when the diaries are filled out in SHG meetings, the focus is on the group's reflection and learning. But it is also possible to build impact assessment from this process. Separately, the facilitator of the impact assessment can sit one by one with a panel of randomly sampled SHG members and fill out a semi-structured questionnaire, using the completed diaries and conversation with the group member to collect data.

Despite successes, there are also concerns that remain. PRADAN is primarily a livelihood promotion organization. In such a scenario, the officers are exceedingly focused on the issues related to implementing livelihood projects, and many a time there is a tendency to be narrowly focused purely on the income enhancement of clients' families. The finer concerns of building capabilities, bringing about impacts on the broader well-being of the women involved and setting up sustainable systems are sometimes sidelined. PRADAN's mission does mandate PRADAN to look at the broader well-being of the families rather than just incomes. At least in the short run there was a choice to be made: whether to pursue the empowerment approach and fall behind on income enhancement targets, or just push for targets. It was indeed a difficult choice to make. Given these factors, it is not surprising that there was initial resistance to the idea of introducing ILS.

ILS is a process-intensive tool, taking a lot of facilitation time in SHG meetings. The system does not reduce time commitments in the field. Some field officers, who had hoped that ILS would be a time-saving device, were disappointed with the tool, especially through the initial stages which were particularly time-intensive. Experience from one project site also does suggest that ILS could be time-saving as well; but after the SHG members have used the diaries for a continued period of time, say about three or four months. Since the pictorial methodology reduces most of the facilitation work, even local village SHG leaders are able to use them and generate discussions in the SHG. To that extent the involvement of the field officer is reduced. But the initial investment of time is still a challenge.

Many a time the members would come back for the next meeting, not having looked at what they did the previous week, and many would not remember what had done. So in the next meeting quite a lot of time would be spent revising the earlier module. For some of the officers, this was a frustrating experience. These experiences, compounded by the fact that they were quite busy, led to a situation where many of the field officers were on the verge of rejecting ILS.

On the other side, many officers who had been personally interested in the idea followed up the system earnestly. Their observation was also that even if ILS does not reduce time commitments, it helps the professional use time more effectively in providing structured inputs to members based on a comprehensive curriculum designed around the lives and livelihoods of those members. Those who have been using ILS regularly do state that over a period of time that their facilitation skills develop, and that it takes less and less time.

Keeping in mind these time challenges, it was decided that ILS should be integrated seamlessly with the day-to-day operations of the staff, so that neither staff nor clients would feel any additional pressure from its use. The advantage of this integration would be that the time pressure would not be felt. The officers routinely spend time in the groups for training, planning and supervising implementation. Many of these tasks can be effectively done through ILS. To facilitate this process, we have produced a group promotion manual that integrates the ILS pages at the various stages of group promotion. The ILS pages get filled out with no extra time or effort. In the initial stages the ILS pages are pictorial training modules and later they become more and more reflective as the issues move from simple to complex.

But there is a word of caution here. Adequate time has to go into educating the staff on the processes that go along with the pictorial workbooks. Pictures are not the be all and end all. Pictures have to be accompanied by sensitive facilitation, keen and patient listening, and effective debriefing. Uncomfortable moments are not to be sidestepped or glossed over, but confronted in order to enhance the learning value. In short, it means that the field officer on the spot should be able to for the moment set aside his/her agendas and focus attention on the agenda generated by the members, which may not be purely about income generation. It is not the matter of just additional time required but a matter of a readying oneself to be guided by the agenda generated by the group that may be concerned with much broader issues than what one is pursuing. That is a commitment that the facilitator has to make even while introducing the tool. ILS thus presupposes that we are ready to listen to what the community wants to say and are willing to be flexible in the time taken and in our approach.

Conclusions: scaling up ILS?

Scaling up ILS to more SHGs, in the same field location and to more locations, is an issue that we are concerned with now. Since there were a number of positive experiences of the ILS diaries enabling intense reflection and learning, it was felt that this aspect of ILS could be spread to all the PRADAN locations.

Nevertheless, similar to the Participatory Rural Appraisal(PRA) tools that assume a certain amount of facilitation skills and process sensitivity on the part of the practitioner, there are certain minimal preconditions that must be satisfied for ILS to be implemented more widely in the field. ILS assumes that there is an organized group activity going on in the field that is housing ILS. Unlike PRA, ILS is not a one-off activity, but an ongoing process. It is by design not an extractive process, so there has to be a group existing in the setting where it is being done, so that the learning that is generated can be captured and any necessary action can be initiated.

Scaling up ILS must therefore be preceded by group formation. So if there are programmes or processes that do not have a component of forming and sustaining groups, ILS may not be very effective. As a corollary it might be correct to say that those community development programmes that have group formation as a basic approach could use ILS as a tool to assist them in group promotion and strengthening, facilitating member learning, and enabling group action and empowerment. The caution here is that the organizers may need to be prepared to allow the process to move beyond their initial mandate or goals, or the goals for which they are funded. So additional time requirement, at least in the initial introductory stage, the orientation of the field staff and their need for facilitation skills would need to be factored into the planning.

One of the steps that PRADAN has taken to increase the outreach of ILS is to develop a standard operating procedure for group promotion integrated with

ILS. After this was introduced, ILS spread to about 300 new groups in two states, Chhattisgarh and West Bengal. At present the teams are using the group workbooks, and plan to gradually shift to the member workbooks.

Another initiative that is being used to facilitate cross-learning is supporting SHG members to teach each other. Using the pictorial methodology, it becomes easy for women who have already done ILS to train other new members. Seeing promise in this approach, now we are in the process of identifying SHG leaders who can be put through more systematic training on ILS so that they can be used as extension agents.

An important principle in scaling up is to ensure that the system should be able to run without any sophisticated inputs, such as, in this case, the time of the PRADAN field officer. We are discovering that ILS has a lot of potential to draw on women's own wisdom. But we will have to wait and see whether it can evolve to a level where the SHG members themselves will be able to carry forward the ILS processes. Scaling up ILS demands constant review of the tool and trimming down if necessary; intense training and orientation of staff and the SHG women; demystification of the facilitation process; and involving group leaders in the process. ILS is an extremely powerful tool, but requires long-term commitment from the organization using it.

ILS has the potential to become self-spreading, which would require the creation of a critical mass of practitioners. But these are early days. Currently more deliberate and systematic efforts are required to take ILS to more locations and programmes, and create ILS around a variety of themes. Donors and NGOs who profess to the agenda of women's learning and empowerment should make efforts to adopt ILS into their programmes. What ILS needs now are champions who will spread the word. Over a period of time and reasonably large-scale usage the tool will get distilled and the core design principles will become clearer. There are a number of questions that still need answers. How do we deal with the need for aggregation for impact assessment? Is the methodology that PRADAN has adopted, that of having a separate system for impact assessment, the most appropriate? Does ILS require more facilitation or less facilitation? What are the themes for which ILS would be most suitable? How does the interest of the women in using the ILS workbooks sustained over a long period of time? Who meets the cost of printing the books on a large scale? PRADAN's experience does throw light on many of these issues, but it will take continued use over a longer period for the solutions to become clearer.

What is required is to have faith in the basic principle that the poor women have the agency to determine their own path. They have the right to set their life goals and strive to achieve them. ILS is a tool that has enormous potential to manifest this agency and build on the women's internal resources and capabilities. If these key tenets are adhered to while different agencies and people work on ILS, it can emerge as a very powerful instrument for women's learning and empowerment.

CHAPTER 6
Evolution of the Internal Learning System: a case study of the New Entity for Social Action

Sundaram Nagasundari

This chapter discusses the experience of a network of Indian NGOs, the New Entity for Social Action (NESA), in adapting ILS, a participatory methodology (PM) which combines programme evaluation and participant learning functions through the use of pictorial participant diaries at different levels. Since 1998, NESA has been participant in and practising various evolutions and innovations of the methodology. ILS has been used in NESA's work with *dalit* and *adivasi* women and children, in natural resources management, microcredit and HIV/AIDS.

The chapter first discusses the evolution of ILS within NESA, looking at how it was adapted to meet NESA's objectives for the empowerment of marginalized communities. It goes on to discuss the impact of ILS among the communities that NESA works with, before reflecting on some of the key issues that emerged in the process of evolving the methodology to meet different objectives.

NESA works to secure life with dignity among *dalits*, *adivasis* and other vulnerable communities in the three southern states of India, Tamilnadu, Karnataka and Kerala. It is a unique network of 40 constituent members comprising individual organizations, networks and community-based organizations (CBOs). The constituents of NESA are united by certain non-negotiables based on the rights of marginalized groups to secure life with dignity. It also upholds the values of transparency, accountability and inclusiveness in decision-making. NESA partners share their expertise through training and sensitization, and lobby for policy changes. Incorporating participatory methods to facilitate and support programme planning and implementation has been a priority among NESA partners.

I was appointed as a trainee to work on the introduction of ILS to NESA, in partnership with Helzi Noponen, who developed the methodology (see Chapter 4, this volume). My work also formed part of my postgraduate studies, which focused on the potential of ILS as a monitoring and evaluation tool. Subsequently I was promoted as programme officer for ILS and was provided with support to develop the tool within NESA. My role in ILS implementation is orienting NGO leaders and senior field officers, supporting NGOs to develop impact assessment indicators, developing *sangam*[33] and organization-level diaries, field-testing indicators and supporting NGOs in the implementation and consolidation of organization diaries.

Evolution of ILS in NESA

ILS is a participatory impact assessment and planning system developed to analyse the impact of microfinance and livelihood programmes by community members using pictorial diaries. These diaries give comprehensive pictorial representations of a range of indicators symbolizing the life and situation of the community. Through participating in ILS, community members develop a greater awareness of their own context, depict various possibilities for creative action, and are supported to analyse the impact of such actions. Noponen introduced this tool to one of NESA's partners for use in their microfinance and livelihood programme. Understanding its significance, NESA decided to introduce ILS to all sectors, and orientation in the methodology was given.

NESA envisioned ILS as a tool to enhance the ongoing programmes of its partners for the conscientization and empowerment of marginalized communities through participatory methods. To meet these aims, NESA partners evolved the visual diaries that had been used in different sectors during the pilot phase, so that they included indicators on a range of different human rights, including untouchability practices, child rights and gender equity.

NESA as a network also had an important use for ILS beyond community learning in the context of programme work. Working on diverse political and economic rights issues related to untouchability, atrocity, violence, access to land and common property resources (CPRs), NESA decided that it needed to capture and track social changes over time. ILS was a tool for the kind of impact assessment that NESA needed, involving the analysis of multiple variables by local communities themselves. In effect NESA envisioned that the best monitors of rights abuses would be community members themselves. ILS could provide an effective documentation of issues on which accurate information was very scarce. NESA hoped that this new knowledge would help in their advocacy and lobbying and bring about policy changes at national and international levels.

While the adaptation of ILS for a single NGO with intervention programmes in microfinance and livelihood support was a relatively simple process involving stakeholder analysis, adapting it to the needs of a network composed of very different members was much more challenging. NESA's partners have dissimilar capacities in terms of time, and human and financial resources and they also have diverse focuses. NESA adapted ILS for the human rights programme by developing rights-based indicators. These indicators were initially developed by senior staff of the NESA partner NGOs and some CBO members; then they were field-tested with the community members. Indicators were finalized by sector, with each sector convenor working with a small core group comprising the ILS coordinator, senior staff and field animators.

To build a common platform for using ILS, NESA organized orientation workshops in 2001, the first with key partners and the second with all partners. That we were able to persuade every single NGO to enter into a common programme of using ILS, and that sector leaders were able to convince sector convenors, is a pointer towards the enormous commitment and focus which existed at the most senior levels of NESA. The role played by the executive director in collectivizing this process and carrying it forward was particularly important

After the decision was taken to implement ILS among NESA partners, three phases of orientation training were conducted in 2001. These supported partner NGO chief functionaries and senior field staff to enable them to understand the conceptual and theoretical aspects of the method and to develop indicators in a practical session.

Subsequently, NESA's policy-making body[34] brainstormed exactly how ILS should be implemented. The tool is adaptable to many of the different levels at which microfinance programmes work: individual, pressure group, group, centre, cluster and federation/branch.[35] The information it generates is useful for local people, NGOs, networks and donors. NESA has both a wide coverage and limited resources. It was decided that NESA would prioritize the implementation of ILS diaries at the levels of the *sangam*, the programme (organization), the sector support team and the NESA central secretariat. This meant that all NESA partners would have both *sangam* and organization diaries. All the *sangam* information would be consolidated into the organization diary. Then the respective sector indicators from each organization would be consolidated in the sector diary, and finally the sector indicators would form NESA's indicator bank. This was the plan, but due to funding constraints NESA has only developed *sangam* and organization diaries so far.

It was also agreed that more indicators needed to be developed to represent NESA's seven key programme areas. Further training was conducted for NESA partners in each sector, which included field animators, to develop indicators for each sector. Other processes were connected to this. In the *dalit* and *adivasi* sector, for example, representatives from 12 networks comprising 175 *dalit* organizations, 63 *adivasi* organizations, and the *dalit* sector secretariat organization participated with NESA in the initial stage of developing a vast number of indicators. A smaller group then spent enormous time and energy in fine-tuning the indicators in consultation with their network and CBO members, testing and developing them through different drafting stages. As a result of this process and other similar processes in different sectors, an indicator bank of 428 indicators was developed. One important unique adaptation of ILS was the identification and agreement of three non-negotiable indicators for each sector, which would be included in every diary at the *sangam* level. This was an important turning point in the process, unique because it helped to interlink non-negotiables of different sectors together and would ensure the interlinkages

> **Box 6.1** Non-negotiable indicators in ILS by thematic area
>
> **Adivasi *sector***
>
> How many of *sangam* members have a scheduled tribe certificate?
> Are we revitalizing our *adivasi* culture?
> Do we have access to collect minor forest produce?
>
> ***Gender***
>
> Is our husband sharing household work equally with us?
> Do we treat boys and girls equally?
> How many of us have a myth that a woman should not eat nutritious food?
>
> ***Child***
>
> How many girl children are attending school until they are 18?
> How many of us give equally nutritious food to girl children?
> How many of our children enjoy a violence-free environment in the community?
>
> ***Natural resource management***
>
> Do we recognize ground water as common property?
> Do the landless have a share in fishing rights in common water?
> How many months does our own production last for consumption?

within the sectors. The non-negotiable indicators for each sector are shown in Box 6.1.[36]

The picture in Figure 6.1 illustrates one of the non-negotiable indicators chosen for natural resource management, in this case access to fishing rights in common waters such as village ponds or lakes.

To measure conditions in relation to this indicator, a five-level scale is used reflecting the landless *dalits'* right to a share of this resource. The five levels are full share, half share, no share, share unknown and resource unavailable. Here full share means the *dalits* are getting a full share of fishing rights in common water; a half share means that at certain times they are allowed to fish in common water, depending upon the landlord's permission; no share means they are not allowed to take fish at any time; share unknown means the landless *dalits* do not know that they have a right to share in fishing in common water; and resource unavailable means that there is no common pond or lake in their village. These five scales are represented in the ILS diary template, allowing *sangam* members to put a tick-mark in the appropriate column. In this way, community members gain awareness about their rights to access CPRs.

Depending upon the issue and how it is best measured, each indicator will have a different scale, including yes/no, count, frequency, five-point scale and

Figure 6.1 Share in fishing rights over common water.

10-point scale for internal assessment of *sangam* functioning. The process of the indicator development exercise itself is significant, because indicators are the mirror or pictorial representation of day-to-day issues, and hence they need to be specific and accurate in capturing real concerns, and to have the potential for awakening the consciousness of communities about their existing situation. This required a high level of clarity and sensitivity about the issues concerned.

The next stage of the adaptation process was field-testing in a trial with different networks and organizations. The field test took place with a small, random sample of *sangams* to find out whether the community members understood the pictures, whether any further indicators were needed, whether existing indicators needed modification or deletion according to local contexts, and the time taken to complete the *sangam* diary.

After the field test, the diary was redesigned and a second version of the diary was finalized for a much longer, in-depth field trial. This took place over six months, in a larger sample of communities and with full orientation of community members. The revised *dalit sangam* diary, which became known as 'Community Eyes',, was prepared for field trial with 400 *sangams* of 8,000 women from 24 NESA partner organizations. Twenty-four organization diaries were also developed. For this trial, another training of trainers was organized for network members and animators to enhance their skills in the methods for introducing the *sangam* diary to the community, collecting information, using different scales and calculations, and analysing information at the community level. They in turn went on to train their field staff. The information collected in the field trial was consolidated in the respective organization diary by the field staff, and these diaries in turn were consolidated in the sector diary.

NESA is now in the process of analysing the baseline information collected by the organizations. After this process, a summary analysis report will be sent back to network NGOs. Another workshop is proposed for discussion on the analysis report, sharing by the practitioners on the impact of using the method, and challenges and constraints faced by them in the process of collecting and analysing.

Impact of ILS in NESA

The field trial of 400 *sangam* diaries had an exciting impact in NESA. This was felt at many levels of the network, from the community through to the partner organizations.

Many community members were energized after using the diary because of acquiring new knowledge, reflecting their own lives and hopes for the future. There are many examples of individuals who have been enabled to make changes in their lives and livelihoods, prompted by their participation in the *sangam* diary process. For example, the human rights indicators in the diary encouraged the women to assert their rights. In one case a *sangam* woman, after seeing the picture on asserting rights to CPRs, prompted her husband to take part in an auction to get a share in local temple land, a CPR which until then had been denied to the community as a whole. Subsequently, other women and men from the same *dalit* community were motivated to do the same. Here, the impact is not only in terms of claiming entitlements to CPRs, but in terms of empowering a woman to prompt a decision to claim a rightful share. Instead of requesting that her husband take part in the auction, she demanded it. This is the case of one woman, but it was repeated in several other *sangams* too.

The field test also showed that ILS is not only useful for empowering the less powerful. It can also have impacts as a pedagogical tool for the more powerful, which gives them space to reflect on their own behaviour. For example, one NESA partner implemented the 'Community Eyes' diary in a non-*dalit sangam*. The diary highlighted village untouchability practices, including the separate glass system for *dalits*, compulsion to do menial jobs and not being allowed to sit on equal terms with upper-caste people in communal areas. After using the diary, the non-*dalit* women's *sangam* immediately stopped using the separate glass system for *dalits*.

Using the visual diaries has also had an impact on the animators who facilitate the diary process. Pictures speak louder than words and images of sensitive issues such as untouchability practices, atrocities, domestic violence and HIV/AIDS are often not openly spoken about during *sangam* meetings. The animators often feel too threatened to discuss them very openly, because they are sensitive things for women to discuss in public. By using visual diaries, there is less work for the mouth, as the pictures themselves create room for discussion. Visual projection makes sensitization very quick and effective.

In spite of the animators spending time and energy in the village in the initial stage of introducing ILS, the detailed information generated by the diaries gave energy and motivation for the animators, because it provided documentation about the entire village in one single diary. One satisfied animator said: 'Now I am very happy that I can give information about the village which I am working in to my director whenever she asks, as the ILS diary gives me this information.'

Beyond the animators, impact is also felt at the level of the organization. The information gathered in the *sangam* diaries was helpful to identify the issues which need immediate focus, identification of excelling and lagging programmes, the reasons behind this and the steps that could be taken. Apart from this, the consolidation of all the *sangam* diaries into one single organization diary gave information which could be used for proposal writing, advocacy and lobbying, and reporting to donors. For example, the baseline information collected through the diary on the number of untouchability/atrocities cases filed, and the share of CPRs received by the *dalits*, are essential facts for advocacy and lobbying. In South India, where no formal records exist in villages, this knowledge, generated from the community, is legal evidence for the existence of such social problems in villages.

The baseline details of the diary give overall social, economic, political and cultural information that can be used to highlight what needs should be met by programme interventions, how such programmes should continue and what strategies they should have. For example, information about child education and child labour can substantiate the need for child intervention programmes in a particular area. Similarly the particulars related to the impact of programme interventions in villages can validate the progress reports of activities to donors.

Reflections

In this section I reflect on the various factors that have affected or contributed to the implementation of ILS within NESA and its member organizations. These are the roles of knowledge, skills and commitment; the role of leaders and risk-taking; the role of the practitioner; the tension between adapting a broad concept by using a diversity of methods; and sticking to one specific methodology or brand. Thoughts on themes are followed by reflections on some of the challenges that arose in this process.

Knowledge, skills and commitment

Knowledge, skills and commitment are the three key aspects that a practitioner needs to have for the success of any participatory methodology (PM). The practitioner should enhance their skills, developing a complete understanding of the key features, principles and limitations of the method before implementation. The practitioner's commitment to the participatory nature of the method is also very significant, and is closely related to the commitment and support of the organization they work in. In the case of NESA, there was a strong commitment to introducing ILS methodology to its partners. The key features of ILS inspired this commitment, because they were in line with NESA's own belief that marginalized communities can assess their own life conditions, track the changes happening and keep records of rights issues. The commitment manifested itself in NESA's support of partners to develop indicators and provide orientation training on ILS. This allowed the continued practising of ILS and the development of further adaptations to new areas beyond its roots in microcredit.

Role of leaders and risk taking

The role of leadership in the process of adapting a methodology is very crucial. ILS was a risk, particularly for a network like NESA; it was a new and relatively untested methodology. NESA's executive director played a major role in taking the risk of implementation. He learned about ILS as an innovative tool which had only been introduced to microcredit and livelihood programmes, but he was convinced about the impact which would be created by the method in more diverse areas related to *dalit* rights, and worked hard to convince NESA partners of this. Apart from influencing partners, he also took the risk of deploying resources, both human and financial.

In terms of financial resources, NESA's work is largely funded by the Netherlands Organization for International Development Cooperation (NOVIB), which supported the initial orientation training programme and indicator development exercises. This included initial training, orientation, fees for the resource person and a series of indicator development exercises. Beyond this, however, the ILS adaptation process was not on their funding agenda, and NESA raised financial support from the Comité Catholique Contre la Faim et pour le Développement to implement the *sangam* diary in 400 *sangam*s, in order to develop a shared commitment towards ILS processes among NGO leaders and others at various levels.

Role of the practitioner

The practitioner of any participatory method should give attention to his/her attitude and behaviour in implementing the method, and this is also true of ILS. It is particularly important to develop the attitude of accepting and learning from feedback, the attitude that they can do it, the attitude of acceptance of critique and challenges. In addition, the practitioner should think that they are facilitating the community to do its own analysis, rather than creating awareness with the theoretical knowledge and skills learnt. In the case of ILS, the practitioner also needs to inspire NGO leaders, staff and the community members with the effectiveness of the methods in order to sustain the programme.

One of the strengths of ILS is that those who have used it have been humble enough to understand and innovate according to the local contexts, instead of forcing the method to be applied as a ready-made tool which is available for universal application. The community and its aspirations need to play a central role in any innovation if the methodology is to be really effective. The practitioner can also add creatively to a method like ILS, fusing it with various elements of other participatory methods available, rather than sticking to the rigidity of one method. This applies not only to blending Participatory Rural Appraisal (PRA) tools with ILS – like the income and expenditure tree which was used in microcredit and livelihood diaries – but also to other elements of participatory theory and practice. Using ILS in combination with Freire's conscientization method is an innovation identified in NESA's work (Freire, 1970). While the pictures in the *sangam* diary can be used to assess people's life situation, at the same time they can be used to pose the problems that the community is struggling with. Here, the pictures can be used as a code to catalyse brainstorming and discussion, in a fusion of ILS and Freirean approaches.

A tool alone will not solve all problems, and there is a need for extensive facilitation by the practitioner to handle the expectations and initiatives stimulated by using the ILS method. For example, the method might have catalysed the community's awareness about human rights issues, prompting them to take immediate action. Such situations have the potential to create conflicts with other communities. Hence practitioners need not only to know the tool, but also to have a deep understanding of the community and long-term vision to help the community to reflect on the root cause of the problem and arrive at good strategies to overcome the problem pragmatically.

Concept compared with brand – recognition of the diversity of tools

PMs are very diverse. Each method has its own values and principles which may be used in different circumstances. For example, PRA has been used by NESA during tsunami relief and rehabilitation to identify the livelihood and education needs of communities and children in 75 villages of coastal parts of India. NESA felt PRA, especially rapid appraisal tools, are the best to use during a disaster like the tsunami, as they have a quick as well as an effective impact in terms of facilitating the community to think about its new life incorporating the principle and practice of community ownership and participation. It also helped the NGOs to understand the communities closely and the various livelihood options possible.

Similarly, NESA plans to introduce ILS to the tsunami-affected victims to track the changes in their lives over a period of time. Here the significant matter is to adapt and use different tools to achieve better results than to focus on the use of a fixed or single-brand solution. So tools should be chosen according to the situation and environment, rather than having an unquestioning attachment to any particular method. The core concept of any PM should be facilitating the community to recognize, reflect and respond. Particular methods which satisfy this concept should then be selected according to the situation. Hence one organization or practitioner should not stick to one method when there is a diversity of methods that could be used.

Challenges

Several challenges were encountered in implementing ILS in NESA and its partners. At the heart of any PM is the core concept of facilitating the community to recognize, reflect and respond to its situation. In order to facilitate this, several further adaptations were made to ILS based upon NESA's experience of implementation.

The initial version of ILS begins with using diaries at the individual level, then moving to *sangam* and organizational levels. NESA started with ILS at the *sangam* level, but I feel that any NGO which is looking for a massive impact among the community should begin with using individual diaries. The individual diary is critical in inspiring and assisting each individual to recognize, reflect and respond. Despite the usefulness of the individual diaries, the repeated comment I heard from the animators in using ILS is the requirement of time and additional effort from their part. Hence careful thought needs to be given to integrating ILS with other programmes, with animators setting aside a certain amount of time in every weekly *sangam* meeting for ILS activity. At the same time, care needs to be taken that the ILS process remains slow, so that it gives space for the community to reflect on each indicator.

In its original form, ILS involves some statistical calculations, which are very important and useful for meeting the information needs of stakeholders beyond the village level. But the process can also be modified in such a way that the community does not have to do all those calculations itself, which experience has shown is sometimes difficult and does not always meet information needs at the community level.

The diary includes numbers, which are more useful for the implementing organization than the community. Even so, measurement scales could be modified to make them simpler in order to avoid complicated calculations. The major learning is that ILS needs to be simplified further so that it will reduce the burden on practitioners in terms of statistical calculations. This would also reduce the number of pages in the diary, which reduces the production costs. For example, NESA developed indicators for all its seven sectors, using separate diaries for each sector. But it was found that implementing all seven of these sectoral diaries would overburden the communities and would duplicate information. To resolve this, it was decided that the sectors should form an indicator bank, and only three diaries should be developed for each of NESA's three main thematic areas: *dalit, adivasi* and children. These diaries would include the non-negotiable indicators of all the seven sectors.. Hence, a NESA partner working with *dalit*s can use the diary developed for the *dalit* community, which will include specific indicators related to *dalit* issues; similarly for organizations focused on *adivasis* or children. The appropriate indicators related to gender, natural resource management and HIV/AIDS will only be included in the three diaries mentioned (*dalit, adivasi* and children), according to the group's situation.

Major learning

The effectiveness of this method is that community members do the day-to-day impact assessment by themselves, and in doing so they recognize, reflect on and respond to daily challenges. Another significant aspect of this method is that it tracks changes over a period of time, which is a process-oriented rather than a one-off approach. In addition, it is an educational and sensitizing tool which can be used to support communities to obtain knowledge on sensitive issues such as rights, domestic violence and HIV/AIDS.

In contrast to other PMs, ILS has the possibility of generating information from individual to community levels. But ILS is a long-term, time-consuming process which needs commitment, resources and sustained action at all levels of participation. Because pictorial representation is very culture- and region-specific, a major challenge in the implementation of ILS is that the diaries need to be redesigned each time according to the region, community, culture and focus areas of the NGOs. This is a major obstacle to any potential efforts to scale up ILS by simple replication.

The evolution and development process of ILS consumed an enormous amount of time for orientation, indicator development, facilitating the *sangams* to collect information, analysis of information by the community, consolidation of the *sangam* diary and the NGO diary, and analysis of the accumulated information. It is essential to spend enough time in the initial stages for the development and sustenance of the method. This huge amount of investment in the beginning is a major limitation. Although NESA developed indicators for all the sectors, due to financial constraints the diaries were only implemented in the *dalit sangams*

NESA's experience in using ILS has some unique features, most importantly having human rights indicators in addition to the livelihood indicators in the diaries. At present, these diaries have been used by *dalits* and non-*dalits*, and will be used in future by *adivasis*, children and sexual and religious minorities. This highlights the important of ILS as a tool that can be used by diverse groups in their day-to-day life. In addition to this, not only women but also men – especially young men – are using the diaries, which empowers them in asserting their rights and enhancing their knowledge. NESA's identity as a network of organizations is an important factor in allowing it to track impact on diverse issues in one single diary, and this innovation is both significant and special.

CHAPTER 7

Road to the foot of the mountain, but reaching for the sun: PALS adventures and challenges[37]

Linda Mayoux

Introduction

The Participatory Action Learning System (PALS) is an eclectic and constantly evolving methodology which enables people to collect and analyse the information they themselves need on an ongoing basis to improve their lives in ways they decide. PALS does this through producing an integrated set of diagrams and participatory processes adapted from a general repertoire of diagram tools and participatory principles and tailored to different literacy and skills levels, specific issues, contexts and organizational needs. Group and higher-level participatory structures form a focus for linking individual and group learning into participatory programme decision-making, local lobbying and policy advocacy. The interlinked goals are both individual empowerment and pro-poor accountability of the wider development process.

This chapter gives my own personal perspective on the PALS 'road journey', explaining how and why the PALS 'brand' of participatory methodology (PM) has evolved in the way it has, and what I see as its main achievements, challenges and ways forward. I begin with the underlying emotional inspiration for PALS, which was the response to anthropological fieldwork with very poor people in India and Nicaragua in the 1970s and 1980s. Following this, academic inspiration came through contact with emerging participatory innovations during consultancy work on participatory research, impact assessment methods and gender issues in microfinance. My own ideas took concrete shape from the late 1990s as a methodology for women's empowerment in microfinance and they were developed in a series of papers for the DFID-funded Enterprise Development Impact Assessment Information Service (EDIAIS) website. PALS as a named methodology was born in 2002 through work on the impact assessment of enterprise and civil-society development with Kabarole Research and Resource Centre (KRC) in Uganda. PALS has since been spread through innovation and detailed adaptation for an increasing number of contexts and issues by NGOs in India, Uganda, Sudan and Pakistan. I conclude by examining the challenges now faced in the attempt to move to scale for lobbying and advocacy, a move necessary to really address the multiple contextual constraints which serve to perpetuate poverty and inequality.

It must be stressed that although I have been responsible for the original ideas, focus, design and documentation of PALS for different purposes and contexts, equally important innovation and adaptation are now being developed by women and men in villages and urban areas in Uganda, India, Sudan and Pakistan, supported by local staff in local NGOs. Their perspectives and stories remain to be documented.

Eclectic beginnings: emotional inspiration and academic searching

PALS is unashamedly a constantly evolving eclectic methodology inspired by a wide range of (fully acknowledged) participatory processes and diagramming methods. Box 7.1 summarizes the main features, some of which are common to most participatory methods, some building on specific innovations and others distinctive to PALS.

My own underlying emotional and personal inspiration came from anthropological village-level research over the 10 years 1978–89 in West Bengal, South India and Nicaragua. Officially focusing mainly on gender and enterprise development, the research rapidly came to include participatory processes in village organizations, leftwing movements, and government and NGO policy processes. As a young and inexperienced female researcher I was initially shocked by the terrible tragedy of hunger, sickness, continually dashed dreams, and hopes and early death faced by many people I got to know. Over time, the more I got to know people, I was also inspired by the strength, heroism and determination of many of the people I met, very poor women and men in their daily struggles as well as local political activists, many of whom risked their lives to challenge oppressive structures and corruption. But I came to question much of the participation in participatory development and also the usefulness of even sincere and well-designed research which did not lead to any tangible benefits for people who gave up their time to work with me.

The mess of contradictory impressions, emotional reactions and conflicting facts bombarding me during this period taught me many things. First, in relation to participation and participatory development:

1. Poor people are not communities or victims or 'good simple people', but just as complex and contradictory as everyone else, as individuals and in the ways they relate to other people.

   Inequalities which cause so much suffering are perpetuated not only by the better-off or by men, but also by poor people and by women. It was not only the fragility of many friendships and the frequent eruptions of jealousies, conflicts and violence and the frequency of domestic violence and dowry deaths which shocked me. It was the fact that women generally blamed the women, and that women collaborated or were even the main perpetrators of the deaths. It was only in time that I came to more fully

Box 7.1   PALS' distinctive features

Goals

To empower people (as individuals and communities, and particularly very poor women, children and men) to collect, analyse and use information to improve their lives and gain more control over decisions which affect them.

To increase pro-poor outcomes, accountability and governance of development programmes, planning and implementation

Process principles

Participation for empowerment

- Based on information needs of people themselves developing their learning, analytical and participatory skills. All diagrams and analysis are done from scratch by people themselves to reinforce skills and confidence to do things (if necessary and all else fails) without outside support (or interference).
- Inclusive process prioritizing the needs of the most disadvantaged and promoting the awareness, participatory and listening skills of the relatively better-off.
- Builds structures for networking, mutual learning and collective action through careful sequencing of individual and group activities and inclusion of institutional analysis.

Action learning

- Learning for future improvement, not policing past failure, through analysis not only of what has happened to whom, but why, followed by detailed discussion of practical ways forward.
- Focus on recording those things which are necessary for moving forward in a way which is accessible to all, including use of photos and video.
- Ongoing action learning. Diagrams include action targets to be tracked over time, as one attractively coloured large wallchart and/or as an individual or group diary.

Sustainable system

- No separate PALS process but integration into existing training and follow-up in staff/community interactions like outreach, monitoring and loan application processes.
- Dissemination through mutual learning. Skills, issues and networks are followed up and reinforced through discussion and action during group meetings and integrated into participatory decision-making structures.
- Additional information needed by programmes and donors is collected as a separate process in purposive studies and donor evaluations which build on the participatory information base, but also use other qualitative and quantitative methods.
- Information from the participatory system is aggregated in participatory planning forums like networking fairs' and/or AGMs as an input to lobbying and advocacy. This maintains dynamism and increases effectiveness in a cost-effective way.

understand and empathize with the complex trade-offs between people's immediate and long-term needs, personal priorities and the public interest.

Unless PMs seek to understand, acknowledge and address individual interests, diversity and potential conflict, they are unlikely to be effective in bringing about positive change.

2. Poor people are rarely stereotypical passive victims of poverty awaiting deliverance by NGOs or governments.

The more I got to know people and had the opportunity to observe processes over time, the more it was obvious that many very poor women and men have strong and articulate philosophies of life followed through with great self-sacrifice and heroism, drawing on local egalitarian cultural and religious traditions as well as more recent Marxist ideologies – far in advance of my own ideas and actions. People constantly learned from and taught each other when skills had a clear and concrete use. The rapid spread of the handicraft industries through women marrying into new villages teaching eager neighbours and passing on contacts with middlemen/women, and of silk labourers developing enterprises together, was in contrast to the very limited use of any of the skills taught in government or NGO training. Processes of change have rapidly speeded up as people take advantage of transport and road infrastructure and television, as well as education. In all these processes NGOs and development agencies are largely absent, irrelevant or dismissed as corrupt, even those officially promoting participation.

Participatory processes need to build on the aspirations and strategies of very poor people, not as reliance on self-help but to identify how and where external support is really needed.

3. Culture and tradition are many-faceted and many-layered and constantly negotiated and renegotiated. Over time it became evident that many of the staunchest public supporters of tradition had very different (and widely known) private lives 'behind the hay in the barn'. Gender issues are particularly complex. Many women in Nicaragua as well as West Bengal turned with great fervour to religious ideologies which treated them as inferior as a refuge from the turmoil, corruption and violence around them. Gender inequalities and violence were taken for granted, as culture, even where (as in the case of Islam) there are clear religious prohibitions against it. But the initial sparks of new social ideas (as well as malicious gossip) spread very rapidly through extensive invisible networks, even among Muslim or Hindu women apparently observing strict norms of seclusion and subservience. In time practices unquestioned as tradition (even where like dowry they are actually quite recent) become replaced by new practices which everyone is doing nowadays (even if only a few people have in fact broken the mould).

Participatory methods need to be culturally-sensitive, based on an in-depth understanding of cultural complexity, not culturally naive, taking at face value interpretations of culture by those in power. Simplistic cultural preconceptions and stereotypes hamper both finding out the truth and discussing ways of addressing challenges.

4. Generalized messages about the people's struggle or women's rights are too abstract to engage people for any length of time, even if they are demonstrably the underlying cause of serious problems. Many women and men are only too conscious of their oppression and do not need lectures from privileged outsiders.

Participatory methods need to help people explore their dreams for the future, identify those which are realizable, analyse linkages between the different challenges they face in reaching them, and identify immediate steps forward.

Second, in relation to research and research methods:

1. The more I knew, the more I knew I did not know. What people said and what they did were often very different, and both changed over time or even from one day to the next in ways they were often unaware of. Even apparently simple facts like daily wage rates which people quoted with ease in survey interviews were in reality negotiated, highly variable and bore little relation to what people received. Unpredictable daily incomes where people sold what they could at any price in order to get a meal for the evening were simply not knowable without daily tracking. Any rapid extraction of simple monitoring indicators is therefore a pipedream; reliable information can only be obtained through helping people reflect and think through their answers in a way that motivates them to do this seriously and honestly. But it is possible through experience to probe, discuss and collect systematic information even on very sensitive and controversial issues like violence and sexuality, which are often omitted as too difficult or culturally inappropriate. This was often necessary to really understand people's experience of poverty.

2. Poor people have a right to benefit from the time they spend with researchers. Many people enjoyed a good informal chat, but many demanded to know if they answered all my questions, what will they get out of it – lots of people had come before and just wasted their time. This is not only a question which determines the reliability of any information given, it is also a moral imperative as a response to empowered challenging by respondents of extractive research processes which do not benefit them.

3. The role of outsiders with greater wealth and education is always difficult and contradictory. Outsiders have much to learn from many people, but only if they stop assuming (or being granted) any automatic superiority. The situation of poor people not listening or learning from training is often caused by leaders and trainers not listening and treating poor people as equal – or even superior – in their knowledge and understanding of poverty. At the same time poverty restricts access to the wider pool of knowledge which poor people need, giving a difficult position of power to trainers and leaders in filtering and presenting this outside reality and its implications.

A second, more obvious and practical, set of inspirations came from the mid-1980s from the range of participatory diagram methods which were then beginning to gain popularity in academic and NGO circles. After 1989 I was grounded in the UK, unable to do fieldwork because of my very young family. This gave me the opportunity to do some teaching, read widely and reflect on my experiences. In the early 1990s I started teaching for the Open University and was impressed by the effectiveness of both the experiential learning and systems/cognitive diagramming approaches in study skills preparation. This approach often produced much clearer thinking and better essays than my more conventional teaching at Cambridge University. My interest in diagramming methods of recording and analysis was also born from necessity with the sudden onset of repetitive strain injury in early 1994, making me physically unable to write or type for any length of time. This enforced shift from linear to lateral thinking and the visual representation of complex issues has in the end been very formative in experimentation with different diagram forms. It also prompted me to become much more interested in photography and video as a means of communication and systematic recording.

In the mid-1990s I did critical reviews of both published and NGO participatory development literature and later specifically participatory diagram methods for the Open University. From this reading it was clear that participatory research methods were no panacea – they suffered from the same dilemmas as other types of participatory development I had earlier observed. Their practice did not necessarily address the methodological shortcomings of more conventional quantitative and qualitative research methods. Shortcomings were particularly acute in relation to gender issues (Mayoux, 1995; Guijt and Shah, 1998). Nevertheless it was also clear that participatory methods, particularly the then emerging PLA version as documented by Robert Chambers (1997) and PLA Notes, represented an attempt to address the challenges of power relations and inequality and give greater weight to the voices and perspectives of the poor. Like many others I became convinced that, when well facilitated, the richness of information gained in a very short time made participatory methods a viable more empowering alternative, or at least a complement to, conventional anthropological or survey methods (Johnson and Mayoux, 1998).

In the late 1990s these two strands of work on gender and poverty reduction and participatory methods began to take more concrete and practical shape in the context of my work on microfinance programmes and women's empowerment for DFID, the United Nations Development Fund for Women (UNIFEM), the Open University and other funders. First, evidence was increasingly showing that savings and credit alone were unlikely to significantly increase women's incomes or address inequalities in households, markets and communities.

Second, this increasing questioning of microfinance had led to growing pressure from donor agencies for impact assessment. However, most existing impact assessments were policing activities imposed by donors and resented by programmes. They often appeared to have limited relevance, reliability or contribution to practical decision-making. Even participatory assessment was often an extractive exercise, consisting of little more than requiring people to spend time attending one-off PRA exercises and focus group discussions to meet the information needs and process requirements of donors and NGOs. There was a need for a new approach to impact assessment which focused not so much on 'policing and measuring the past' but 'improving future practice' (Hulme, 2000).

This led me to argue that there was a need for a methodology for women in SHGs which would help women plan livelihoods more effectively and give group discussions more strategic direction in meeting needs and challenging inequality.[38] This could at the same time, if based on the systematic use of participatory diagram techniques accessible to non-literate women, also provide much of the material for more reliable and empowering monitoring and impact assessment for the new 'improving practice' focus (Mayoux, 1998). From 2000 my work as principal researcher for the DFID-funded Enterprise Development Impact Assessment Information Service (EDIAIS) enabled me to develop these ideas further, not only in relation to microfinance but also to other areas of development.

My work at this time also drew on a number of emerging innovative methodologies which were actually being implemented, and in different ways provided part of what I envisaged as ways forward:

- *Reflect*, using participatory diagrams for literacy and individual and community diaries on an ongoing basis for lobbying and advocacy (see Chapters 1–5, this volume).
- Participatory monitoring system being developed by the Small Enterprise Foundation (SEF) in South Africa and promoted in the Microcredit Summit campaign (Simanowitz, 1999).
- Participatory market research diagram methods for microfinance programmes developed by Micro-Save Africa.
- ILS (Noponen, 2001, and Chapters 6, 7 and 8, this volume) using individual as well as group diaries and recording as a basis for impact assessment and local lobbying.

All these methodologies, themselves evolving and dynamic, continue to inform and inspire the development of PALS.

This phase culminated in 2001 when PRADAN in New Delhi asked me to facilitate and edit a book of papers for a workshop bringing together people working on participatory learning methodologies for women in microfinance (Mayoux, 2003d). This gave me the opportunity not only to learn more about ILS and PRADAN, but also about Area Networking for Alternative Development Initiatives (ANANDI), working on women's empowerment in Gujarat, which would become one of the key subsequent contributors to PALS. Their area networking events (*melas*) for women's empowerment are an effective means of bringing together local experience for training on a large scale, advocacy and lobbying.

Basic road map: from broad ideas to PALS as a coherent system of principles, processes and tools

Focused development of PALS tools and processes beyond my own writing and imagination started in October 2002 with a training workshop on participatory monitoring and evaluation with KRC and its partners in Uganda. KRC was under donor pressure to produce better documentation of their achievements and it was looking for a participatory organizational learning process which would not only produce information for donors but contribute to their main programme goal: empowerment and civil-society development. Some of KRC's partner groups – mainly local NGOs and CBOs – were using *Reflect* for literacy, and were drawing community natural resource maps and body maps for HIV/AIDS awareness. Matrices and tree diagrams were used for awareness-raising around gender and civil peace issues. Staff had also recently been trained in 'appreciative enquiry 'and 'open space' methodologies. The participatory monitoring and evaluation training workshop refined KRC's vision and mission statement using the newly acquired 'open space' skills, and resulted in the first draft manual for the Sustainable Participatory Action Learning System (SPALS), incorporating ideas from both 'appreciative enquiry' and 'open space'. KRC then undertook field training, piloting and dissemination of SPALS principles with its partners, building on the tools with which they were familiar as the start of a long-term capacity-building process to increase participation and equality in their groups.

A second and much larger PALS workshop in May 2003 brought together the pilot experience of KRC itself and local CBO partners involved in developing and adapting PALS, including Green Home and Bukonzo Enterprise Training (BET) which have been part of my own PALS road journey. Funding was found to invite ANANDI to contribute its experience of area networking fairs, and Port Sudan Small Enterprise Development to present experience with Micro-Save's market research tools. It was at this workshop that the main diagrams and processes currently used by PALS participants, shown below in Box 7.2, were brought together and subsequently written up as the first full PALS manual (Mayoux, 2003e and further developed in a series of papers for EDIAIS (Mayoux, 2003a, 2003b, 2003c). KRC then undertook much more extensive training of partner organizations and local community trainers using their own adaptation of the manual.

Reaching for the sun: principles underlying concrete visions and tangible change

Since 2003 PALS has been adapted for a range of issues in a number of countries, largely through organizations attending the second KRC workshop. The next major set of innovations were in relation to gender issues. ANANDI invited me to do a five-day participatory review of ANANDI's approach and gender work, using PALS methods and including PALS training for staff. The review not only

Box 7.2   Diagrams and process in PALS methodology

Diagrams

Road journeys (developed from ANANDI) chart a journey from point a to point b, generally over time. Vision journeys are forward-looking journeys to the future. Achievement journeys look back to the past. The road is divided into stages with quantitative targets which can be tracked. External opportunities and constraints are presented as signposts or bugbears along the way to assess attribution. Action strategies are marked for tracking.

Diamonds (emerging from the second KRC workshop) show distribution around an average. These identify local criteria for an issue starting by contrasting extremes (e.g. most versus least powerful, richest/poorest), then progressively moving to centre ground. Then numbers of people/objects/incidence are marked at each level. Finally, strategies for bringing up those at the bottom are discussed.

Trees (PLA) start from a trunk representing an issue or an institution like a household or community. Inputs are shown as roots and outputs as branches to analyse challenges/ solutions, incomes/expenditures and so on. Both roots and branches can be of different sizes and quantified, arranged, coloured, grouped and ranked for qualitative analysis.

Circles (PLA Venn or Chapati) show the relationships between different elements represented as overlapping circles. Circles can also be quantified as pie charts, of different sizes, colours, fills, lines for qualitative analysis. Action strategies are marked for tracking.

Also used are PLA physical maps, matrices, calendars and many new diagrams that have emerged locally. Quantitative information can be recorded by facilitators in the same way as surveys, except that participants think through responses and retain the original diagram. All diagrams include trackable action targets revisited at a later date.

Process

The following steps underlie the use of individual diagrams and/or sequencing of diagrams in order to move from analysis to action planning:

Step 1 Analysis of difference and inclusion through stakeholder analysis to identify lines of difference, consensus and conflict of interest.

Then with different key interest groups:

Step 2 Visioning change. What are people aiming for? What do people want to be changed?

Step 3 Appreciating achievements. What positive changes have been achieved and how?

Step 4 Identifying challenges. What negative changes are occurring and what challenges need to be addressed?

Step 5 Identifying strategies. How can positive changes be further increased? How can negative changes be avoided? By whom?

Step 6 Negotiating change. How can the different views and potential conflicts of interest be negotiated in practical programme or policy change?

demonstrated the usefulness of the poverty diamond, road journeys, food security calendar and institutional circle maps in 'rapid assessment', but also resulted in adaptations of the diamond for identifying local concepts of empowerment and investigating domestic violence (see Figure 7.1). [39]

The initial visioning for the empowerment diamond was the first time I had encouraged women who had never held a pen before to do individual drawing. This showed how, if left to themselves without staff peering over their shoulders, these women overcame initial hesitation and supported each other to start to put down their ideas – and enjoy the process. For domestic violence the combination of the diamond and the road journey were able in about three hours to help women move from denying any existence of domestic violence to discussing their distressing experiences for the first time, to proposing solutions which were then followed up by ANANDI (Mayoux and ANANDI, 2005). In 2004 PALS was again used with different ANANDI groups to look at very complex issues of intra-household relations. This proved difficult in the half-day available with each group: not only had many of the women never held a pen before, but they had also not thought about intra-household gender inequalities. Nevertheless, from a qualitative research perspective, far more was learned in that short time than from conventional anthropological methods about the considerable variability in women's household situations, how women felt about each other, about gender inequality, family planning and abortion, and a range of other issues (Mayoux, 2004).

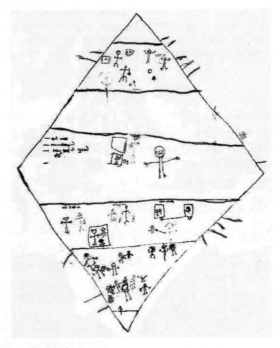

Figure 7.1 Violence diamond.

The work for ANANDI was paralleled by gender work with Port Sudan Small Enterprise Development (PASED) from April 2004 to start a new poverty-targeted microfinance and empowerment programme for women, Learning for Empowerment Against Poverty (LEAP).[49] PALS training has been an integral part of the development of the programme from the start as an awareness-raising, planning and organizational learning process. Over 600 women have now used PALS diagrams. PALS has been very effective in helping LEAP women's centres think through and identify ways forward for the many challenges they face. Women's centres are now using the diagrams independently of LEAP staff (LEAP, 2005). PALS training was also given as part of gender training for Pakistan Microfinance Network. Following this, the Kashf Foundation did some very interesting work using empowerment diamonds (Sardar and Mumtaz, 2004).

The next big step was the development of an effective methodology for individual-level learning to feed into group learning. In 2004 I worked with a US-based NGO, the Trickle-Up Program (TUP), giving start-up grants to very poor entrepreneurs. Their Africa program officer had attended the second PALS workshop and then done a study of three CBO partners of KRC and TUP. This concluded that PALS had resulted in impressive levels of self-confidence, the full participation of all members with no leadership dependency, the effective self-evaluation of progress, and increased collaboration and unity in the group and in households. It had also led to viable solutions to problems being implemented at individual, household and group levels (van Riet, 2004). Importantly, another impact study had questioned the effectiveness of TUP's existing training programme, and recommended that this be given some attention.The collaboration with TUP offered the opportunity to address some of the challenges that were arising and design together the following.

- A training programme for very poor non-literate people fully integrating PALS diagrams, to enable people to decide how best to use a TUP grant to improve their livelihood
- An built-in monitoring system using these diagrams which both benefits entrepreneurs and fulfils TUP's very specific information needs.
- A participatory process which can be self-generating and sustainable through inspiring entrepreneurs to use the methodology as individuals and groups with very limited support from either local staff or TUP.

The training and piloting began September 2004 with Jamghoria Sevabrata (JS), a local CBO and TUP partner working in one of the poorest tribal areas in West Bengal, accompanied by staff from ANANDI. This was followed in December 2004 by training and piloting with Green Home in Uganda, accompanied also by staff from KRC. During these trainings, new local innovations in teaching numeracy (ANANDI) and the symbol-based recording of business information (BET) were shared and included in the TUP PALS manual. The TUP manual has subsequently been further field-tested and simplified. Field reports from TUP and my own probing discussions in May 2005 indicate that the methodology is now effectively used by staff to do their own training of new batches of TUP grant beneficiaries.

The TUP process demonstrated very clearly that even people initially afraid to speak up in front of outsiders could, within the space of a few hours as part of a batch of 15–30 trainees, progress to quite sophisticated road journey analyses of their businesses. This included recording simple calculations on profit and loss using lines and circles. They were then very eager to make their full contribution to group challenge solution trees which could quantify the incidence of different problems and identify solutions. A snowballing process was introduced whereby instead of 30 women all arriving at the same time, they would arrive in groups of 10 at intervals. This meant the first batch received sufficient attention. Those who rapidly progressed were able and very proud to be able to train the next batch as they arrived, their own needs then being followed up once training the last batch had been properly started. This enabled more women to be much better trained, and also developed their confidence that they did not need to wait for the NGO to come next time before starting. For some participants, both non-literate and educated, the diagrams were the first time they had been able to really analyse the complexities of their business decisions. The diagrams have also improved communication between programme staff and participants, enabling people to express themselves much better and promoting a more equal relationship.

These new methodologies and processes have now been incorporated in the most recent KRC manual for its Microfinance Association Programme.

Moving beyond base camp: challenges of scaling up

The PALS journey so far has been slowly but steadily upwards and outwards. In all partner programmes funding limitations have restricted my personal involvement in PALS to at most five- or six-day staff field training. These simultaneously train programme participants and pilot local adaptations, sometimes following a separate programme evaluation. Trainings are followed by production of a tailored manual for the specific organization, with the issue and context based on any new innovations from piloting and the broad pool of diagrams and processes coming from the original PALS documentation and other participatory literature. The manual is then sent to programme staff to use as best they can. Programmes have so far generally been too busy training and disseminating PALS along with their other work to systematically monitor the use and impact of PALS. This chapter has therefore relied on scattered information on numbers of trainees in some training sessions and anecdotes from the more visible groups. Full documentation of local innovation and critical evaluation remain to be done.

The PALS road journey encourages people to vision and dream and 'reach up for the big sun circle at the end of the road'. It has so far been most successful in relation to individual and group empowerment, significantly increasing people's learning and analytical skills, self-confidence and group participation. The diagrams, basic process and concepts are easy for people at all levels to understand and use even after only a half a day's training, although more sophisticated diagrams and analysis result from a longer period. Local staff and entrepreneurs have been able to continue this process, innovating with the diagrams and showing other people in their groups. The poverty diamond, for example, has been used in India, Sudan and Uganda for poverty targeting, investigating the impact over time and social inclusion, and has resulted in groups developing concrete strategies for including the poorest in their communities. PALS is now spreading quite quickly to new areas, groups and issues, through the enthusiasm of those involved and as an integral part of programme activities.

However, reaching nearer the sun may mean not just journeying along a pretty country lane, but learning to climb a mountain without a clear path. There is inevitably a very difficult balance between:

- participation – facilitating open exploration of tools and ideas and methods;
- leadership – guiding a process and standardizing diagrams to produce both usable information for programmes and the most informative analysis for participants to help them improve their lives.

A few spontaneous local adaptations have not worked so well. But the TUP process highlighted what could be achieved in a short time once diagrams are properly designed and piloted. PALS must inevitably be a staged process over a couple of years, from initial exploration and innovation to more systematic analysis, planning and documentation. It takes time to develop self-sustaining skills, capacities and participatory structures at both participant and staff levels while maintaining the focus on concrete actions for empowerment. Until local skills are sufficiently developed, detailed manuals need to be adapted for each specific issue, then continually revised in the light of experience and changing needs.

The biggest challenge is the move to scale for lobbying and advocacy – to move beyond mountain base camp. The nature of poverty means that poor women and men can only do so much through self-help, even when supported by committed NGOs. Significant improvements in their lives will require changes in the economic, social and political context, including women's property rights, informal-sector regulation and global trade agreements. This will require not only further expansion of PALS, but a credible aggregation of information fed into strong networks of informed people. Quantitative and qualitative data can be collected and extracted from PALS diagrams and process observation, then aggregated and documented by groups or staff in the same way as data from survey questionnaires or interviews. But how far KRC's current work with the Ugandan government on large-scale integration of PALS into its poverty resource monitoring and tracking process will be able to maintain the empowerment focus in the current political situation is unclear. A systematic combination of PALS with ANANDI's lateral learning fairs to collect aggregated information in an empowering way is planned for LEAP. More systematic use of visual media – photography and video – are also envisaged to increase communication at all levels. However, design, initial facilitation, and higher-level analysis and documentation of aggregated PALS data require the same levels of experience and skill as more conventional research methods. These research skills are still to be developed in the organizations involved, involving both participants and staff.

Perhaps the most difficult challenge of all will be, not expansion or aggregation of reliable information, but ensuring that the findings influence policy-makers. This will require reversing donors' thirst for easy short cuts which target nearly all the resources towards macro-level expert-determined strategies, one-off quantitative impact assessment or at best financially sustainable programmes for the better-off enterprising poor. It requires an adequate investment of effort and resources into developing the capacities and networks of those at the bottom of the power and resource hierarchy to make an ongoing and informed contribution to decision-making and increase the accountability of development institutions. This is an inherent and inseparable part of any serious agenda for pro-poor development and good governance.

CHAPTER 8

Keeping the art of participation bubbling: some reflections on what stimulates creativity in using participatory methods

Dee Jupp

Elsewhere in this publication, it has been acknowledged that the scale-up, spread, roll-out of participatory methods carries risk. While 'How to' manuals and tool kits for participation have had an extraordinary and impressive impact on raising the profile of participatory methods and encouraging their wide geographic spread, there are dangers in using them unquestioningly (particularly when they appear to have a good pedigree), in assuming they are appropriate for use even in very different contexts and kowtowing to the pressure of participation by command perpetuated by funding agencies and other powerful interests. If participation is to stay and not suffer the indignity of relegation to the scrap-heap of development fads, creativity, innovation and customization must be continuously encouraged to maintain interest and inspire facilitators and participants alike.

Happily, the challenges which fuel the much needed creativity have become more diverse over the years as people have pushed the boundaries and proved that what was deemed impossible is possible. Challenges have arisen in a variety of guises; for example, where issues to be reviewed are sensitive, where participants are considered extraordinary and where resources are limited. There are also important opportunities to enrich participatory approaches by poaching ideas from other disciplines and situations where risk-taking is positively encouraged and creativity promoted. In the following sections, I describe some of those situations which have spawned '*Eureka*'[41] moments when modifications, fusions and creations in participatory methodology (PM) have happened. Rather than replicating these approaches, I encourage you to learn from these situations to actively seek out new challenges and opportunities which will stimulate your own creativity.

Sensitive issues as a challenge for creativity

In the early years of Participatory Rural Appraisal (PRA) practice, it was happily being used in a variety of typical and relatively safe contexts: preference ranking for crop varieties, ranking of health service provision; mapping of physical and natural resources; changing trends in schooling, seasonality of crop prices and infestation and so on. But was it possible to use it to discuss sensitive issues such as gender relations, sexual health and behaviour, human rights abuses, bribery and corruption, debt, crime and security, conflict?

Instinctively the feeling was that it was not possible. These were issues that touched people emotionally and personally, and could put people in jeopardy if confidentiality was violated. But the potential value of bringing these issues out into the open, giving permission to speak, setting the scene for demanding public accountability and the prospects of generating opportunities for mutual support by airing sensitive issues were extremely alluring. The onus had to be to create methods and space, which would enable voice and, at the same time, protect individuals. The following provide some examples of innovation shaped by the sensitive nature of the field of enquiry and the challenges they encountered.

Human rights

In 1996, I and a group of Bangladeshi facilitators (Promoting Participation Team, PromPT) were engaged by the Ministry of Law, Justice and Parliamentary Affairs (PromPT and IDHRB, 1996) to undertake a participatory investigation of the perception of and extent of human rights abuses at village level, and seek means to build mechanisms to protect and safeguard human rights. This was clearly a huge challenge and, as far as we knew, without precedent. How were we going to broach the subject of human rights among villagers who did not use the concept? How were we to get people to talk openly about issues that they either accepted as the norm or habitually hid from public scrutiny?

After much discussion, we arranged for an artist to draw over 30 picture stories which showed such diverse situations as kidnapping, mistreatment of second wives, acid throwing, teasing teenage girls, beating, false arrests, dowry and preferential feeding of boys over girls.

In participatory sessions in villages, these easily interpreted pictures were shuffled and laid haphazardly on the ground with no hint of weighting given to the seriousness of the incidents being depicted. Different groupings of men and women of different ages were then asked to interpret the pictures, asked if incidents like these ever happened in the village and to rank them according to the frequency with which they occurred. They were then asked what action had been taken in each case.

A second series of pictures of people who might be called on to help were laid out and villagers selected those they would most likely seek help from. They were then asked if they could not get the help they wanted from their first choice to whom they would then turn. Flow diagrams were thus created, which, in turn, naturally evolved into matrix ranking exercises to review the efficacy of different forms of dispute settlement.

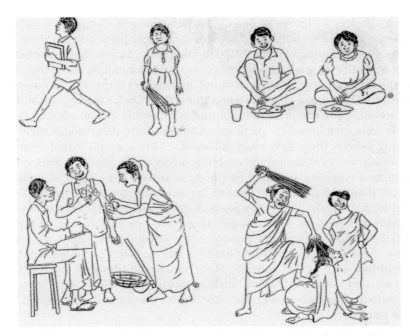

Figure 8.1 Picture stories. Pictures showing differential treatment of girls and boys, differential wages for men and women for the same job, and woman beating daughter-in-law.

Forty-two villages and nearly a thousand villagers were involved in the study. The most common rights abuses were noted, in ranked order, as 'no access to equitable justice', 'dowry', 'child labour', 'domestic violence against women' and 'restricted access to health care services'. On subsequent sharing with village and regional leaders, the police and lawyers, less resistance was observed than normally encountered with research findings, as the audiences were confronted with the direct opinions of the villagers. In one session with police (police abuse was ranked ninth among the rights abuses), a senior officer said, 'Yes, we are sick, we can't cure the disease of others. We abuse human rights even when we are supposed to be the protector.'

After the study, the facilitators reflected on the process and felt that this study had stretched them as never before. The visual methods had won the trust of the participants and had introduced the concept of talking through the pictures. The constant use of the third party in discussions, referring to the pictures rather than to actual incidents that had happened in the village, allowed participants freedom to talk from experience with less fear.

Corruption

Bribery and corruption is endemic in many institutions in Bangladesh, not least of all in the banking system. PromPT was commissioned to undertake a listening survey by the Swiss Agency for Development Cooperation (SDC) in Dhaka in 1997 to establish the views of small entrepreneurs regarding bank credit services (Jupp and PromPT, 1997b). Here again, a challenge was presented: to get normally passive and powerless clients to talk candidly about the service and the behaviour of the bankers as well as to reflect on their own compliant behaviour. Mind-maps provided a minimum structure for participants to assess reasons why they did not avail themselves of bank loans and graffiti/dream boards were established for participants to post 'wild ideas' about their ideal banking service. Force-field analysis (Lewin, 1951), a simple visual technique to examine the constraining and enabling factors which affect the achievement of a desired objective, was used by clients to analyse the current state of loan services. Bankers were asked to write cards (anonymously) describing the formal and informal ways in which they assess creditworthiness. This exercise revealed widespread nepotism, bias towards larger loan provision and waiving of regulations for good customers (presumably those willing and able to pay bribes). At the conclusion of the study, bankers and banking policy-makers were confronted with actual outputs from visualized analyses by the small entrepreneurs and their own banking profession. They were forced to acknowledge that bribery was the second most prevalent dissatisfaction with credit services.[42]

Similarly, when parallel studies of urban and rural users' perspectives of NGO financial services for the poor were conducted in Bangladesh (Jupp and PromPT, 1996), the challenge was to encourage borrowers to talk openly about the loan service and behaviour of the NGO field officers. But they frequently indicated that 'If we say something bad about the organisation, they will be angry and stop giving us credit', and indicated to the facilitators that they had been told by the NGOs giving them credit not to discuss anything with outsiders regarding the organization or loan-giving procedures. It was also apparent that malpractice was escalating, with the mushrooming of NGOs providing credit as a means to their own self-sufficiency (pushed by the threat of reduction of external funding and the funders' demand for organizational sustainability). Not least of all, there was growing collusion among NGOs to provide credit to repay other loans so that officers' recorded repayment rates would be demonstrably high (over 90 per cent).

The credit movement was at its zenith and any criticism was perfunctorily sidelined. It was important to develop methods of enquiry to probe these sensitive issues. We used the 'proportional investment and repayment source' chart,[43] where participants were provided with 10 stones, seeds or coloured sticky dots, which represented the total value of their loans, and asked to distribute these among different ways of getting cash to make repayments on the loans. It was found that 16–32 per cent of loan repayments were made from sources not related to profits from the investment financed by the loan – a fact that, at the time, was hotly denied by NGOs. The investment charts, which also used the idea of distributing stones proportionally among the different types of investment made, indicated that investments were generally not made in the way declared when getting the loan or, indeed in the way claimed by the NGOs. For example, 'As one man placed all ten dots in cow purchase, his daughter, standing nearby, said "Oh yes, that was the money you paid for my dowry"'(Jupp and PromPT, 1996). Controversially at the time, the methods revealed that less than 5 per cent of rural borrowers experienced financial profit from their loans. 'If we fail in our business, the credit organization does not worry. They only worry if we fail to make repayments.' Some rural women told the facilitators to ask the NGOs to stop giving so many loans. They were in considerable debt and felt pressurized to take more and more loans (Jupp and PromPT, 1996).

Reproductive health

In 1997, the Marie Stopes Organization commissioned PromPT (Jupp and PromPT, 1997a) to undertake a qualitative and quantitative baseline study on the reproductive health needs of female factory workers, commercial sex workers (CSWs), clients of commercial sex workers and poor urban women, in order to provide improved services at its seven health clinics situated in major cities in Bangladesh.

Although much work has been done subsequently with such groups all over the world, particularly related to the HIV/AIDS pandemic, there was very little experience of using participatory visualized methods probing sexual issues with these groups at the time.

Participants were mostly illiterate and worked long and atypical hours. In addition to the familiar visual methods of matrix ranking (of contraceptive

Figure 8.2 Conducting fieldwork on reproductive health. Meeting commercial sexual health workers under their makeshift shelter at dawn in Bangladesh.

preference and health-seeking behaviour), body-mapping, seasonality and daily routine analysis, new methods were devised to help the participants review their sexual activity. For example, small cut-out puppets depicting people from a range of professional and socioeconomic backgrounds were provided from which participants selected and ranked typical partners according to numbers of this type of partner they had had sexual contact with. Body-mapping was done as individuals, either drawing their own pictures or using prepared images and placing coloured stickers on the parts of the body where they experienced most pain and discomfort. Approximately 40 per cent of major illnesses experienced by female factory workers and 96 per cent by CSWs were found to be related to reproductive health. Of CSW clients, 60 per cent indicated that their priority health problem was in the genital area and a further 15–20 per cent indicated this to be a second priority. Men were provided with pictures depicting bachelorhood and marriage and were encouraged to use stickers to indicate the total number of sexual partners they had had at each period in their lives.

These were completed anonymously in privacy and then mixed up and shared with the whole group for discussion. All participants indicated that they had had premarital sexual relations and nearly 90 per cent with more than one woman. All married men included in the study had had extramarital sexual relations. The discussions also revealed the extent of the practice of men having

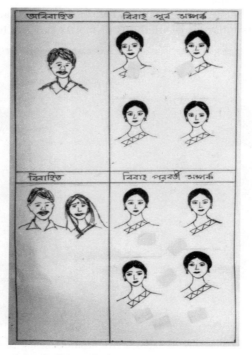

Figure 8.3 Sexual partners before and after marriage.

sex with men. The shared revelations were extraordinary for the men themselves, but also resulted in a sea change in the way HIV/AIDS and sexual health education and awareness were conducted in Bangladesh. The traditional view that the CSWs were to blame and that brothels should be shut down to avoid the spread of HIV/AIDS was discredited and the policy-makers were forced to accept that extramarital and homosexual sex was extensive. Awareness campaigns were redesigned to reach the general population.

Nothing like this had been done before. As long as individuals' privacy was maintained there seemed no end to the possibilities of exploring issues previously assumed to be taboo. The CSWs, usually fearful of harassment, arrest and media exposure, were prepared to spend long periods of time on these participatory exercises, late at night or at dawn. Even though a project of a major international NGO had recently paid them to participate in a questionnaire-based study and insisted that our study would have to follow suit, the team found only one incidence where payment was required. Why? Because the participants felt that they benefited from the visualized discussions and had been open to talk about issues previously considered too private. 'This is for us, you have come for us', was the sentiment frequently echoed. In fact, some even refused offers of tea and snacks, such was their commitment. These discussions paved the way for positive behaviour change enabling participants to be fully involved in analysing for themselves the benefits of change, both the steps and means for change and to establish collective support for change.

Peace-building

Some 30 Somalis (specially flown out of wartorn Somalia and gathered from the wider Somali diaspora) attended a peace building workshop held in Kenya and sponsored by Diakonia (Jupp, 2002). Although they all desired stabilization in their region in order to enable development, they represented different perspectives and factions and many had traumatic memories and had suffered emotional upheaval during long years of bitter conflict. This presented another challenge for dealing with sensitive issues. In order to bring issues out into the open without embarrassment or creating tension among the holders of diverse views, a giant mind-map (Buzan, 1996; see also below) was constructed across a whole wall of the venue. At the centre of the mind-map was the problem; a political stalemate and constitutional crisis affecting the Puntland region, and the only guidance given was to place causes of the problem on the left of the chart and effects on the right. Participants added in their own 'graffiti' in their own time (sometimes secretly) and gradually established and developed links and relationships between ideas. The final product spoke for itself.

The various issues at stake were visualized for all to see, but without judgement, and enabled a common understanding and a basis for determining action to deal with the issues and break the stalemate. The mind-map stayed on the wall throughout the four-day workshop as a reality check as the peace plan was crafted.

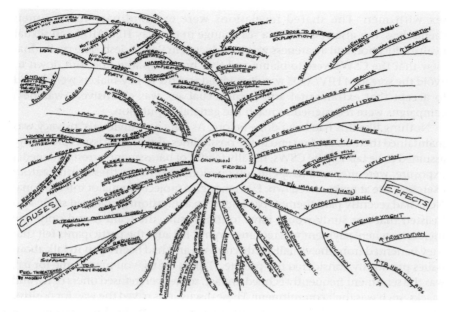

Figure 8.4 Peace building in Puntland, Somalia: a mind map.

Finding ways to listen to extraordinary voices

Just as PRA in the early years had been used in safer sectors, it had also almost always been used with the a general population of adults, usually defined by activity: farmers, mothers, group or club members, water users and so on. What about using it with people who were on the margins? What about using it with different age groups? What about using it with people who spoke rare dialects? What about using it with people with disabilities? These were people whose voices were least often heard and who are often the most difficult to meet, have the least time, are shy and inhibited, distrust outsiders and avoid participation for a variety of reasons.

The challenge involved redesigning participatory methods that could be used in these circumstances, but equally importantly, training acilitators who could work in awkward, uncomfortable, stressful and difficult conditions. Thus, we held extensive self-reflection sessions prior to working in such conditions in order to reduce prejudice and judgemental behaviour among facilitators, enabling them, for example, to meet CSWs at dawn in brothels or crouched in large drainpipes in Bangladesh and at bars and in taxis in Tanzania, to involve themselves in play sessions and theatre workshops with street children in Tanzania and Bangladesh, to accompany Bangladeshi factory workers on their way to and from work and to be taken to hidden locations in downtown Kingston, Jamaica to run sessions with dons and their gangs.

Cooperrider (1996), working with a social action foundation in Chicago, promoted the idea that children should interview adults. Some of the most

Figure 8.5 Street boys in Tanzania, drawing their dreams and fears.

interesting interviews producing the best data were those conducted by children. Cooperrider attributed this to children's ability to 'be surprised, inspired and inquire into our values and possible worlds', and went on to note 'a spirit of inquiry we (adults) need to redeem'. My own experience has borne this out on many occasions. For example, the street children in the Tanzania study revealed much about their fears and aspirations and the specific risks they face in their everyday life.

Children in urban slums of Jamaica produced insightful plans for the future of their communities. During poverty situation analyses in rural Jamaica, children were considered a nuisance at PRA sessions until facilitators routinely carried papers and crayons with them and encouraged them to draw what they liked and disliked about their community. Gradually, these children's drawings became integral in all sessions as they revealed another dimension of living in poverty. One particular example of how children's views led to immediate action occurred when very young children drew pictures of the things they disliked on their way to school. The most important image was of stray animals, which frightened them to such an extent that they found excuses not to go to school. Within days of sharing these pictures with the adults of the community, all stray animals were removed and community norms established to ensure that schoolchildren could walk to school without fear.

Poaching and fusion as sources of creativity

Other disciplines have been a great source of inspiration for participatory development. Elaine Dundon (2002) notes that 'relying on one source of information [for innovation] is like going fishing in a large pond and sitting in only one spot all day, hoping fish will come to you. What is needed is a bigger hook and movement round the pond.' In this section I provide examples of a few approaches which I am familiar with and which have used a 'bigger hook' to catch ideas from other disciplines and which have been adapted successfully in participatory development.

One of my own personal favourite pieces of poaching is the use of transactional analysis (TA) (Hay, 1992) in helping field workers and researchers to analyse their attitudes and behaviour as facilitators of participatory processes. Eric Berne first introduced TA in the 1950s as he set out to simplify Freudian principles for use in the practice of health and healing. He translated the 'id', 'superego' and 'ego' into child, parent and adult ego states respectively, terms that carry more personal meaning than Freud's categories. Berne put forward the idea that we all operate in all three states and these have nothing to do with our actual age. We can be a critical or nurturing parent in some circumstances, a playful or demanding child in others and, in yet others, a reasoning adult. TA refers to the fact that the dominance of one ego state can affect the relationship one has with another person. For example, taking a critical parent stance on an issue leaves little opportunity for the other person to adopt any other position than one of the admonished child. A relationship of mutual respect is achieved when both participants are able to adopt an adult-to-adult stance. It is this state that is the preferred interaction between external facilitator and participant.

In Bangladesh, I used this idea to prepare a number of role-plays where a 'facilitator' was given a particular role to adopt towards a 'participant', e.g. criticizing a rural mother's hygiene neglect as the cause of her child's diarrhoea ('critical parent') or sympathizing effusively with a destitute widow ('nurturing parent'). Observers of the role-play reflected on how the role-playing 'mother' or 'widow' reacted to the behaviour of the facilitator and noted that they seemed forced to react in childlike ways which diminished their power in the relationship.

Like TA, appreciative inquiry (AI)(Cooperrider and Srivastva, 1987) has been poached frequently. Originally developed by clinical psychologists, it has subsequently been used in human resource management and team building, and more recently in participatory development. The process focuses on conversations highlighting the positive and is sometimes referred to as 'inquiring with the heart'. It often follows the 4D cycle of conversations: 'Discover' which focuses on valuing the best of the current situation; 'Dream' which envisions what might be; 'Design' which discusses what should be; and 'Deliver' which deals with the practicalities of making change happen and focuses on future innovation and action. Deborah Duperly Pinks (personal communication) had come across this approach in her psychology studies and adapted it successfully with demoralized and demotivated inner city communities in Kingston, Jamaica. She asked community members to recall the last time they felt alive and engaged and to draw these experiences on paper. Sharing these drawings led to raised energy levels and reminded everyone that there were positives in the community that could be built upon. Tendencies to bring up past failures and current obstacles had to be continuously warded off by the facilitator redirecting attention to the magical moments. .

I have used AI in a number of participatory workshops, particularly where morale seemed low, problems insurmountable and where participants seemed to be in a rut. A notable occasion was working with government education departments in the eastern Caribbean where they were used to negative evaluations and working in a mode of fault-finding and fault-fixing. Educationalists and administrators were astonished by the diversity of exciting stories that emerged through AI. The energy devoted to these sessions was unprecedented and senior officials commented that they had never previously tapped these seams of innovativeness from the grassroots experience before. Similarly, in a workshop in 2002 with Afghan NGO workers, the participants' faces said it all: they were worn out, exhausted and had all experienced first hand atrocities and deprivation. We went through an AI exercise and participants found that they were able to reconnect with their old motivated and committed selves and see opportunities even in the current situation.

Like AI, the positive deviance concept posits that understanding why things go right and replicating the conditions which had generated small successful deviant practices is more useful than a preoccupation with problem-solving. This concept was first promoted in Hewlett Packard by its personnel manager, who used the process of amplifying positive deviants in an attempt to become the most successful research laboratory in the world. The manager searched out small grassroots initiatives from within the organization rather than relying upon externally driven transformation. These initiatives provided local and workable answers to many of the company's existing problems and sharing this indigenous knowledge led to huge gains. Save the Children staff (Sternin, 2002) adopted this approach to understand issues of child malnutrition in Vietnam. They asked villagers to track the weights of children in the village and focus particularly on the feeding practices of poor families, whose children were nevertheless well nourished. How did these positive deviants feed their children? The Save the Children staff helped these deviant mothers to teach others their secrets about how to provide better nutrition.

The facilitators at the Jamaica Social Investment Fund (JSIF) (personal experience) were encouraged to ask communities to identify communities exactly like theirs in terms of resources but which appeared to be harmonious and better developed. Exploration of these positive deviant communities provided important insights, particularly concerning issues of social capital. In the 'Views of the poor' study in Tanzania (Jupp, 2003), participants were asked to take photographs of houses and assets of people in the village whom they admired and reflect on what was different about their lives. The photographs were of those who shared many of the same background characteristics (tribe, land ownership, religion, education, etc) as the photographer, but had been able to utilize their resources more effectively, often as a result of higher stocks of social and psychological capital. This analysis of positive deviants gave some families inspiration for change.

'Fishbone' or 'Ishikawa analysis' was devised by Kaoru Ishikawa, a Japanese quality control statistician, and was originally primarily used in commercial organizations as a systematic means for teams to analyse the root causes of problems. It is called a fishbone because its construction resembles a skeleton of a fish. The problem to be reviewed is the 'head of the fish' and each bone of the fish represents different categories of problems. Brainstorming around these categories helps the team to analyse the causes of the problem under discussion. This technique is much more fluid than the problem tree demanded by logical framework exponents, as ideas can be loosely linked around themes and linear cause–effect relations are not required. Like the tree diagram used by Stepping Stones, its organic form is attractive and meaningful for participants and fun to construct.

The JSIF encouraged communities to use this method to examine why earlier community projects had failed as well as current constraints on community development (Jamaica Social Investment Fund, 2000). Communities found these constructs elucidating and this became the most popular way of reviewing problems, as evidenced by the dominance of displays of fishbone diagrams in the two community expos held in Kingston in 2000 and 2001 to demonstrate community action to politicians and the general public.

Mind-mapping, pioneered by Tony Buzan, involves creating a diagram comprising a web of related ideas, which radiate from the central or core idea. It supports creative thinking and unfetters the mind from conventional and restrictive linear thinking. Buzan (1996) argues that the mind actually operates with multiple thoughts and in multiple directions at the same time, and that our use of language and numerics, albeit essential in communication, inhibits full creativity. Mind-mapping is often an element in Future Search workshops (Weisbord and Janoff, 2000), which specialize in working with large numbers of participants. As mentioned above, one of the most enlightening mind-maps I facilitated was the one created as part of the peace and reconciliation process for Somalia.

'Value of time' is a standard technique for estimating time savings in the economic analysis of transport projects in developed countries. It is based on a questionnaire study of travellers' transport choices and estimates from the choices made (cost, time, comfort, safety, etc) how much value people put on travel time saving. Until recently, the approach was regarded as unfeasible in developing countries where illiteracy is high and transport choices limited. This meant that economists tended to base their economic feasibility analysis of transport projects on the more easily calculated vehicle operating costs alone. This, however, heavily biases investment decisions in favour of better-off areas. It was therefore considered critical to find a way to modify the conventional methods of valuing travel time so they could be used to ascertain the value of poor travellers' time. As a result the benefits accruing from their time-savings (albeit small per individual but substantial in terms of numbers of travellers) could provide robust arguments in favour of pro-poor infrastructure development.

My colleagues at IT Transport (IT Transport, 2002 and 2005), have conducted three studies in rural Bangladesh, Ghana and Tanzania and have shown that it is possible to determine the value of time savings in rural situations in developing countries using modified stated preference ranking techniques. Travellers are asked to examine the same journey using different means of transport or combinations of transport and rank their preference. In the Africa studies, the team developed a variety of visual techniques to make it possible for illiterate people to clarify the choices they can make. Children who had not directly experienced some transport options were able to imagine the advantages and disadvantages from photos and discussion.

The extent to which travellers are willing to pay for time saved in travelling can be computed. Economic methods are then applied by researchers to the value-time savings identified in the preference ranking exercise in terms of national wage rates. These methods had to be modified to take into account the lack of wage employment, the diversity of rural work and subsistence patterns, time use and multi-purpose travel. This modification was largely informed by using participatory methods of enquiry to contextualize people's preference ranking responses.

So successful have these studies been in demonstrating the usefulness of 'willingness to pay' based value of time studies that other applications – siting of markets and water pumps – are being planned as components of economic analyses.

Figure 8.6 Using a questionnaire survey on transport choices.

Performing arts use a variety of techniques, which theatre in development exponents have been adapting for many years. My daughter, who is a performing arts student, keeps me well supplied with ideas for using in participatory sessions. Her favourite theatre technique is the 'Yes, let's' exercise which requires everyone to suspend judgement and embrace a suggestion for doing something (in theatre arts such things as 'Yes, let's pretend we are aeroplanes' but in the development context it might be an icebreaker or common agreement to give attention to an unusual idea, such as 'Yes, let's think through a wild idea', or 'Yes, let's listen to what the children have to say'). Character development in theatre arts often uses experiential exercises to develop awareness about power relations. A method referred to as 'hierarchies' helps theatre students review emotional hierarchies, for example, increasingly intense manifestations of fear and positional hierarchies, for example, experiencing what it feels like to be junior pupil, sixth-former, teacher, head teacher, governor. An adaptation of this has proved useful for facilitators of participatory approaches to reflect on their behaviour and attitudes. It is also useful for communities to think through issues of power dynamics and develop empathy for different people's emotional experiences. Joanna Thomas used the theatre-inspired trust game to extraordinary effect with prisoners in the maximum security prison, Pollsmoor, in South Africa. As part of the 'Change is possible' programme, workshops were arranged in which gang members were forced to confront themselves. In one session, they were asked to fall backwards off a table into the arms of other prisoners. Many commented that they had never trusted anyone in their lives before.[44]

Fun, experimentation, risk-taking and resource limitations as creative stimuli

'What makes me innovative is the energy and focus created when people get absorbed by a method I have introduced. Their enthusiasm inspires me to think what I can do differently next time and how I can make it even better' Bimal Phnuyal (2005, personal communication).

What distinguishes excellent facilitators is their willingness to continually improve, adapt and create new ways of finding out. These are the people who, like Phnuyal above, constantly strive to make the experience for participants meaningful and different, who learn from each encounter and from the multiple realities of their participants.

As a consultant I am often asked to work on short contracts with strict budgets. While this has obvious constraints and can be frustrating, I would also claim that it has forced me to be extremely creative. The fact that I almost never have resources to write manuals or guidelines means that the approaches used are always fluid and evolving. Without the millstone of a big outlay in materials I can use local materials, access local resources and can ditch any earlier iteration which I might have otherwise held dear. I am free to invent and innovate for every new circumstance and this is very liberating. Of course, this also means that clients have to have trust in me.

The design of the 'Views of the poor' study in Tanzania (Jupp, 2003) was innovative because of resource limitations and a willingness of the donor, SDC, to take risks. In the early evolution of the terms of reference (TOR) it was proposed that this would be a small-scale assessment of the poor to 'provide glimpses of the other reality'. In-house reviewers threw in the inevitable arguments of lack of representativeness and the need for definitions and frameworks or constructs for poverty. Jointly, we worked hard to loosen up the TOR and expectations to enable the study to become genuinely the views of the poor. Fortunately, the two key persons involved in SDC, Peter Arnold and Gerhard Siegfried, had both experienced PMs first-hand and were able to defend the flexibility of the TOR and trust the consultant.

Several risks were taken. Staff of SDC and development partners were used as facilitators even though they had never done any field research before; throwaway cameras were provided to householders, who had never held a camera before, to take photographs of what they liked and disliked about their lives; and the study centred on spending complete days with selected households in an attempt to understand the other reality.

The new researchers (SDC and partner staff) were given a brief orientation, which focused on behaviour and attitudes rather than techniques and methods. The intention was to demystify the research process and emphasize participants' natural communication skills associated with immersion in new and unfamiliar situations. No label was given to what they were doing (this was not Participatory Rural Appraisal or the Participatory Learning and Action System), so there was no question of whether they were doing it right, no standard techniques, no manuals. Instead they were encouraged to just have conversations, get to know, find out and experience for themselves. It was suggested that they would encourage householders to use photos, drawings and stories, but there was no prescribed format. Facilitators gave camera users[45] very basic tips. Some photos were of sky or feet but the majority were surprisingly good quality.

The concept of spending a whole day with households worked well. Facilitators were able to work with the householders (fetching water, cooking, agricultural activities) so that the normal daily routine was largely maintained. This meant that the householders were more at ease accommodating the facilitators and chatted freely over joint tasks, and facilitators gained more insights into the deprivations experienced by the householders. Triangulation through conversations with different members of the family at different times was possible. The experience for the facilitators turned out to be unexpectedly transformative. Their first-hand insights and experiences gained during this brief exercise continued to be drawn on in policy discussions for many years. In the words of one researcher, 'Sincerely speaking the picture was not in my mind before the study... it seems I had never been in contact with such poor family members in the past. I understand that I am also coming from rural areas but didn't expect them to express the way they did' (Jupp, 2004).

Enabling the spread of innovativeness

Although the branded participation methods have been instrumental in bringing participatory approaches to a wide audience, it is essential to keep on discovering new ways of finding out. What started out as innovations have frequently lost their edge by routinized and unquestioning adherence to manuals and guidelines and have consequently gathered opponents who are increasingly sceptical about the superficial nature of many manual-driven participatory practices. It is not innovation but innovativeness (processes and means) that needs to be nurtured.

In conclusion, here is a brief reminder of ways you can promote innovativeness.

- Wide exposure and openness to **a variety** of participatory approaches.
- Maintain a **healthy irreverence**: it is important that facilitators rebel against attempts at indoctrination with a particular brand of participation.
- Use **generic language** to describe different contexts in which participation is used (e.g. participatory monitoring and evaluation, reflection process) rather than brand names and acronyms.
- Spread the **principles** of good participatory practice rather than the practices. For facilitators, coaching and self-reflection on attitudes and behaviour are more important than training in techniques.
- Grasp **opportunities** which require innovation (sensitive issues, hard-to-reach participants, poor resources).
- Embrace and develop half-baked ideas; **take risks**, try out and trust that the process will be iterative and should naturally evolve; avoid trapping yourself into method scripts which limit creativity; pilot emergent ideas, factor in time to debrief and reflect on what works and what does not, and modify as you go along.
- Create environments where facilitators and participants **want to invent**. Support play and having fun. Risk being thought crazy.
- Support **intuitive processes**, and if you have to, look for sources and roots for this after.
- Squash **repetition**. Do not allow facilitators to use the same approach over and over. It makes them lazy and the quality of participation always suffers.
- Look outside the discipline of participatory development and **poach** good ideas.
- As Walt Disney said, 'If you can dream it, you can do it!'

CHAPTER 9

HIV and AIDS, the global tsunami: the role of Stepping Stones as one participatory approach to diminish its onslaught

Alice Welbourn

Introduction

In December 2004 catastrophe hit the Indian Ocean when the tsunami killed nearly 300,000 people. Whole communities vanished. They were the poorest, living on societies' margins, both literally and metaphorically. There was a passionate international response to this catastrophe. Horrified, millions donated to appeals as its extent unfolded. This year, a silent disaster continues, rolling out around the world: the equivalent of 10 such tsunamis through deaths from AIDS-related illness and 16 tsunamis through new HIV infections. Although the immediate physical devastation will not be as great, with 40 million people globally now HIV-positive entire communities have also vanished. In sub-Saharan Africa, forests have disappeared because trees have been turned into coffins. Many farms have reverted to bush, because farmers spend all their time nursing sick relatives. Life expectancy in Botswana, a most prosperous African country, has dropped from 45 to 30. There is thus a massive, critical need for effective and meaningful approaches to address this global tsunami of HIV/AIDS.

Participatory approaches could surely help. However, many organizations wanting to scale up good-quality participatory interventions have faced challenges: demands from donors to provide quick-fix, short-term interventions; lack of funding for training or follow-up; and assumptions that one quick intervention per community should suffice. A particular challenge has been to find ways to encourage people to talk about HIV, sex, death – things most people just find very tough.

This chapter charts the development and fortunes of one participatory HIV/AIDS approach, called Stepping Stones, which, despite these challenges, is still widespread 10 years after publication. I start with an overview of its basic elements, then describe its creation, adaptations and spread. I then explore some of the funding challenges, and conclude with reflections and wider suggestions.

What is Stepping Stones?

The idea

Stepping Stones is a training package on gender, HIV, communication and relationship skills. Launched in 1995 and written as a personal response to my own HIV diagnosis, it built on and employed a wide range of participatory methodologies (PMs), including role-play, mime, body sculptures, drawings, discussions, debates, song and dance. No formal education is required, making the workshop process accessible to all. First developed with a multi-faith Ugandan community, many organizations internationally have widely adapted and translated it. One key attraction of the package is that people can relate easily to it through their own life experiences, which underpin all the exercises. Rather than imposing messages from above, this approach puts them in charge. Stepping Stones is designed to enable women and men of all ages, individually and collectively, to explore their social, sexual and psychological visions and needs, to analyse their communication blocks and to practise different ways of addressing their relationships with others. Workshops aim to enable people to change their behaviour through the stepping stones which the sessions provide. The package is eclectic, enabling people to explore the multiple issues affecting sexual health, including gender inequalities, lack of choice in household decision-making, money, alcohol use, traditional practices, attitudes to sex and violence, power imbalances between adults and young people, and attitudes to death and our own personalities. Although used mainly in HIV prevention work, Stepping Stones seeks to enhance lives, supporting participants to find their and others' lives worthwhile enough to want to preserve and look after.

Reasoning and purpose

Globally, most women and girls are socialized to look after their relatives, but are rarely encouraged to care for themselves. Financially and legally they also usually depend on others for material support, even though they may themselves contribute the most domestic labour, child care and food production. In these ascribed roles, women often become conditioned to compete for scarce resources against other women in their own communities, rather than supporting one another. Many women, particularly in poorer communities around the world, feel overwhelmed by their workloads, worn down by their subservient position and, perhaps hardest, feel that this is their rightful place in society, that somehow they are to blame if they are mistreated, and that they have no power – or right – to alter the status quo.

Similarly, in many parts of the world, many men, old and young, feel let down, ignored or rejected by their elders, that life has nothing to offer them, through poverty, lack of qualifications or of work opportunities. Often young men feel damaged and unsupported by a system in which they see no role for themselves. A common reaction to this sense of alienation in many societies is for males to act in brash, uncaring ways, to turn to alcohol and violence, or to feel suicidal or uninterested in preserving their lives. Such issues as love, care, trust, condoms, alcohol or other drug use, or the morals of gender violence often never enter their vocabulary.

Stepping Stones supports people to see possibilities in their lives which they had not previously considered. By enabling people to understand how our societies make us feel the ways that we do about our lives, and by then enabling people to articulate their hopes and fears to one another, Stepping Stones provides opportunities for participants to develop the understanding and belief that they can take control of and responsibility for their own lives, rather than feeling that their problems are their own fault, or their lives entirely governed by others. Participants then move on to practise skills that can start to turn these new realizations into reality, and to develop individual and joint strategies to improve the quality of their lives.

During the sessions, participants explore the range of factors that determine the quality of life, including physical, material, psychological, social and sexual wellbeing. Stepping Stones supports participants to form a strong bond, recognizing the values and contributions of all a community's parts. It works simultaneously at different psychosocial levels, enabling individuals, their peers, their partners, their wider families and neighbours to work on these issues concurrently. In this way, behaviour change, not only for HIV prevention, but also for multiple interrelated issues, can begin to take place in communities where workshops have been run well.

Content

The original Stepping Stones package was designed as 18 sessions, around four themes (see Table 9.1), over 3–4 months, for four parallel groups of older and younger women and men, meeting simultaneously.

Table 9.1 Stepping Stones themes

Theme 1 Group cooperation • positive and negative feelings about sex • what does love mean • taking risks • blaming others	***Theme 3*** *Why we behave in the ways we do* • hopes and fears for the future • exploring why we behave in the ways we do in sexual situations • pros and cons of alcohol use • pros and cons of traditional practices • issues around household income and expenditure • accepting and taking responsibility for our actions
Theme 2 HIV and safer sex • facts and feelings about HIV and people with HIV • learning about condoms	***Theme 4*** *Ways in which we can change* • assertiveness and rehearsing for reality • 'I' statements • trust • preparing for death • requesting community support to change the future

Each session lasts around three hours, with between one and two sessions a week, accommodating participants' availabilities. The timetable encourages participants to practise what they have learnt between each session and monitor these experiences in the sessions. To maximize attendance, the sessions seek to entertain as well as to challenge and explore. Sessions begin with a review of the previous session. Next comes a warm-up game, normally a fun introduction to that session's subject. Physical actions in these games help participants to remember key learning points. The main exercise(s) then follow, each lasting up to 40 minutes. A wind-down game helps bring participants back to reality. Stepping Stones progresses from easier sessions with less emotional content, to more challenging sessions, addressing taboos such as gender and age norms, and death. It was never intended as a manual in which people might dip and pick, so it works most effectively where the road map of the progressive exercises has been closely followed.

Challenges

One central tenet of participatory learning approaches is that we work on issues which openly concern community members, and do not impose our own agendas. But HIV challenges us, since it breeds on the combined taboos of gender, sex, religious morals and death. Each of these is hard enough to raise anywhere, so how participatory can we be and how manipulative do we need to be?

Although some have rightly suggested that the original Stepping Stones package focused too much on HIV for participants who had not yet considered its relevance to their own lives, the original manual did differ significantly from other contemporary HIV methodologies, since participants could realize how much HIV connects to many general concerns. Theme 3 addresses the hopes and fears of young men and women for their futures. Here the manual really began to diverge from most contemporary HIV packages. Unsurprisingly, from there on, many facilitators found it very challenging, if they had not yet had the chance to address these issues personally in their own lives. But conventional scare tactics, or simplistic, externally generated IEC (Information, Education and Communication) messages,[46] with scant perceived connection with local experience, could not address such complex emotional issues. Such approaches just undermine those who have no choice over what happens to them in their lives; they often produce blame of HIV-positive people, making others scared of us, as if it must be our fault that we have been foolish enough to acquire the virus, rather than helping us all to understand its true complexities.

Stepping Stones creation

The initial plan

Stepping Stones is in a series of booklets and videos produced by the Strategies for Hope (SFH) project, at that time linked to ActionAid.[47] The series aims to promote informed, positive thinking and practical action on HIV/AIDS by all sections of society. In 1993 SFH decided to produce a booklet on women and HIV. Although I then knew little professionally about HIV, with my background in gender, health issues and Participatory Rural Appraisal (PRA), combined with my own newly diagnosed HIV status, the series editor risked hiring me. Soon I suggested that we might develop a training package on both women and men and their interactions.

Sources of advice and influence

The Stepping Stones package benefited from the wonderful contributions of many advisers from Uganda, Norway, the UK and elsewhere advising on content, style, design and illustrations. Redd Barna (Norwegian Save the Children) was working in Buwenda, Uganda, the location of the first workshop. They had developed the community's trust, and most basic needs, such as food security and primary education, were addressed. Rose Mbowa and three former drama students facilitated this first workshop. Partly prepared in outline beforehand, it was then developed and fine-tuned in situ, with long meetings each evening after daytime sessions with the community, analysing what worked, what did not and what else was missing. The video team drew out marvellous vignettes illustrating day-to-day issues in participants' lives and the many connections to HIV.

The package was further influenced by experiences from diverse countries and disciplines, through books, contacts and my own personal experiences. These included a 12-week workshop in the USA with gay men who identified themselves as addicted to sex, and explored why and how they put themselves at risk physically and psychologically (Kelly et al., 1989); British women's assertiveness training workshops (Willis and Daisley, 1990); work with the police on their attitudes to sexual violence in Zimbabwe (Taylor and Stewart, 1991); the Freirean use of theatre to confront exploitation and oppression in Latin America (Boal, 1992); conflict resolution work with young offenders in British prisons (Fine and Macbeth, 1992a, 1992b) and with young people in Soweto, South Africa (Quaker Peace Centre, 1992). All these sources influenced the package.

Other threads that contributed were through my involvement in the PRA/PLA movement (Pretty et al., 1995; Cornwall et al., 1993; Scoones, 1995), and links with the creators of internationally based gender and communication training manuals (Guijt, 1995; Williams, 1994; Chandler et al., 1994). Discussions with Kirsten Røhme, who worked in a Norwegian rehabilitation centre for patients recovering from trauma, were very helpful, as were two good packets of training materials on HIV and family planning (Dixon and Gordon, 1990; Lynch and Gordon, 1991). My PhD research in Kenya (Welbourn, 1984), based on 15 months of living with a poor, isolated agricultural community in Kenya, about 50 miles from the nearest tarmac, also influenced the material. Finally, my own HIV diagnosis – and through that, meeting other HIV-positive people and hearing about their experiences from them – provided all kinds of insight into the issues which no reading or workshops could ever provide. Now many of the ideas in Stepping Stones have become more commonplace. Thankfully this reflects the growth in understanding of the complexity of sexual and reproductive health issues and the influence of gender inequities in particular.

Why the emphasis on gender and age?

Before developing Stepping Stones, I already had a strong interest in the social construction of authority, through gender, age and access to and control of material culture. This developed during my PhD research and subsequently in using PLA tools to examine issues of socioeconomic intra-communal differences (Welbourn, 1991). Unless outsiders seek to find out from different subgroups in a community what issues concern them, they normally only meet the wealthier male elders and miss out on huge concerns faced by poorer and younger men, and by women. The whole area of rights of inclusion and participation of different community members was one which, until then, had been largely neglected by many development practitioners, who felt threatened by gender and child rights issues.

By contrast, in most sexual and reproductive health programmes, men have been neglected. Yet health practitioners are now increasingly realizing that gender is a crucial ingredient, not only in behaviour change, but also in the diagnosis and treatment of many conditions (Gender and Health Group et al., 2005), and that little can change for women unless men change also. But when Stepping Stones was first developed this was largely an unknown concept and most HIV work was being targeted at people who were seen in some way to be 'abnormal' members of society: at that time, gay men in the West and in the South, sex workers, whose 'unacceptable' ways of behaving needed 'controlling'. So Stepping Stones was different in explicitly focusing on established heterosexual relationships between men and women and not on the margins. (I did not address same-sex relationships in the workshops, since I had no valid personal experience on which to draw. However, sexual orientation is a key gender issue and we recently ran an exchange workshop between African Stepping Stones trainers and the Associacion des Hombres Contra la Violencia in Nicaragua, which focuses on challenging homophobia and its links to gender violence,[47] in order to develop work on this issue.)

Spread and adaptation

No package is of any use unless it is accessible. Stepping Stones, distributed by SFH through Teaching-aids at Low Cost (TALC), is fortunate. With around 15,000 English- and French-speaking, mainly African, contacts, SFH channels profits from sales in free and widespread distribution to others who cannot afford them. In 10 years from September 1995, TALC sold 6,000 English and French manuals and distributed 4,815 free. They also sold and gifted around 4,000 videos, in English, French, kiSwahili and Luganda. All original production costs have been recouped through sales. The reputation of other SFH materials and TALC has helped to promote Stepping Stones, as has its website.[48] Thus, despite not being widely promoted, many NGOs have translated, adapted and used it in their communities, and it clearly meets a need many programmes. One NGO worker recently stated:

> I think this is the best methodology that I have had the opportunity to work with in my more than 20 years of experience working directly with women and men in poor communities ... I am very motivated to continue promoting, together with you, this way of working which I am sure will contribute much to slowing the advance of the HIV/AIDS pandemic in Latin America. (Rosa Isabel Garza Caligaris, consultant to the HIV/AIDS Campaign, ActionAid Honduras)

But using Stepping Stones properly is not a quick fix. It requires time, good training, skilled facilitation, care, negotiation, prolonged follow-up and more time. A drug might perform excellently under ideal laboratory conditions, but less well in the real world, where many factors may influence its use. Similarly, under the initial laboratory conditions of Buwenda, Uganda, with highly experienced, trusted facilitators and a well-motivated community, participants reported some remarkable changes after the workshop. But how replicable are these changes elsewhere, with less able facilitators, less locally suitable adaptations, or less trust of the outside agency? Many factors can hinder the effective transfer of such a package.

Nonetheless, many agencies in around 50 countries have adapted Stepping Stones for themselves. We know of adaptations for non-rural community contexts: for students in Zambia, Namibia and South Africa, for urban South Africa and Russia, for wholly Muslim communities in The Gambia and Bangladesh, for people in prison in Morocco and for pre-drug-using communities in Myanmar. Additional modules on sexual and reproductive rights, teenage pregnancy, STIs, contraception, infertility, abortion, puberty and menopause, sexual problems and gender violence[49] have been written.

These local adaptations are crucial to the organic development of the package, to keep it alive and directly locally relevant. The length is a major challenge, and adaptors often omit certain sessions, especially the one on preparing for death. This is emotionally very challenging and some potential users of the package have initially refused to use it because they feel so shocked by facilitating conversations about death, a taboo often far greater than talking about sex. However, in contexts like Zimbabwe and The Gambia, where this session was initially dropped, and use of any of the package was in some cases even jeopardized because of this session, it has subsequently been reinstated, as trainers have realized its crucial relevance to the position of women in society, particularly when widowed. Others have also remarked that their own shortened versions have often grown as long as the original package.

Stepping Stones has also been badly used. In particular we feel disappointed when we hear that organizations have adapted it to impose their own – often moralistic – views on participants, rather than facilitating a process whereby participants are enabled to make their own decisions about what will work best for them. We also feel disappointed when we hear that participants have become elite groups in their communities, through not sharing the basic ideas of the workshop with their friends; or when sex workers in those communities have felt ostracized. These outcomes were certainly not intended by us.

Funding and donor issues

Multiple funding sources

Like other SFH publications, Stepping Stones had multiple donors, primarily Redd Barna, Charity Projects and the Swiss Agency for Development Corporation (SDC). Further contributions from ActionAid, Oxfam, United Nations Development Programme (UNDP) in Senegal and the World Health Organization (WHO) completed its budget of nearly £114,000 over 16 months. Multiple funding sources were necessary and intentional, since I wanted the package to be owned by many, rather than just one agency. HIV was already such a huge issue that I felt it would need widespread effort.

The challenges of continued funding

However, challenges in funding the ongoing use of Stepping Stones programmes over the years have developed. Here is one story as I understand it.

A big NGO received funding from a large government donor to develop training capacity among staff in several African countries, to start facilitating Stepping Stones workshops in those countries. The donor agency sent two consultants, who had not, to my knowledge, themselves used Stepping Stones. Their brief was to assess the progress of the organization's whole HIV programme, including the Stepping Stones component.

The consultants produced a report for the donors. An employee of the donors, who has since left the organization, told me:

> The problem that Stepping Stones has experienced is due, I believe, to a review conducted by ****** and ****** on ***** in 200*. They assert that 'Stepping Stones has been adopted with no convincing evidence that it is an effective tool for behaviour change or that it is relevant to stigma reduction initiatives'. [Their first recommendation was to] 'Discontinue all ****** funded Stepping Stones work by ****** or ****** partners unless persuasive independent evidence of efficacy becomes available by end of July 200*.

After this recommendation, this donor stopped all funding to this particular programme for Stepping Stones. Partners about to start workshops suddenly had no salary or project budget.

I next learnt that another NGO, quite unconnected with the one above, approached the same donor for funds, including Stepping Stones in its proposal, as it had done successfully on various previous occasions. This time this donor informed them that it no longer funded Stepping Stones work at all.

It is true that Stepping Stones does not have a formal evidence base for its effectiveness, despite the wildfire way in which it has spread and been adopted by NGOs operating in many diverse environments. However, so far as I am aware, there is also no other comparable community-based training package in use on this scale around the world which does have such a formal evidence base (Jewkes et al., 2006).

Stepping Stones has been widely and independently bought by organizations in over 100 different countries across Africa, Asia, North and South America and Europe. When the package has been used well, accounts of its effects on the individual lives of trainers, facilitators and participants are remarkably uniform and positive. Many report that the training has had a profound effect on both their personal and professional lives.[50] They explain that they now realize that HIV can happen to them too, and that this has shifted their attitudes towards HIV and people with HIV. Stepping Stones is also listed by several UN agencies in their recommended resources for community work.

Peter Piot, UNAIDS director, has stressed that in the face of this global AIDS pandemic we need to base our work on 'evidence-informed' rather than 'evidence-based' action. Therefore, it would seem that the UNAIDS director is not calling for the 'persuasive independent evidence of efficacy' which the consultants recommended, or which the donor agency appears to need before funding Stepping Stones further. Who is right? Who has the right to judge what is right?

One possible solution would be for this donor to fund a formal evaluation. But these are always costly, lengthy and complicated. Alternatively, the donor could have consulted other Stepping Stones users elsewhere, before stopping its funding. A third solution might have been for the agency to conduct a literature search of the effects of Stepping Stones on communities elsewhere. So far as I am aware, none of these options has been pursued to date.

Political climates, upward accountability and their negative impact on creative thinking

There is another, even more worrying issue here. Increasingly, many donors expect us to define clearly in advance what all our outputs and outcomes are going to be, and whom funds will be spent on. So there is no investment in creativity; there is no faith in us as creative agents of change, nor in the people with whom we might work, as independent thinkers who might come up with new good ideas for themselves, based on their own experiences, along the way. The imposition of a set agenda which allows no room for exploration or experimentation is stifling critical opportunities for learning.

The story above is just one of many about donors' increased calls for rigour, accountability and inflexibility of funding. While donors should be accountable to their citizens regarding what they fund, there is an urgent need for donors, practitioners, academics and communities, including HIV-positive people themselves, to meet and agree on an acceptable, affordable, flexible and transparent framework to assess PMs like Stepping Stones. That framework should ensure that the processes reflect, first and foremost, the true realities of people's lives, particularly the lives of those most affected – HIV-positive people and their carers – rather than the donors' perceptions. That framework should accept that a critical mass of anecdote can also be highly accurate, and that rigour also needs to reflect realities. We need to start demanding accountability from donors, with basic standards of behaviour, especially with regard to phasing out funding, rather than stopping it abruptly, to ensure that staff members, their families and communities are not suddenly left without a salary or a planned workshop.

Decision-makers in donor agencies need better training; and we need to insist that if donors want convincing evidence before they will fund a well-established programme further, that they be prepared to fund that research also. We need to demand that key donor agency staff and the consultants whom they hire have themselves had some first-hand experience of the grassroots lives over which they are making decisions, for instance regular compulsory immersion programmes (Irvine et al., 2004).

HIV: costs compared with investment?

Meanwhile, there are also donors who still, despite all the statistics and projections and the increasing concerns of the business world about the impact of HIV on its global markets, do not think they need to fund HIV work at all, because in their view, HIV does not have anything to do with their own particular interests. Yet my question is: 'What will happen to the work you fund if good work on HIV is not going on alongside it?' When it comes to funding to keep HIV-positive people alive, politicians and UN bodies alike talk about the costs involved in raising enough finances to pay for drugs. Yet none of them talks about the costs to individuals, communities, countries, our global society – and world business – of not investing in those drugs to keep people alive and healthy.

Yet we participatory practitioners do not help ourselves. We do not talk about the positive effects of our efforts in financial terms. Stepping Stones has recouped all its original budget. If we think about the numbers of individuals in communities around the world who say that they have benefited from its contents, I would like to hope that the original investors in that package feel good about that investment and their leap of faith in this creative process.

Reflections, lessons, challenges

As practitioners we have particular responsibilities when we try to address aspects of all our behaviour which are so deeply rooted that the idea of change is deeply frightening. When it comes to HIV, we need to remember that we are dealing with global taboos. I still cannot think of a harder issue to get people to talk about, to address and to change in their own lives, on the scale that HIV is currently demanding of us. So I suggest we need a radical reassessment of our work, to address this challenge. Below I summarize some ideas which might support more effective sustained change.

Freedom from organizational planning structures and creativity produced by donor flexibility

Stepping Stones took much longer to produce than originally envisaged, and than any normal organizational planning would allow. But the relative independence of the SFH series and the ongoing trust of the series editor in the design process were critical. Without this leeway, it is very doubtful that the original manual would have been as effective as it has been. Inputs from many advisers were also key in producing a package that was far more eclectic than others at that time. Third, since several donors and NGOs were funding it, they too had a communal stake in the package and were therefore ready to use it themselves and recommend it to others.

Methods and messages: one size does not fit all

Each participatory approach will only appeal to and transform the lives of a few at any given time. Educationalists are now realizing that different children learn in different ways and that teachers need to present new concepts, both through various subjects and through varied teaching methods, so that children have a greater opportunity to learn than they could when fewer traditional, narrowly defined teaching methods were used. Thus teachers now diversify their techniques, through movement, touch and actions, as well as sight and sound, to reach a broader range of students through a wider use of all our senses.

Yet we in the development world seem to have been slow to realize this. Perhaps we should all be thinking much more creatively about people out there as individuals rather than as the masses and about how we learn. Perhaps we should more consciously be finding ways of making sure that we have a variety of interventions available to choose to pick up, run with and develop, rather than assuming, as we so often do, that there must just be one perfect package out there, one perfect method, that can be spoon-fed, to sort out the same issues for everyone.

Thus, I do not believe that any one training package, board game, photo novella, rap song, film or talk, no matter how great it is, and no matter how life-changing it may be for some people, is going to persuade most people to change the way they behave for good. Life is far too complicated for that. Instead, I believe that as good agents of change we need to ensure that there is also a steady flow of new ideas to complement the classics, new ways of looking at things, use of new media, so that we can all go on learning, can go on seeing the world in a different light, can go on developing new perspectives on old conundrums.

It is only human for people to get bored with the same old messages, even if they are ones which appealed and rang true for them in the first place. Older and poorer people are much better at repairing old objects than are younger or better-off people in general. But if we look at messages, we see people of any background wanting to hear new music or new stories, adding them to those they already like, rather than just sticking with a limited repertoire.

Investment – not subsidy – needs sufficient funds

In the media we often hear about the importance of investment in business and industry. Yet we rarely hear of investment in development, as if it is a foregone conclusion that funds from donors, which we instead call grants, have no worth. The general public in the UK and the USA believes that there are huge funds available for Africa, and also that funding anything in the third world is like pouring liquid gold down a drain. This is partly because of the way in which issues are presented by politicians and the media, without explaining the conditionalities imposed by donors; and partly because of our own poor ability to present the success stories which funding good programmes has generated. The very words that we use create a firm – but very false – division between the developing world and the rest, suggesting that those of us who live in the West or the North somehow are more advanced than the majority of the world.

We need to shift paradigms and challenge our own countries more to realize that development is not a constant drain on the rich, restraining their own progress towards the domination of competitive world markets. Actually it is the mindset of all of us which is at fault. Thus development should instead be described as cooperation, for instance (as GTZ describes it in its name); and this process of engagement should be seen as a critical investment in the future survival and prosperity of all the planet.

Perhaps we should also be aware that investment in people's creative thinking, through training and participatory methodologies which enable anyone to take control of their own lives and plan for their own futures, is every bit as valid and important as investment in goods or objects. This concept of investment in people, through education, health and basic needs provision, certainly seems to have been pivotal to economic development in East Asia.

Moreover, investment in people needs to be enough to ensure that the intended work is viable. Most good participatory work with which I have been involved has been chronically underfunded. This has not only hampered the development of the work itself, but has also placed a huge drain on energy, as staff and communities have spent much time worrying how to keep their ideas afloat. Adequate resources to enable the creative thinking processes of community members are crucial to good development work. Without them, volunteers can do amazing things on very little – but even volunteers have to eat, to earn an income, to maintain their morale and feed their families.

Holistic approaches

I suggest there is also something to learn from the way that global businesses have realized that they need to make their products and advertisements appeal to other parts of people's lives, in order to maintain their profits. Thus, in buying a fizzy drink, for example, customers get the feeling that they are buying a whole life-style. This is a common marketing ploy these days, which many of us deplore. Yet it certainly resonates with social science research findings of the 1970s and our own views as creators of PMs, recognizing as we do from a community perspective that all aspects of our lives are interlinked and overlapping, and that the newspaper we read is likely to connect with the clothes we wear, the books we read, the radio programmes we listen to or people we spend most time with. One recent award-winning example of this is the 'Snake' condom campaign among Aboriginal groups in Australia, in which the condom is shown as a part of the attractions of young Aborigine identity.

Last but not least, we all need to wake up to the fact that HIV can affect us all. There is still great emphasis on targeting sex workers, gay men or drug users: people already placed at the margins of society. While the issues facing these three groups do certainly need special attention, this sole focus has often served to heighten existing prejudice against them. This has also made others complacent about the risks they also face. Now that UNAIDS cites marriage as a risk factor in HIV acquisition for women and girls in Africa and beyond, traditional views on targeting specific populations are inadequate. Stepping Stones broke new ground in that it was written on the assumption that anyone in a community could be HIV-positive and deserves equal rights and respect alongside everyone else. As with all participatory approaches, we will produce our best work when we begin with questioning our own values, attitudes and actions. With HIV, perhaps more than in any other issue in our lives, we must begin – and continue - to challenge ourselves.

CHAPTER 10

Using numerical data from participatory research to support the Millennium Development Goals: the case for locally owned information systems

Sarah Levy

Introduction

Between 1999 and 2003, I was part of a team of researchers based in the UK and Malawi which developed an innovative approach to generating national statistics using participatory methods. The aim of this approach was to support development at the macro level, by informing national policy decisions with evidence – including numerical evidence – from participatory research. It was different from previous approaches in that it was designed to generate statistics from participation that would be representative of the country as a whole: reliable national statistics (Barahona and Levy, forthcoming).

I would argue that generating statistics from research using participatory methods is important if the aim is to support actions at national level which will contribute to human development, for example, by informing the poverty reduction programmes required to meet the Millennium Development Goals (MDGs). However, the approach produces one serious problem: it does not lead directly to development activities in the communities visited by the researchers, nor does it produce any sort of immediate benefit for these communities. Barahona and Levy (2003) argue that the approach is valid, and, with the right measures in place, avoids the extractive nature of traditional methods of data collection. Nevertheless, a conflict continues to exist between research that is designed to inform national policy (even that which respects participatory principles) and processes which contribute to development at the local level.

This chapter suggests a way to resolve this conflict by going a step further than we have done so far. While collecting information that allows policy-makers to take evidence-based decisions, we could also enable communities to improve decision-making processes and to support development at the local level. For example, communities might identify problems in their areas and, with the help of statistics, they might persuade local governments to improve things. Statistics can be very powerful tools for advocacy. Participatory approaches can now provide much of the relevant numerical data, although care must be taken to avoid bad practice.

The chapter draws on my experience as part of a team from the University of Reading which was invited to evaluate a large-scale, free agricultural inputs programme in Malawi (Levy, 2005). When we began work in 1999, the programme was known as 'Starter Pack', and it provided inputs for nearly 3 million rural households. Later, it was scaled down and became known as the Targeted Inputs Programme (TIP).

The second section describes how our approach evolved through studies involving researchers from different traditions (participation and statistics). One such study, in 1999–2000, focused on the relationship between Starter Pack and sustainable agriculture (Cromwell et al., 2000). Tough debates between these traditions, a fruitful exploratory consultation phase and an intensive methodology workshop in which we adapted our approach for the main phase of the study produced lessons for the design of future studies.

The third section presents a study which took place in Malawi in the 2001–2 main agricultural season (Chinsinga et al., 2002). The techniques used in this study allowed us to generate national-level statistics on complex issues by combining key statistical principles with participatory research methods. The study produced reliable results, and did so in a timely manner, feeding into important national-level policy decisions. However, the data were analysed back in the office by the researchers, so the communities who took part did not see, let alone own, the results. They could not be used to lobby for changes at the local level.

The chapter goes on to look at a study that was carried out in Malawi in 2003 (Chinsinga et al., 2004), in which some data analysis was carried out with the participants who had provided it before the researchers left the communities (fourth section). This was a step forward, in that important issues were highlighted and could be followed up by the participants after the study team had gone away.

However, the problem with most research studies, including those using participatory methods, is that they come and go, leaving little or nothing of what they produce with the communities that provided the information. This way of working is not satisfactory. The last part of this chapter argues that governments and donors should now consider the case for establishing permanent, locally owned information systems. It looks at the potential that exists to develop such systems, at both local and national levels. Finally, it considers what such systems would involve, and calls for a serious analysis of their costs and benefits.

Evolving methods through a clash of cultures

What was it that led us to develop an approach that could generate national statistics using participatory methods? In 1999, our team was made up of people from numerical backgrounds, including statistics, but with some experience of

Participatory Rural Appraisal (PRA) and Participatory Learning and Action (PLA). For the Malawi work, we recognized that much of the information we were interested in was too complex to collect using questionnaires, so we joined forces with practitioners of participation. For instance, to study Starter Pack and sustainable agriculture we worked with Elizabeth Cromwell of the Overseas Development Institute (ODI), London, her Malawi-based research partners and members of two NGOs. Our aim was to explore the issues with participatory approaches, but to produce nationally representative information to enhance the credibility of the findings when presented to policy-makers.

Our first discussions were tough: the statisticians on our team wanted a large-scale study in some 40 sites selected using probability-based sampling to give a representative picture of Malawi. The researchers with participatory backgrounds said that it would be impossible to work in so many sites, because they would have to sacrifice in-depth exploration of the issues. A compromise was eventually agreed: the study would have an exploratory consultation phase, in which teams would work in three sites where they would spend a week trying to understand the key issues, experimenting with methods and identifying ways of measuring indicators. Then, in the main phase, a PRA lasting three days would be carried out in 30 sites.

The exploratory phase proved to be a rich learning experience. On the teams' return from the field, a workshop was organized to compare results. We looked at what had been learnt about the issues, which methods had worked and which had had to be abandoned. We homed in on the methods that seemed to be capable of replication in a large number of sites. We tried to get a balance between qualitative information and numbers, by incorporating techniques ranging from transect walks and focus group discussions to trend analysis of factors influencing the sustainability of farming over time and indicators of sustainability matrices (Cromwell et al., 2000).

At one point during the workshop, we realized that the ranking matrices with which the teams had experimented in the exploratory phase would not be capable of producing the desired results in the main phase of the study because different items and numbers of items were being ranked in different sites. Carlos Barahona (a statistician) pointed out that this meant that data from different sites could not be compared or aggregated to produce national results. We would have to predetermine the set of indicators to be ranked, which we could do on the basis of the initial consultations, so that the outcomes could be compared and the data aggregated to national level.

We realized during this workshop that the need for comparability and national-level aggregation also implied that we had to collect information in the same way in each site. Thus, after a fully flexible exploratory phase, a degree of standardization was introduced for the main phase. We produced a field manual with precise instructions for the teams about how to proceed, and a document for recording the information produced in each site (a debriefing document). However, standardization only applied to the key questions and to recording key data; the aim was not to restrict participants' discussions.

Targeting the poor in Malawi

In the 2001–2 agricultural season, the TIP distributed only 1 million packs. The government's intention was that these would go to the 'poorest of the poor. This was to be achieved by a process of community poverty targeting which aimed to empower communities to identify the TIP beneficiaries (Chinsinga, 2005). In Government of Malawi and donor circles, the assumption was that if TIP aimed to target the poorest of the poor, then the poorest of the poor would indeed receive the packs. But the 2000–1 TIP evaluation had suggested that community poverty targeting was not working, and that the communities involved were unhappy about it.

Therefore, in 2001–2 the evaluation teams decided to check whether the packs were reaching the poorest of the poor, and if not, why not? Did the communities have good reasons for their actions? Was targeting in Malawi doomed to failure? Or was it that the programme was doing something wrong, and this could be corrected? To answer these questions, we joined forces with a Malawian team led by Blessings Chinsinga of the University of Malawi to design the 'TIP Messages' study (Chinsinga et al., 2002).

Design of the study

We decided that such complex questions could only be answered by consulting people in the communities which had been asked to do the targeting, and that the most efficient way of doing this would be to use participatory methods. However, we also needed to be able to produce numerical information (statistics) that would be representative of the country as a whole. So we needed an approach that went beyond traditional PRA techniques to allow the numerical data recorded in each participatory study site to be aggregated and analysed at national level. This meant introducing statistical principles into the design of the study.

The approach that we developed involved integrating statistical principles and participatory approaches right from the beginning. The selection of villages was done by a professional statistician using a probability-based sampling method.[51] At village level, we aimed to avoid the problems of conflict between participatory approaches, which rely on volunteers to participate, and the need for representative samples of the village population by asking a group of volunteers acting as key informants to produce information on every household in the village (i.e. a census). This would create the conditions for any numerical data generated to be aggregated between sites without the need for within-village sampling.

In order to be able to aggregate the numerical data which we collected from the different study sites, we also needed the information recorded in each site to be comparable (as in the sustainable agriculture study). In other words, it must be collected in exactly the same way in each site. But the information would be coming from participatory discussions, which need to be flexible. How could we resolve this potential conflict?

The answer that we found was to require the researchers to standardize certain elements of the work (those that would produce numbers) but allow maximum flexibility in the discussion of the issues. An example of this was our approach to the discussion of food insecurity. When raising the issue of food, its importance to people and the problems of food shortages the facilitators encouraged a wide-ranging and flexible discussion. However, when it came to trying to find out how many people in the community were food insecure, we used common definitions of food security and insecurity to allow comparisons between sites. We agreed to use the following definitions in all study sites.

- Food secure (FS): households that have enough to eat throughout the year from harvest to harvest.
- Food insecure (FI): households that have enough food to last from harvest up to Christmas but not between Christmas and the next harvest.
- Extremely food insecure (EFI): households that have a longer period of not having enough to eat. These households start facing severe food shortages before Christmas.

We used Christmas as a reference point because it is a clearly identifiable event that participants could recall, and it coincides with the onset of the 'hungry period' (January to March/April) before the main season harvest in April/May.

From previous studies which assessed how the poor perceive poverty in rural Malawi (Chinsinga et al., 2001; van Donge et al., 2001), we knew that food security is seen as a key indicator of poverty. We therefore decided to use food security as a proxy for poverty, with EFI approximating the 'poorest of the poor'. Although it could be argued that this was an oversimplification, our aim was to find an uncomplicated way of dividing the community into groups to reflect people's perceptions of poverty (Levy, 2003).

Community mapping with cards

The participatory technique that we developed to enable us to generate numerical data on every household in the village was community mapping with cards. This proved to be an extremely powerful tool for producing numbers that can be analysed at village level and – if sampling is done appropriately – at any other level (small areas, districts, regions and the country as a whole). It should produce very reliable data, as the approach is visual and involves in-depth discussion and crosschecking.

What is community mapping with cards? It begins by asking for a group of volunteers to produce a map of the community. This is similar to a social map, in that it shows the key features in the community – geographical, institutional and so on. The main difference is that each household must be marked clearly on the map and given a number. Along an edge of the map, the households are listed by name and number. In order to do this successfully, the participants involved in the mapping exercise need to include people from all sectors of the community, so that members of the group have sufficient knowledge about all households in the community and can act as key informants. A limitation of the approach is that it is probably only feasible in small, rural communities.

Once the map has been completed, a card is produced for each household on the map. At the top of the card, the number of the household is written. In the Malawi study, the cards were then used in discussing different topics. For instance, the same group of participants that did the social mapping was invited to discuss the food security situation in the village and then to place each household in a pile according to which food security category it belonged to, using the predefined categories of FS, FI and EFI. The facilitator then marked all the cards in the FS pile with a food security status (FSS) of 3, all the cards in the FI pile with a FSS of 4, and all the cards in the EFI pile with a FSS of 5. Similarly, information was recorded on the households' TIP status (TS): whether the household had received a TIP pack or not. If the household had received a pack, its TS was recorded as 1; if it had not received a pack, its TS was recorded as 2.

On return to the office, the research team was able to produce statistics on the percentage of FS, FI and EFI households in each village, and for the country as a whole. The study estimated that 32 per cent of households in Malawi were EFI in 2001–2. It was also able to produce tables at village and national levels showing the relationship between receiving a TIP pack and food security status. These showed that the community targeting process had been generally unsuccessful in targeting the most food-insecure households (Barahona and Levy, 2003). The reasons for this lack of success were examined in the next part of the study (see Section 3.3).

The use of the cards allowed us to record a considerable amount of information about households in the village, following – or as part of – in-depth discussions of each topic. Thus, we ended up with the sort of household information normally collected by surveys, but with the advantage that it was the product of discussion during which people would challenge and correct each other. The type of information collected was limited to information in the public domain (not information of a sensitive or personal nature), but this is also a limitation of most surveys.

Using the household cards to study complex issues

During the TIP Messages study, the study teams went on to use the household cards with three other groups of participants who had not been involved in the social mapping. The aim was to understand why community targeting was not succeeding. The three groups were made up of volunteers representing different types of stakeholders in relation to the process of selecting TIP beneficiaries in the 2001–2 season: the village authorities who had selected the beneficiaries, the beneficiaries and the non-beneficiaries. The study team asked each group (separately) to discuss what criteria should be used to select beneficiaries to receive packs. As a result of the study's exploratory consultation phase, we already had a list of possible criteria which the groups could discuss and add to. The participants were then asked to consider every household card and say whether it should have qualified to receive a TIP pack according to one of the criteria for eligibility.

The data recorded on the cards by the three separate stakeholder groups was analysed by the researchers on their return to the office. They produced both national and disaggregated statistics showing what percentage of households met each of the criteria for qualifying to receive a pack, and what percentage of households did not qualify. This numerical data could not have been produced in a reliable manner using a survey, as the issues involved were too complex to explore using a questionnaire.

The numerical evidence had serious implications for the policy of targeting free inputs, as follows.

- Communities did not think that packs should only go to the poorest one-third of households (EFI); their approach to targeting was more complex, involving a number of criteria and producing an 'eligible proportion' of around two-thirds of rural households (64–68 per cent).
- There was considerable agreement between the different stakeholders on the two-thirds targeting level, but a small percentage (4–8 per cent) of households were included because of their relationship to village power structures, and there was disagreement between stakeholders in some 30 per cent of specific cases. This meant that even if enough packs were provided for two-thirds of households, there would still be allegations of unfairness in the selection of beneficiaries. In order to get full agreement between and within the communities, around 80 per cent of households would have to be given packs.
- There was much variability between and within regions, so even if it could be agreed that 80 per cent represented the right level of targeting nationally, at this level there would be oversupply of packs in some areas and shortages in others.

The general policy conclusion from this data analysis was that the 1 million packs supplied in 2001–2 (sufficient for around one-third of rural households) was not enough. The communities entrusted with targeting did not share the view of the policy-makers and donors that free inputs should go only to the poorest of the poor. Nor was there agreement between village-level stakeholders about who deserved to benefit. Thus, unless it meant only the exclusion of a small percentage of households considered ineligible by all stakeholders, poverty targeting was doomed to failure in relation to TIP.

Benefits and limitations of the study

The numerical data from this research study using participatory methods and its policy implications were presented to the Government of Malawi and the donor community. It helped produce the decision to scale up the free agricultural inputs programme to over 2 million beneficiaries in the 2002–3 season, although the principal reason for increasing the number of packs distributed was the food crisis which hit Malawi in early 2002. In this sense, although the participatory research was not part of a process supporting development in the communities visited, it did help to produce a direct benefit for them in the form of greater access to agricultural inputs, which led to increased food production in the 2003 harvest (Levy, 2005).

However, the TIP Messages study missed an opportunity to carry out an analysis of the numerical data that were recorded on the household cards with the participants. All the data were analysed back in the office and presented in a report to policy-makers which the communities that provided the information did not have a chance to read or discuss. Lack of feedback is common in evaluations and other types of research carried out by external teams, mainly because of budget constraints. However, with hindsight, it would have been possible to build in some time – while the teams were still in the villages – to analyse the information on the household cards with participants.[52]

Analysing numerical data with participants

In a study which was carried out in May–August 2003 as part of the evaluation of the winter-season free inputs programme (Chinsinga et al., 2004), we attempted to do just that. As before, the study design included statistical sampling to select villages and used the community mapping with cards tool at the village level. The household cards allowed us to explore whether packs had been allocated to the intended beneficiaries, and whether any packs had gone missing before reaching the villages. While still at the site, the study team constructed a 'Table of mismatches' from the information on the household cards for discussion with the participants. These tables were basically matrices comparing actual receipt of packs with registration as beneficiaries (i.e. entitlement of households to receive packs); they also showed how many of the packs on the register had failed to reach the villages. Chinsinga et al. (2004) note that:

> The Table of mismatches provoked interesting discussions with the participants at village level. In the majority of cases, they provided an opportunity for participants to air their views on Winter TIP logistics because they had, for the first time, a clear visual presentation of what transpired during registration and distribution. In many cases, the participants took this as an opportunity to urge the local leaders to be transparent and accountable when administering programmes of this nature. They argued that their pleas for transparency and accountability were vindicated because what the local leaders thought was effectively concealed, had been exposed by the Table of mismatches.

Whether or not it is feasible and desirable to analyse the data collected in such studies while still on site, for discussion with participants, depends on the nature of the information. In some cases, the information may be too sensitive, or it might lead to conflicts which the researchers would not be able to mediate after leaving the village. However, in cases where the information collected is in the public domain – as with the sort of information that can be recorded by community mapping with cards – there would appear to be no reason why analysis should not be carried out locally and handed over to the people who provided the data. Although people may be generally aware of a problem, numbers can often help put pressure on leaders, as the experience with the table of mismatches indicates.

In this example, the study team analysed the data on site and discussed it with those who had provided the information. An even more attractive option, which we would like to develop as part of future research, would be to carry out the data analysis with the participants. Where literacy and numeracy are weak, this might involve using beans, stones, sticks and other visual aids of the sort frequently used by PRA and PLA practitioners. These could be used by participants as tools for counting symbols or codes recorded on household cards and building matrices, tables, graphs and charts from them.

Further research is needed on the type of participatory methods that would be effective both for generating statistics to be used at the national level and for enabling the communities that produce the information to analyse it and use it for local decision-making and advocacy. Different issues require different approaches, depending on how the information is to be used and at what level it will be analysed. It is important to remain flexible, rather than provide a set of recipes for this type of work. Nevertheless, it would be worthwhile exploring which approaches and tools work best for different types of research questions. Well-designed participatory research studies should with good facilitation be capable of producing data that allow at least some level of analysis by the participants. Putting data into the hands of the people most affected by events, developments and policies, and helping them to produce their own data analysis, should increase their power to lobby local and national decision-makers as well as help to build the case for action at community level.

Locally owned information systems: a vision for the 21st century

The need for change

In recent years I have become increasingly convinced of the need to rebuild the information systems that exist in developing countries, incorporating new indicators and new methods of data collection and management which better respond to the needs of development in the 21st century. The current systems and approaches are based on methods that were seen as modern 60 years ago, but are no longer in tune with our information requirements. The systems continue to collect the same sort of data year in year out without any major assessment of their relevance to changing national policy or local development objectives. Participatory research continues to be isolated from mainstream government statistics, and Geographic Information System (GIS) data and remote sensing tools are underused.

There are now strong reasons for designing more appropriate information systems.

- The MDGs and other development approaches and initiatives have changed our approach to development by placing greater emphasis on poverty reduction. Poverty is understood to be a complex issue, but in the national statistics it is still measured with income and expenditure data from household surveys. The Malawi studies have shown that participatory methods can be used to generate national statistics for measuring poverty and many other complex issues.
- Participatory methods that can generate national statistics can also provide an effective and efficient way of collecting information about education, gender equality, child mortality, maternal health and most of the other MDGs (with the probable exception of HIV/AIDS, which is a sensitive issue).
- There is increasing emphasis on the decentralization of government and a growing recognition of the role of community-based organizations (CBOs) in development. If decentralization is to succeed, it must include decentralizing information systems and empowering local communities through access to information, including numerical data. In other words, there is a need for locally owned information systems which will help to improve decision-making processes and support development at local level. They will also increase people's power to lobby for progress towards meeting the MDGs.

What locally owned information systems would involve

At present, most national information systems in developing countries are centralized, top-down affairs designed to produce key national statistics, mainly using surveys and censuses. While national coordination will continue to be necessary in order to produce national statistics, I would argue that in the 21st century we are in a position to build systems that are decentralized right down to the village level and are responsive to local needs, but which are also capable of generating reliable national statistics. What would such a system look like?

At the lowest level, a CBO in each village, set of villages, semi-urban or urban area would be given the responsibility for coordinating information collection and analysis on a regular basis. In each area there would be a resource centre where the CBO would display key local indicators and other information (quantitative and qualitative). These resource centres would over time build up a historical data series, allowing them to monitor progress (or lack of progress) on reducing poverty and other goals, and to highlight problems and bring them to the attention of local and national authorities. In one case in Nepal, it was reported that a community first established such a resource centre (where it displayed information collected with a technique similar to community mapping with cards), and then renamed it the rights claims centre when it found that the information could be used as a powerful tool for advocacy (Bimal Phnuyal, personal communication, 2005). In this case, there was not only local ownership of the information system, but empowerment of the local community.

The principal methods used for collecting and analysing the information would be participatory, but the research methods used would be flexible, including survey instruments if these were the best way to meet the needs of the stakeholders.[53]

There would be two other key players in addition to the CBOs: NGOs would provide facilitation and would train CBOs in appropriate participatory methods, and the national statistical office (NSO) in each country would be responsible for ensuring that key indicators were measured in a comparable way in all sites, or at least in a number of sites that would be selected using statistical principles to ensure a representative national (or subnational) sample. For this purpose, the NSOs would need to be trained in the application of statistics to participatory data collection. For the system to work, it would be important to draw on the different types of expertise provided by NGOs and NSOs, in participatory methods and national statistics respectively. In my view, it would not be helpful to ask NGOs to take on the role of national statisticians, designing national data collection systems, or to ask NSOs to become experts in participatory methods. In most cases where this has been attempted, the result has been disappointing. Each type of organization has a role to play, but cannot be expected to become experts in a completely different field overnight.

Both NSOs and NGOs might also need to play roles (at different levels) in controlling the quality of the information produced by the CBOs. This would be needed for two reasons: first, CBOs will face a steep learning curve, and may not be able to produce good-quality data immediately; second, some CBOs may be tempted to alter particular indicators in order to make a case for assistance (e.g. by exaggerating poverty data).

It would also be necessary to build in an element of oversight by external actors such as NGOs to ensure that the rights of marginalized people were not violated through locally owned information systems. Communities often ostracize sex workers, drug users, gay people, divorced women, people with HIV/AIDS and religious and ethnic minorities (Alice Welbourn, personal communication, 2005). It would be necessary to ensure that the rights of such people were not ignored or abused.

What sort of data could be collected by locally owned information systems? Much of the information would respond to local needs, but the system would also allow regular measurement of a set of core indicators in a standardized fashion, and these indicators would be capable of aggregation at regional and national level to inform policy. For example (and this is by no means a comprehensive list), the core data could include the following.

- Indicators of poverty and hunger; enrolment in primary and secondary education (by gender); data on child mortality and maternal health; indicators of disease, safe drinking water etc. All these are key areas covered by the MDGs. Most of these could be collected using participatory community mapping with cards, with the data recorded on the household cards for analysis at local and national levels.

- Information on crop production in rural areas, including type of crops and estimates of quantities. The CBOs organizing the locally owned information systems could compile this information in partnership with Ministry of Agriculture employees and local farmers.
- Information on rainfall patterns. This could be collected in the traditional fashion (rain gauges), but would involve local communities in the process and give them ownership of the findings.[54] CBOs could set up and maintain the information collection points with guidance from the National Meteorological Service (NMS).

Each point in a locally owned information system (or at least the sample of sites from which information would feed into the national system) should be GIS-referenced. In return for channelling data into the national system, communities should receive feedback from those doing the analysis at national level in the form of access to national-level information via computer or through a local government office. For instance, in the case of rainfall data, the CBO would feed its information into the system and in return it might receive remote sensing information from the NMS. Meteorological data on short-term predicted weather patterns and long-term trends would help local communities to take decisions about farming and the sustainable use of the environment.

Funding issues

Many people reading this chapter will probably think to themselves: 'That sounds great, but it would be too expensive.' Before leaping to this conclusion, it would be worthwhile making a serious analysis of the net cost of establishing locally owned information systems and of the benefits likely to be generated at local and national levels in terms of improved information and closer linkages between research and development.

On the cost side are the initial infrastructure and training that would be required for NSOs, NMSs, NGOs and CBOs; and the running costs (principally maintaining resource centres, making modest payments to CBO members for their time and covering the expenses of data collection). However, these should be compared with the not inconsiderable costs that are currently incurred by NSOs, NMSs and NGOs to produce data on similar topics, usually in an uncoordinated and irregular fashion. At this point, it is hard to predict whether the costs of locally owned information systems would be higher or lower than those of the centralized systems that they would partially replace.

Conclusion

This chapter has presented innovations in participatory methodologies which took place as part of research in Malawi at the beginning of the 21st century. We have shown that these innovations allow us to generate numbers from participatory research that can be aggregated for analysis at national level, feeding into national policy-making. However, more needs to be done to develop the approach so that the numbers can be analysed at community level, feeding into the processes of local development. Numbers from participation are a powerful tool for advocacy at the local as well as the national level.

The development of such methodologies also gives us an opportunity to reform out-of-date, over-centralized information collection systems. The development challenges of the 21st century – among them, meeting the MDGs – require new approaches to the production and ownership of information. If we want to empower poor people to take part in reducing poverty and promoting development, we must end the monopoly of information by central governments. The development of participatory methods capable of producing local as well as national statistics means that the potential now exists, even in remote and marginalized communities, for people to produce their own information. The results have the potential to be more reliable than those produced by outsiders. To governments and donors I would say: this is an opportunity that should not be missed.

CHAPTER 11

Participatory village poverty reduction planning and index-based poverty mapping in China

Joe Remenyi

Introduction

This chapter is about innovations in poverty analysis and planning in China that have roots going back almost two decades. It gives an account of the political and institutional challenges of introducing participatory approaches, and provides lessons about making participation at the grassroots meaningful and practical for a huge bureaucracy. These innovations marked nothing less than a revolution in local governance of publicly funded poverty reduction interventions, including the unprecedented involvement of poor communities in village poverty reduction (VPR) planning and poverty mapping.

This exercise was based on an extensive set of field experiments that were core to an Asian Development Bank (ADB) technical assistance programme, County Poverty Alleviation Planning (CPAP). The purpose of this work, done in partnership with the body responsible for Chinese national poverty policy, the Leading Group Office for Poverty (LGOP), was to identify a minimal set of poverty indicators that could be used to target the poorest villages, facilitate participatory VPR planning and measure progress in poverty reduction.

China has achieved much in terms of poverty reduction in recent years, but at the turn of the century many felt that a more concerted effort was needed to benefit the very poor. A more targeted approach was needed because of leakages in the flow of funds and a growing realization of the demise of top-down solutions. Traditional views of poverty and methods for measuring it had limitations in distinguishing the poorest and identifying pockets of poverty.

In contrast to the more usual methods of measuring the incidence of poverty, the indicators developed in this research programme were those that poor villagers selected as best describing their experiences of poverty. From the many dozens of indicators discussed with villagers, a village-level index showing the incidence of poverty was constructed, dubbed the Participatory Poverty Index (PPI). This index is a means by which poor villagers can self-assess and monitor the progress that is being made in relieving the incidence of poverty in their community.

This chapter, written by one of the researchers who developed and tested CPAP and the PPI, describes the processes that the research team followed as the methodology evolved, discussing important influences and experiences that emerged from the development, testing and spread of the PPI methodology. The chapter finishes with some observations on issues that have arisen from the manner in which the framework for participatory poverty reduction planning has been applied and adapted by local government officials and village people in poor counties in rural China.

Listening to the poor

My first exposure to Chinese poverty policy implementation came in 1991. I had been invited to participate in a poverty assessment and impact monitoring training programme for senior agricultural scientists from southwest China. The training programme was part of the Ford Foundation's brave experiments in inclusive development under the Yunnan Upland Management (YUM) programme.

The YUM programme had many parts, one of which was a focus on action-learning based training, through which some remarkable innovations were introduced into provincial and village-level poverty planning and project implementation procedures, including participatory problem analysis with poor villagers, provincial and LGOP officials; locally sourced professional and technical assistance to facilitate the solution, the identification and technology transfer in partnership with poor farmers; experiments in community-controlled natural resource management, especially in relation to potable water and irrigation; and province-level governance innovations to strengthen the capacity of mainline ministries to incorporate farmers' problems into their annual work-programme priority-setting procedures.

It is almost impossible to overstate the importance of these innovations. In rural China, long-entrenched traditions and values give rise to the view that the poor are to be blamed for their poverty, and are ignorant and unscientific people. Most local officials are highly sceptical that any benefit might be gained from consultation with poor villagers. Ford's YUM programme was grounded in a rival belief, championed by the Foundation's Environment and Agriculture programme officer, Nick Menzies. He was missionary in his conviction that poor farmers are the true experts on rural poverty. Training in poverty analysis and participatory strategies was part of the support structure that the YUM programme brought into its unique mix of innovations in bottom-up development.

I had come into the YUM programme on the tail of a global research programme on income generation programmes with poor people in the informal sectors of economies in Asia, Africa and Latin America. The results of this three-year research programme were published as a book (Remenyi, 1991) that Nick Menzies read. He found himself intrigued by the participatory methodology (PM) and the theoretical framework it used, labelled the poverty pyramid.

I had designed the poverty pyramid framework to allow me, or any researcher, to quickly make sense of the flood of information that comes from poor villagers when one takes the time to sit and listen. The poverty pyramid classifies village households according to their sources of livelihood, from the poorest of the poor, whom I called the vulnerable poor, at the base, to the near poor at the top. I used this functional framework to structure the training programme that I presented to YUM scientists in Yunnan and to emphasize the importance of maintaining a rigorous fix on how productivity in each stratum of the poverty pyramid could be increased.

The poverty pyramid proved to be a robust framework, engaging to poor villagers who seemed to find the picture it gave of their community insightful, and highly informative for those of us interested in understanding the reasons why poverty persists in the villages visited. The usefulness of a well-structured reference group of village experts – including the local teacher, the local barefoot doctor, the village accountant, the village women's group chairperson and prominent village entrepreneurs – as a rapid and simple source of indicative information was confirmed over and over. This was a key moment on the path that led to the CPAP framework for participatory VPR planning and mapping.

In coming years my involvement in the YUM programme opened doors to a succession of complementary involvements in poverty programmes across many

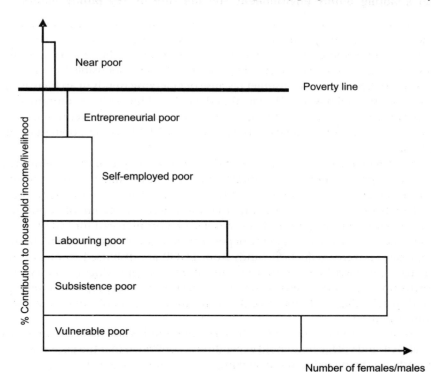

Figure 11.1 The Poverty Pyramid.

provinces in China. In the course of these engagements I was struck by the number of local Chinese officials and development professionals who knew of the Ford Foundation's work in promoting participatory methods in development. From what I could see, the Ford programme had made an amazingly influential impact on the environment needed for more participatory, consultative and inclusive approaches to development.

The ADB's CPAP initiative, in which participatory poverty mapping was further developed from 1999 to 2001, directly benefited from this environment. The scaling-up of VPR planning across much of rural China carries a heritage that flows directly from the work initiated by Ford under YUM. Virtually all of the CPAP team had been involved in one or more ways with Ford's support for YUM, or a related Ford programme. The ripples of change initiated by YUM and its related programmes remain strong in China. Without them, the environment into which CPAP and the participatory VPR planning methodology it recommended was released would not have been as receptive. Moreover, the capacity of local LGOP officials and their collaborators to adapt what they received is as important a part of this heritage, as is the basic appreciation of participation as a strategic methodology in development planning.

An enabling policy environment and the role of key policy actors

The Chinese share a great and wholly justified pride in the transformation of their country from one where chronic poverty was the norm in the 1960s and before, to one where chronic poverty is the exception in the 21st century. But the new millennium was greeted by Chinese officials responsible for national poverty policy with some disquiet because of emerging trends of an increasing incidence in rural poverty. The fact that the political hierarchy is committed to abolishing chronic poverty in rural China is a crucial and powerful enabling factor for reform of the delivery of resources for VPR to target populations in China.

If one had to describe the nature of the governance system that determined key poverty alleviation interventions on the eve of the millennium, it would not be a description of a bottom-up and open process. The Chinese policy process had institutionalized an ingrained commitment in favour of top-down bureaucratic administrations. For example, a report prepared for LGOP (ADB, 2002), describes the current mode of poverty planning as 'trickle-down'. In this approach, poverty reduction funds from LGOP are disbursed towards rural villages, but pass first through provincial government offices, county and township offices and enterprise structures. Relatively small proportions of total funds reach villages, despite recent reforms in the system of rural production administration.

Towards the end of the 1990s, official Chinese and World Bank research into rural GDP and village household expenditures confirmed that the pace at which poverty was being reduced was slowing, if not in full retreat (ADB, 2000; Chen and Ravallion, 2004; LGOP, 2000; LGOP et al., 2000; Li et al., 2003a). As senior officials in China and key donors realized that past trends in poverty reduction were not being sustained, a bandwagon of pressure formed to convince the LGOP and the China State Council that more of the same was no longer a viable option for national poverty policy. The challenge of chronic poverty in China is fundamentally different from what had gone before. The remaining pockets of hard-core rural poverty demand more than minor refinements to past approaches to VPR.

The LGOP accepted that the causes of chronic village poverty were not well understood, and that under past approaches to VPR chronically poor people were being bypassed as provincial and township officials diverted poverty funds away from poor villages into what they saw as better investments in development. The folly and negative consequences of past policies and practices, especially the headlong push by local governments into township and village enterprises, were becoming increasingly obvious. As the number of failed enterprises mounted, with little or no benefit to chronically poor counties and villages, the national return to poverty reduction spending was further and further eroded.

Opposing the received wisdom of the trickle-down model, the LGOP and the State Council gradually came to recognize that poor villages must be targeted directly. In May 2000, the State Council declared that the national poverty policy for the new millennium would be revised to establish a closely targeted programme of VPR (China State Council, 2001). The new policy would direct national poverty funds directly to county level, giving county officials the responsibility of addressing chronic poverty, and achieving sustainable income and employment generation in poor villages.

However, policy reform on paper is always easier than policy reform in practice. China's problem was that its traditional approaches had not established the bureaucratic procedures or the practical frameworks to suddenly make poor villages the core of national poverty policy; and the entrenched views of those charged with implementing policy continued.

The LGOP approached these challenges by seeking assistance from the ADB. Together they agreed to fund an action research programme, CPAP, to identify key reforms and processes that would be needed to implement the new policy of VPR. Implementing CPAP meant supplementary investments for training in participatory approaches and capacity-building for participatory village development planning. Sustained poverty reduction would also require some innovations in village-level governance and public-sector support for investment, to lift the capacity of poor villages to be self-reliant.

Principles for participatory VPR planning and mapping

Late in 2000 the search began to identify a practical framework for CPAP. How could the reality of poverty at the grassroots, especially chronic hard-core poverty in village China, be measured, monitored and addressed? From the very beginning, the LGOP was adamant that the CPAP framework had to be based on participatory methods of problem analysis, solution identification, activity designs and budgeting, the scepticism and biases of provincial and county level staff in Poverty Alleviation and Development Offices (PADO) notwithstanding (ADB, 2002).

The CPAP research group was drawn from China's most important university for expertise in participatory approaches, led by Professor Li Xiaoyun,[55] pioneering champion of participatory approaches to development in China. I joined his team as the ADB's international specialist on pro-poor development planning.

As seen from the previous section, CPAP was part of a wider movement towards the evolution of locally based planning in China. But this trend was not without opponents, so it was important to be cautious in developing reformed planning frameworks. The State Council was keen to ensure that the shift towards locally based planning should be accomplished with a minimum of conflict from proponents of the status quo. This was to be achieved by minimizing proposed reforms to the existing LGOP governance of national poverty alleviation policy and practice in China. Nonetheless, the increased emphasis that was to be given to participatory, bottom-up procedures did imply some changes in governance which would create forces for change that would be resisted in some quarters and embraced in others.

Steering a path through wider political processes at the same time as searching for a practical framework required the research team to establish some key principles to guide its work.

1. The research process must begin with agreement on some basic concepts, including what it means to be poor; how this understanding can be translated into a practical strategy for mapping poverty across villages; and, crucially, how the recommended framework can be structured to ensure that the exercise of poverty mapping will also reveal the key reasons why poor villages have remained poor.
2. An action research format is essential to ensure that villagers are partners in the process and the final outcomes.
3. The poverty reduction framework must be practical and replicable within the budget constraints of the LGOP.
4. CPAP must not only be village-friendly, but must also attract the support of key village representatives in order to make poverty reduction efforts sustainable.
5. The framework must be dynamic, to facilitate ongoing learning and understanding the many ways in which poverty is experienced by villagers in their own circumstances.

These principles and the context that gave rise to them shaped the subsequent stages of developing, testing and refining the VPR planning and mapping methodology. In the three years to the close of 2002, the research team pursued these principles and the questions that arose out of successive field visits and CPAP component trials.

Describing poverty in rural China using common indicators

The research project began with a week of team meetings in Beijing. Key to these meetings were team seminars that allowed for individual presentations on what each team member believed they knew about poverty in rural China. In the course of these informal day-long seminars, we sought to get to know one another and to provide opportunities for sharing meaningful experiences from working at field level in poverty projects. Time was devoted to the consideration of field research methods that team members had found especially productive. We made formal presentations on topics in which each of us specialized, including the use of the poverty pyramid framework, approaches to Participatory Rural Appraisal (PRA) and community participation. Individual team members drew attention to published literature directly relevant to CPAP, including unpublished reports written for donors by team members. This first stage was crucial for team-building, and constructing a shared team understanding of what we believed we knew of chronic poverty in China. The second stage of the project saw individual team members preparing drafts of the basic components of CPAP, readying these for field-testing.

The third stage, field-testing, would ultimately generate the raw material needed for VPR planning and the construction of PPIs. Among the components of CPAP to be pilot-tested in participatory poverty assessments at village level was a long list of potential poverty indicators. Fieldwork, in the form of participatory data collection exercises, proceeded in three steps: to gather data on up to a dozen or more poverty indicators for each pilot village, to report on the outcomes of participatory poverty analysis exercises, and to generate a matrix of development opportunities identified by villagers.

Initial fieldwork saw three teams dispatched to a range of poor villages in Hebei Province. We took to our tasks knowing that policy, governance and institutional responses would also need to be tailored to ensure the greatest probability of successful poverty reduction interventions. Data were collected through a lengthy process of village consultations, PRA-style information gathering, and small-group poverty problem analysis. In the first instance, villagers were challenged to identify what they believed to be the best poverty indicators. A key resource at the original village consultations was the list of poverty indicators drawn from our desk study of the literature. Villagers were taken through a time-consuming and detailed explanation of the meaning of each indicator and how each might be used to tell us about the incidence of poverty in their village.

By the end of 2000, several hundred village studies had been undertaken using open village meetings and smaller focus group meetings. From these it became clear that a consistent shorter list of eight key poverty indicators could be distilled from the longer list presented to each village meeting. This was confirmed after further consultation between team members, considerable thought about the data before us and a return to the field to confirm with villagers the accuracy of the eight indicators we had isolated. The indicators covered three key types of poverty: livelihood poverty, infrastructure poverty and human resource poverty.

Livelihood poverty is in many ways related to the low productivity of subsistence agriculture that has traditionally been identified as a cause of poverty in rural China. It did not come as a surprise, therefore, to find that villagers give high importance to their food security situation as an important element of how they experience poverty. What was a surprise, however, was the unequivocal manner in which poor villagers distinguish between subsistence poverty, arising from food insecurity, and cash-flow poverty. Poor villagers are very concerned to improve their access to additional sources of cash and confirm that for them poverty is often associated with the persistence of a liquidity crisis at personal, household and community levels. Poor villagers also confirmed that when they do accumulate additional cash or in-kind income beyond current requirements, one of the first ways in which they improve their livelihoods is by up-grading the quality of their housing. Moreover, villagers keenly follow such indicators and can identify which households have experienced rises or falls in their grain production, which have had access to more or fewer sources of cash flow in the past season, and which households have upgraded their homes in the course of the previous year.

Infrastructure poverty is an issue that affects everyone in a poor village. Access to a ready and convenient source of potable water, for example, affects the household availability of able-bodied labour power in all households. It is one of the great anomalies that in rural China, where the supply of labour is typically the most abundant factor of production, a high household dependency rate, caused by a shortage of able-bodied adults relative to the number of dependent children, frail, aged and disabled or chronically ill people in a household, is one of the more important causes of household chronic poverty.

Villagers also attach high priority to the existence of an all-weather access road to the nearest significant market. This is connected to livelihood as well as infrastructure poverty, indicating the concern that poor villagers have for improving their opportunities to generate additional sources of cash receipts. Other benefits of better communications and more convenient transport are valued, but these are secondary to the impact that a good-quality all-weather road can make to the quality of village livelihoods following increased cash flow from sales to new markets.

Feedback from villagers made it clear that human resource poverty has two critical elements that are critical to how poverty is experienced at the household level. First, poor villagers recognize, unequivocally, that extended illness of the adult women in a household is a root cause of chronic poverty. In this sense poverty is not gender-neutral and villagers were quite aware of this fact. The daily grind of poverty serves to confirm to poor villagers that failure to maintain women in good health, for whatever reason, has serious adverse consequences for household welfare.

The second indicator of human resource poverty identified by poor villagers reflects the very high priority given, even by the poorest households, to education as an investment in a better future for their children. Poor villagers do not willingly keep their children from attending school, and see education as an important means by which their children can have a better quality of life, and so increase the probability that in their retirement they, too, will have an effective safety net.

Table 11.1 shows the eight core poverty indicators in these three areas of poverty that were selected by poor villagers.

Following the identification and ranking of indicators by villagers, village-level open-ended meetings were held to further explore villagers' perceptions of potential solutions to their continuing struggle with chronic poverty. In this part of CPAP, villagers were asked to distinguish between three levels of poverty reduction interventions that they would like to see implemented. The first level included those interventions that the villagers claim to be able to manage by themselves for themselves, subject only to permission from local authorities to proceed. The second set of interventions covers those that villagers cannot implement without modest additional resources from outside authorities, public or private. The third level refers to all those poverty reduction investments that villagers cannot see happening without substantial inputs from external agencies, especially the government sector.

It was at this stage that a serious discussion took place between the CPAP team members on how we might best use and interpret the data from the field trials. A particular source of debate concerned how to use the prioritized list of poverty indicators to develop an index that would allow the LGOP and its partners to target interventions at the poorest villages and to plan interventions that were likely to work. Increasing the probability of success is an important goal of participatory poverty analysis and development. Moreover, each of the eight indicators seemed to offer new and important insights into both the root causes of chronic poverty and possible escape routes. It would be a tragedy if

Table 11.1 Eight key indicators for three core types of chronic poverty

Poverty indicator	Measure
1. Livelihood poverty	
a. Cash receipts per person per year	Yuan
b. Grain production per person per year	Kg
c. House quality (roof and exterior walls)	% brick
2. Infrastructure poverty	
a. Access to an all-weather access road	Days without access
b. Easy access to quality drinking water	Hours spent collecting water
c. Access to reliable electricity supply	Days with interrupted supply
3. Human resource poverty	
a. Women's morbidity	Days lost to illness, females >12 years
b. Children's education	% of eligible children in school

this new information could not be integrated into extant LGOP-led VPR planning procedures.

I, along with several others, was inclined to accept the views of villagers on poverty at face value and to allocate each indicator a similar weight in developing a PPI. But Li was adamant that this would not do justice to the information that villagers were giving us about their poverty. Gradually it dawned on us that what was lacking was an easy method for ranking each indicator and for inserting these rank orderings into a framework that also conveyed information about the relative importance that villagers give to each of the three types of poverty into which we had classified their responses. The method we developed enabled us to construct the PPI. The combination of qualitative and quantitative elements for each indicator enabled us to do poverty mapping across villages in a consistent and comprehensive manner.[56]

Developing and using the PPI

The PPI is a self-assessment based index that requires villagers to rank their personal experience of poverty on the basis of the eight poverty indicators listed above, the first three of which are proxies for livelihood poverty, the next three for infrastructure-environmental poverty and the final two for human resource poverty. The personal estimates are then discussed in open meetings by the villagers until a single set of numbers and weights is agreed for the village in general. In the course of their personal assessments and subsequent village-wide assessments, villagers rank the eight indicators and the three types of poverty according to the importance that they attach to them. Each indicator is scored out of a possible maximum score of 5, from the least important to the most important, in their village's experience of poverty. By incorporating the weights for each indicator and each type of poverty, the PPI indicates what the villagers believe are the dominant ways in which poverty is experienced in their village. Hence, the most important types and characteristics of poverty are embedded in the PPI according to the rankings made by the villagers.[57]

The importance of calculating the PPI in this inclusive manner is that the resultant process of village poverty mapping not only engages poor villagers in a dynamic problem analysis of poverty, but also highlights key sources of chronic poverty, as seen through the eyes of poor villagers. The process is intended to enable villagers to communicate to county, township and provincial officials what, in their view, are the areas where they need most help to overcome the constraints of low productivity, inadequate access to cash flow, core environmental and infrastructure deficiencies, or human resource asset problems that are the root cause of chronic poverty.

Opportunity analysis is the third aspect of the VPR and PPI processes. This phase has become subject to the greatest subsequent adaptation by local officials. In the original CPAP trials, villagers were asked to identify the sorts of interventions that they would like to see happen for sustainable pro-poor village development. Our pilot trials indicated that villagers' responses to this challenge could generate an opportunity matrix for each village, the results of which could then be compared across neighbouring villages and used to facilitate regional development planning on the basis of cross-village pattern mapping. By examining the opportunity matrix for each neighbouring village, patterns of need as seen by villagers would emerge. These could then be considered by the provincial planning commission as it prepares regional development plans.

The opportunity to undertake this level of integration of the PPI and CPAP into pro-poor VPR planning has not materialized. Instead, local authorities have tended to substitute the opportunity matrix phase of CPAP with a more prescriptive menu of VPR interventions, villagers' assessments of needs and opportunities notwithstanding. In the best cases, the menu of options will have arisen from the application of CPAP-style participatory poverty assessments. In the majority of cases, however, the opportunity matrix is an aspect of CPAP that has not, as yet, been adopted by those responsible for VPR planning (Remenyi and Li, 2004).

Adaptations and scaling up

CPAP became the LGOP's recommended framework for VPR in 2001. By the end of 2002 several hundred village consultations had been completed as part of the LGOP's programme to implement national poverty policy reforms in favour of targeted poverty reduction. A national training programme in CPAP was designed and rolled out across all LGOP training centres, including a CPAP training manual (Li et al., 2003a). More than 10,000 copies of the training manual were printed and distributed with funding from the Australian Government Overseas Aid Programme (AusAID). By the end of 2004 the CPAP process for VPR planning, or a modified form of it, had been replicated in more than 1500 villages (Li et al., 2003b).

There are some important governance and village-level institutional innovations implied by the CPAP and PPI processes. Typically these have given rise to the establishment of village-specific development implementation groups (VDIGs). VDIGs are separate from the village committee, though membership is almost always overlapping, with common members drawn from the local party hierarchy and village government.

Scaling up CPAP across poor counties in China has involved a national programme of trials and pilot exercises. In addition, a nationwide programme of training and capacity-building for participatory approaches to VPR has been implemented by LGOP, with special assistance from AusAID, the Japanese International Cooperation Agency and other donors. As a result, by mid-2005 all provinces in China had adopted forms of VPR planning that take their roots from CPAP. There are now literally thousands of Chinese villages where modified forms of CPAP have been applied and VPR implementation groups are functional.

However, the modifications to the way that CPAP has been applied in given village situations have been substantial. The modifications made in individual locations are indicative of a Chinese bureaucratic sector that does not easily shed its prejudices. At heart the Chinese public sector remains risk-averse, is suspicious of the ability of poor villagers to run their own agenda successfully, and fearful of the possible flow-on effects of radical change in grassroots development planning on popular pressure for even more local government reform. Consequently, where CPAP has been piloted it has not often included the full poverty mapping exercise or involved the calculation of a PPI for each and every village. To do so is likely to have challenged the status quo too much. Instead, modifications of CPAP have tended to be restricted to limits placed on public-sector funded VPR project choices. Villagers have been free to choose from a menu of VPR options prepared by local officials. They have not been free, as noted earlier, to construct their own VPR opportunity matrices.

In some instances the menu of possible poverty reduction interventions that has been put before villagers has involved a PRA exercise of some sort, but mostly this has not been the case. One can speculate why this has happened. There are restrictions on participatory interventions because there is every likelihood that there are no funds available to do village PRAs, or to travel to remote hamlets to organize and mobilize local people. Moreover, in many counties and townships, influential officials continue to view the consultative process through jaundiced eyes, preferring to proceed on the basis of their understanding of why poor villagers are poor. In the absence of data to the contrary, who is to say that they are wrong? So long as there is a dearth of data to show otherwise, local officials in rural China will continue to cling to views that reject the possibility that poor villagers might better understand what is needed to abolish chronic poverty in their village than educated local officials and responsible public-sector gatekeepers.

Support of villagers for the use of the truncated CPAP framework is strong and readily explained. Typically local officials have not only placed a menu of possible VPR interventions before villagers, they have also attached to the menu the guarantee that a minimum annual budget will be spent on their choices in the coming three years. The budget may be modest, possibly as low as 100 Yuan (£7) per person per year, or as high as ten times this amount. Whatever, the promise of public money actually being spent in the village to the direct benefit of villagers is a strong incentive for enthusiastic village approval (Taylor and Plummer, 2004). Past experience of villagers in poor counties is that the benefits of national poverty fund expenditures rarely reach down to the village, let alone the poor household level. It is relatively easy, therefore, for local officials to shore up support for their views, the views of villagers notwithstanding, by guaranteeing to spend a minimum budget on village selected priority projects, subject only that this budget must be spent on one or more of the options presented in the menu of interventions presented to villagers.

Despite this, the radical nature of the reforms that China is implementing in converting national poverty policy from a focus on province and township to a focus on villages should not be underestimated. The reforms are generating governance changes that are altering the political landscape from the grassroots. There is evidence that what we now see is only the beginning of what will prove to be a much larger downsizing of the public sector and the devolution of responsibility for local government to village communities. Poor villagers and local government officials are only gradually realizing that this process of devolution and smaller government is inexorable. VPR planning, using the PPI and the broader CPAP framework, may well be assisting poor villagers and local officials to better understand and come to terms with changes in the interactions between the private and public sectors. By following the participatory VPR processes that are at the heart of CPAP, it is likely that local communities are creating a data-supported appreciation of the sources and causes of chronic poverty that will, in time, enable local government officials to continue to embrace, albeit gradually, additional features of the full set of VPR planning procedures in the PPI and CPAP frameworks.

Conclusions

Despite the variety of approaches to measuring poverty (income, entitlements, skills, assets), all share a common framework, external to the target population, based on poverty measures indicative of a received wisdom. These objective indicators relate to levels of deprivation in key consumption areas, environmental factors core to sustainable livelihoods, and community access to institutional structures described as essential to a healthy level of economic activity.

CPAP-based VPR planning and participatory poverty mapping (PPM) is distinguished from these objective approaches to measuring the incidence of poverty by the substitution of self-assessment procedures for the external imposition of a predetermined set of indicators. Self-assessment enables poor household and village members to take charge of the way in which their poverty is described and quantitatively assessed. PPM allows poor households and poor villagers, as a community, to choose those indicators that, in their view, best describe how poverty is manifest in their lives. Despite possible common foci for poverty indicators – for example, income per person – the PPM process allows individuals and households to distinguish between the material (subsistence production) and financial (cash receipts) sources of income per person, and to attach a weight to each component to ensure that the decomposed income indicator more correctly reflects the importance that poor households attach to each component.

The results of a PPM exercise may not, therefore, use indicators that are different from those that the more usual methods employ to describe poverty. However, the implications and the interpretation of the results of self-assessed poverty mapping are fundamentally unique and rich in terms of the lessons that can be drawn to guide the design of anti-poverty interventions. A significant effort is needed to bridge the gap between how development agencies measure poverty and the reality of how poor people experience and understand their poverty. PPM is a means to this end.

CHAPTER 12

Navigating the trade-offs in the use of participatory approaches for research

Carlos Barahona with contributions from Dee Jupp, Helzi Noponen and Alice Welbourn

Introduction

This chapter explores the tensions that develop when participatory approaches are modified to produce information that is used outside the local settings with the intention of informing decision-making. It explores a series of experiences where participatory approaches have been used at a local level, with different degrees of benefit and use by the individuals or groups involved, and where external stakeholders have attempted to bring together the information from different individuals or localities in order to use the aggregated information for decision-making purposes.

Why might someone want to use participatory methodologies (PMs) to analyse local conditions and then aggregate to inform decision-making? It is important to remember that participatory approaches are about changing power relations, opening spaces for those whose voice is often not heard, facilitating the analysis of complex issues by the people directly affected by those issues and eventually generating actions. The temptation to use such approaches for informing decision-making at the higher level probably comes from their perceived success at local level. Why should decision-makers not take advantage of the information that those approaches have the potential to generate? It could also be argued that the use of reliable information for decision-making will eventually benefit the localities where the information was generated, so the cooperation of local communities or individuals in gathering such 'data' is justified. Or is it?

How people acquire, process and use information is linked with the way they interpret the world, with the philosophy that underlies their system of analysis. At the risk of generating strong reactions, but with the intention of illustrating an important contradiction in the use of participatory approaches for research, it could be argued that participatory approaches, and many of those using them, have been influenced by qualitative disciplines, which follow the interpretative philosophy of analysis, tend to take a holistic view of what is being analysed, and would probably favour a deductive approach.[58] In contrast, the demand for and the credibility attached to aggregated information that helps in decision-making are often led by people who come from an inductive tradition that falls more comfortably within a realistic paradigm.[59] The challenge of reconciling these two strong traditions is not the intention of this chapter; however, it probably lies at the foundation of some of the case studies explored here.

For example, recurrent questions from practitioners of participatory approaches who want to influence decision-making processes by using results from these approaches are how they can demonstrate the external validity of their findings, how they can claim that they can be generalized, and how can they ensure the credibility of the information thus generated. These practitioners seem to be convinced about the effectiveness of participatory approaches, know through their experience that they generate useful, reliable information but appear to feel a need to respond to the challenge posed by outsiders about the credibility and reliability of their conclusions. Others from more radical participatory research traditions are content to have facilitated popular knowledge and awareness that leads to action, and are less concerned with these validity and credibility issues, perhaps to the disadvantage of their causes. The fact is that credibility, 'generalizability and external validity are concepts that belong to a philosophy of analysis different from that underlying the concepts of participation. In accepting the challenge of reconciling the two traditions referred to above, advocates of participation need to understand and learn to use the tools used by quantitative approaches.

Barahona and Levy (2003) discuss the principles that allow statistics to claim that the information generated through the use of statistical methods is representative and generalizable. We argue that it is possible to integrate statistical principles and participatory approaches based on our experience in Malawi (see Levy, Chapter 10 this volume). But what compromises are needed for this integration? And do the gains offset the losses? These are questions whose answers should help practitioners of participatory approaches to decide whether to play the quantitative game or not.

The case studies below[60] are used to illustrate the trade-offs faced by some initiatives that are attempting to play this game. They also highlight some of the problems and dilemmas that anyone attempting to rise to the challenge is likely to face, independently of their own awareness of the issues. No claim is made about the case studies being representative or generalizable, but they provide interesting examples of how the challenges are being met in practice.

Comments

In this case, the demand for an evaluation process that aggregates data from the grassroots groups comes from an external agent, originating from the need to provide the head of the donor with data which can be trusted, not just felt to be good. The grassroots groups did not originate the process of evaluation; it was facilitated through a process of listening and negotiation by an external agent,

Box 12.1 Case study 1 Reconciling flexibility and standardization

Samata land rights movement in Bangladesh

Dee Jupp

Samata is a land rights movement in Bangladesh. It evolved from a small local organization, which directly intervened in the struggles of the landless for their right to unused government land over which they had legal entitlement but which had been appropriated by land grabbers. It is a people's organization founded on the belief that unity is power and has achieved enormous success through mutual support, direct action and advocacy to acquire and retain land resources for the extreme poor.

Samata's reputation has attracted the attention of bilateral donors and considerable funding. A mixed blessing, it has brought both enormous challenges and opportunities. Samata is not and should not be made to be an NGO, but the donors are more familiar with NGO workings and have well-defined expectations which do not transfer well to a people's organization.

Samata is a membership organization and its agenda and direction are wholly determined by the membership, albeit supported by salaried mentors, trainers and advisers. Its groups meet entirely for their own ends, not as vehicles for service delivery by others. Before the major funding, there had been no formal system of impact assessment and success had been gauged by positive outcomes of various struggles. Donors liked Samata for its dedication, its grassrootedness and its potential to become a key civil-society force for change. But they were in a dilemma about how to evaluate its impact and effectiveness. As one donor put it, 'We know in our hearts that it is doing good work but not in our heads.'

Whatever the evaluation process, it was imperative that it had to be first and foremost for the use of and valued by members. Here then was an opportunity for a genuinely grassroots-driven process. Donors and management of the advisory services would have to take second place and find ways to use the evaluation process for their own purposes. It was realized that Samata members had been meeting week in week out for as long as 10 years, even though only a very small percentage of their membership (and sometimes none at all) ever actually acquired land. There was clearly another intrinsic value to membership, which had not been acknowledged.

A participatory listening exercise was conducted with groups with the simple objective of finding out what benefits members felt from membership. A huge range of benefits emerged. These were mostly related to members drawing strength and confidence from each other in the attainment of a range of rights and entitlements. It was found that the benefits could be clustered into those relating to political capital accumulation (including issues of voice, platform, good citizenship, exercise of franchise) social and human capital (including mutual support, external relations, respect, access to and influence on health and education services), access to economic resources (including land and water bodies, financial and technical services) and capability (groups' capacity to manage their activities themselves). It was found that benefits also tended to follow some kind of pattern dependent on the age of the group, and over a 10-year lifespan, groups moved from an awareness of their rights through confidence and capacity-building to independence and self motivation; a classic empowerment continuum.

The range of benefits have now been tabulated as 132 indicators described in easily understood Bangla and supplemented by pictures. Each group (presently 18,000) will go through these once a year at a time which suits them and assign a 'happy' or 'sad' face to each indicator depending on whether they feel they have achieved this or not. The self-reflection process (*protipholan* in Bangla) takes the group about four hours first time round and is anticipated to be much less in subsequent years. It provides an opportunity for the group's members to analyse their activities and progress themselves and define future action. To date, groups unanimously claim that they find the process inspiring and their willingness to spend so much time on it is a testament to this.

For the purposes of external reporting and performance management, a desk exercise is undertaken comprising the assignment of scores to the 'happy faces' in order for the group to be evaluated in terms of its overall development as well as attainment in the four dimensions of political, social and economic capital accumulation and capability of the group. A variety of statistical analysis can be performed on these data for management and impact analysis which satisfy the funders and programme managers. However, the groups themselves are never under any obligation to follow prescribed patterns of behaviour or development. Their progress is wholly dependent on their needs, their situation and their experience, although they say that the *protipholan* helps them to recognize gaps and weaknesses.

Thus, this is an example of scale up which standardizes the range of benefits which a group might experience but imposes minimal structure in terms of participatory methodology (except the scoring chart) and does not require groups to follow the same routes to achieve benefits. It embraces the diversity of pace and context that affect different groups in becoming empowered.

with cooperation from the groups and their advisers. Because of the tactful approach used and the commitment to make the evaluation process participatory, the resulting process seems to have opened spaces for reflection and action at grassroots level; it uses participatory tools as aids and anchors for the discussions; and the information produced is of direct benefit to those involved in the discussions. In addition, a strong feeling of ownership of the process and the information generated has been reported. In terms of participatory practice the process seems a success. In terms of information we can see how the process of analysis has the potential to move elegantly from data to information and from information to knowledge. But what compromises have been made?

Perhaps the main compromise is related to the adoption of a uniform process for the self-reflection exercise and a unique instrument to guide the evaluation across all the groups. This instrument is described as a set of 132 indicators, evaluated using the same scale of happy or sad faces. This imposes a limitation to the type of analysis that can be carried out during the self-reflection meetings and the level of detail that is recorded about the assessment of each of the indicators.

What are the losses derived from this compromise? It could be argued that the self-reflection groups are at risk of losing the flexibility of a process of reflection that should address their own group concerns; that the process of scoring the indicators with happy or sad faces can become mechanical and the richness of the analysis can be lost by focusing on the data side of the self-evaluation. If this happens, the participatory nature of the evaluation and its benefits at local level would be lost, as the data collection aspect of the process would take priority. However, if the participatory process is well managed, the self-reflection activities will not be restricted to simply completing forms, and discussions or further analysis that spin off from the guided process would ensure that the process continues to be productive at the local level.

What are the potential gains? Apart from the results of a participatory process at local level, if all groups address the issues in the same manner, record the results carefully and gather them together by a system that minimizes the potential inclusion of errors, the managers will be able to aggregate the information and process it using standard statistical tools. There are several advantages to this way of collecting information. First, because each group uses the information for its own purposes, the incentives for providing distorted information are reduced to a minimum and the quality of any resulting data set is likely to be much better than that of information collected through traditional methods such as surveys.

Second, an interesting new opportunity is created. The standardization of the process allows interaction between groups, so they will be able to compare their experiences on the basis of a common instrument. This opens a new level of analysis for the members of the groups and their management structures.

There are also new risks introduced to the process. One is that the management does not make use of the information and the process is cut short and only delivers local benefits. It would be a pity if something like this happens, but the risk here is one of not reaping all possible benefits and not one of loss of benefits that already exist.

A technical risk is that the management could attempt to gather information on all the 18,000 groups and overstretch its resources. Although managing such a large amount of information is not beyond the capacity of a qualified data manager, well-designed systems are needed to ensure that the quality of the information is high. The organization of systems to collect forms, the process of entering and then cleaning the data, although boring, are not trivial. A quick calculation would suggest that on average results from 72 groups should be processed every day of the year (assuming 250 working days in a year), a task that is not impossible if well organized but that requires good planning and some basic data management skills. The managers of this information should question whether they are interested in gathering information from each and every group. A sampling strategy, probably along the lines of a longitudinal, panel study of groups, would be an alternative. This would fulfil their data requirements with less demand for resources.

Case study 2 The Internal Learning System

Professional Assistance for Development Action (PRADAN) is an NGO working in India where it has implemented the Internal Learning System (ILS) (see Narendranath, Chapter 5 this volume). PRADAN (2005) describes the ILS as:

a participatory learning and impact assessment tool for Self Help Groups (SHGs) based on pictorial workbooks [diaries]. These enable women to track and analyse events in their lives and use the understanding to make changes therein. SHGs can use this data to take stock of where the group and its members are. It helps PRADAN promoters and women interact in the context of the status of individual families rather than programmatically.

ILS was initiated by the Ford Foundation, and evolved over a number of years within a NGO context. The concept was to develop a participatory monitoring and evaluation system for micro-finance NGOs that would be internally driven (Noponen, 2005 and chapter 4 this volume).

This case study looks at ILS as used by PRADAN, and how it has adapted participatory approaches to deliver benefits at a number of different levels.

Box 12.2   The Internal Learning System

Helzi Noponen

ILS was originally designed as a longitudinal panel survey built over time in an interactive facilitated process. It is also enriched before, during and after the use of ILS instruments with individuals, by qualitative methods such as in-depth open-ended interviews, focus group discussions (FGD) methods and Participatory Rural Appraisal (PRA) exercises. It has been developed to meet the learning and information needs of donors and NGOs for programme evaluation, and local people who are often illiterate. Individual and group diaries, and a range of other largely pictorial tools, are used to catalyse learning.

It was designed 'to be a monitoring and evaluation system that is internally driven responding to the on-going needs of development organizations and their participants to learn about program impact – what is working and not working, and why, so that changes could be made in a timely manner' (Noponen, 2005).

A careful and critical mix of qualitative and quantitative approaches helps remove an inherent danger for a hybrid such as ILS. The danger is that trying to blend contrasting elements and features of each approach misses the very strengths of each. ILS also tries to balance tensions of context-specific methods (typically qualitative) that seek out nuances and in-depth meanings specific to the unit of analysis, and context-neutral (typically quantitative) methods that seek consistency across many specific contexts for generalizable results.

For example, in ILS I have created a hybrid form of PRA by grafting on to the ILS pictorial formats key elements of in-depth qualitative PRA exercises, such as income and expenditure tree exercises and production calendars, satisfaction rating scales and ranking exercises. I first devised simpler ways to record information from traditional PRA exercises, in which respondents do not have draw symbols or navigate complex tables. In their traditional form, PRA exercises require a great deal of staff time and facilitation skills when done in situ starting from blank slates and using hand-drawn elements as the need arises (contextual approach), that make them unfeasible to do on a repeated basis (i.e. over time) for a large programme population.

The outcomes of PRA exercises are not usually preserved or held by participants so that they can reflect on their progress over time – it is predominantly used as a one-off tool. Often, outcomes are not directly tied to immediate planning exercises that make use of the knowledge gained to improve decisions about credit use or livelihoods. The ILS PRA exercise format and the responses made are preserved in the participants' diaries. Participants can use the knowledge gained in the exercises in making ongoing decisions about livelihood and credit use as they track changes in their household situation over time.

In ILS, elements of PRA exercises, especially likely possible responses, have been distilled or frozen into standardized pictorial icons or small symbols. This reduces the amount of staff time and facilitation required and also imposes a standard structure for consistency in probing and response across a sample of participants that can be numerically coded for quantitative analysis (a move towards a non-contextual approach). These response categories, however, have been developed through feedback from many previous, contextually focused PRA exercises carried out among the target group in the process of designing and testing the modified ILS version of the PRA exercise (an example of a sequential mixing of a largely qualitative method with ILS).

Despite these inbuilt features attempting to merge features of each approach, the danger of emphasizing quantitative over qualitative aspects could still exist in ILS, as many organizations desiring to adapt ILS tend to focus only on what is most obvious: the use of pictorial diaries in participants' hands. They tend to place less emphasis on other less visible but key features of ILS such as the rich, iterative and cumulative learning process for participants, field staff and managers that surround the use of the diaries.

The ILS process is less visible and more difficult to control in terms of quality than the ILS diary content. How well do field officers understand and promote the value of learning over time among participants? Do they seek fuller and richer understandings on development issues being tracked in the diaries? Do they encourage participants to use the goal-setting, problem-sorting, priority selection and planning formats?

One of the strengths of ILS is that it is an ongoing embedded system. Unlike a one-off survey, PRA exercise, or case study, ILS exercises are repeated over time and available at all times for reflection by participants and staff. Do field officers only work towards getting participants to complete the diary entries so that implementation targets are reached or data captured for impact reports, or do they encourage sharing experiences and reflection on progress, especially outcomes, of past plans? The challenge is for organizations to motivate staff and provide them the time, space and training resources to use ILS in a rich learning process that empowers participants and provides even more in-depth understandings for staff on their life and livelihood development. Otherwise, the best features of ILS are underutilized.

Comments

As in the case of Samata, the development of a system capable of aggregating information for decision-making was driven by an external stakeholder interested in facilitating decision-making at the macro level but with a commitment to enhancing the internal process of learning and the action of partner NGOs and programme beneficiaries.

The ILS approach borrows from the strengths of participatory approaches and traditional survey methods, and in doing so creates a hybrid that is well suited to the objectives for which it was designed. At the centre of ILS there is a detailed approach to the development of the diary, the instrument that is used to collect information. This diary is developed through a series of iterations based on consultations with local participants and relies heavily on pictorial representations. The reported level of ownership of the diary by the women who use it, and its suitability to engage in the analysis of important aspects of their own lives, make the diary an ideal vehicle to facilitate participation and action. (for more detail, see Narendranath, Chapter 5 this volume)

It is here that ILS faces a crucial challenge. The diary could become a vehicle to stimulate participation, analysis and action (local dimension); or the diary could become an instrument for the collection of data that is seen by local participants as belonging to an external agent (remote dimension). ILS emphasizes the importance of striving towards the first function of the diary, and for this purpose systems of training and support for local participants and facilitators are established.

Although ILS is a participatory approach, in the case discussed here it focused its data-gathering activities on individual members of SHGs as well as on group-level information.[61] With this it breaks the pattern of group work often associated with participatory methods. This is very refreshing, because in doing so it refuses to try to make the problem fit the tool and innovates in such a way that many of the advantages of participatory approaches are maintained. ILS does not throw the baby away with the bath water, as it still uses some group activities and analysis facilitated by NGO staff.

The process of information gathering, analysis and action is effective at the local (individual and group) level and achieves what most participatory approaches aim for: analysis followed by action. At the same time, because of the structured way in which information is gathered and recorded by the local participants, it creates the possibility for joint and comparative analysis of information between local participants (intra- and inter-group), while addressing the objectives of the remote stakeholders. It facilitates data collection that can yield useful information for decision-making at the macro level.

While the information, if managed appropriately, has the potential to generate reliable, externally valid and representative results, there is a further condition that needs to be satisfied. If the information is not a census of participants – the ILS development team sensibly and deliberately took the decision to collect information on a sampling basis – the method of selection of the sample of participants needs to rely on statistical sampling.[62]

The ILS design includes a level of standardization in the way it organizes activities, conducts the information-gathering exercises and registers this information. This conforms to the need for the comparability of information across local participants. As with the Samata case, the trade-off here is one between flexibility and in-depth analysis as against the structure and standardization required to satisfy the demands for information of the remote stakeholders. ILS has the potential to generate data suitable for aggregation and analysis using statistical tools.

What do these cases tell us?

These two case studies have some common traits.
- They both impose a level of standardization on the participatory process.
- They have the potential to involve every group or individual affected by the activities of the movement or organization, while at the same time offering the possibility of sampling for the collection and analysis of the information that can be used at higher levels for decision-making.
- They have adapted participatory tools to fit the issues of interest.
- The process is not restricted to a data collection exercise, and the information that is acquired for aggregation would be a by-product of meaningful local activities. But more importantly, the local process and the data collection seem to evolve within a symbiotic relationship.

Perhaps this is possible because there is already a strong movement or programme that has built local capacity, so the participatory evaluation has appropriate structures to rely on and produces information whose benefits are valued by the individuals who belong to these structures as both staff and programme beneficiaries.

Case study 3   Ethical issues

There are ethical considerations in trying to construct the kind of methodological hybrid discussed so far. There have been a few efforts to look at these ethical issues, but the risks are potentially high. The following case study presents one of the aspects associated using participation for research and how sometimes the participants may be disempowered through the process of research.

Box 12.3   Participation as a coping strategy for survival: disempowerment by and of researchers

Alice Welbourn

As an HIV-positive woman I have become not just someone professionally interested in participation, as a matter of conscience, but also someone personally interested in participation as a means of psychological survival. Around the world and throughout time many people who have experienced deeply traumatic events, whether they be earthquakes, train crashes, alcoholism or road traffic accidents, the death of a child or the horrors of war, have responded to these events in their lives by trying to put something back. The response to an HIV diagnosis is no exception. Many others whom I have met, from all walks of life, have decided that the only way to cope with their diagnosis is 'to try to make sense of it all', 'to make sure others don't go through what I went through' and not just to survive, but to thrive. There are also many others who are highly dedicated, who volunteer to support causes for other reasons. But here I am focusing specifically on people who become activists in a cause which has touched them personally.

The right to participation is enshrined in Article 27 of the Universal Declaration of Human Rights. (The right not to participate is also there, in Article 20. So this means that no one should be forced to participate, if they don't want to.) In the world of HIV there is something called 'GIPA', which stands for the 'greater involvement of people living with HIV/AIDS'. The idea behind this is that we have the right to be involved in all decisions which affect our lives. This was a principle which was created at an international AIDS conference in Paris in 1994 and to which many organizations subscribe – in theory. But in practice, the International Community of Women Living with HIV/AIDS (ICW), the global network of positive women to which I belong, regularly finds this principle either overlooked or ignored. We find that if anyone is invited to a meeting, it tends to be a positive man rather than a positive woman; if a positive woman is invited, she tends to be cherry-picked by the organization as a guest speaker to tell her story, rather than to be involved in the real discussions which follow. This often means that, in her role of honour, she can feel nervous or awkward about making any criticisms about the organization's work. And young positive women, whom this virus is now hitting hardest, find it particularly hard for their voices or views to be heard as equals in decision-making foray.

During the week of the workshop which led to this book there was a workshop happening in the same building. Academics from around the world were meeting to discuss vulnerability and AIDS. That afternoon I played hookey from our write-shop for an hour to attend one session where two speakers in succession quoted from HIV-positive people whom I know. The first quote was from an HIV-positive young African engineer, a member of our network. Her quote appears in a book which we published,[63] on the basis of her and other young positive women's research of their own experiences, which is how this academic knows of it. The second quote was from a gay HIV-positive lawyer, also a passionate speaker. Neither of those two HIV-positive people was at the meeting to tell their own story or to contribute to the discussion about the issues which are affecting their lives. Nor was there a representative from any other international HIV-positive people's network present in the room. I left the room before the session finished, holding back my tears, wondering what else we have to say or do to get the world to realize that participation is not just a privilege but a right, not just a box to tick but a fundamental survival strategy for so many of us.

I know that if I show my anger the battle will be lost – women are not supposed to get angry. I know that if I process my feelings from where they are now and turn them into humour, I will probably get further with explaining the situation to others, but this takes yet more energy, which at present I cannot find. I am glad that my HIV status has made me open my eyes in some small way to the manner in which all of us, perhaps all the time, manage to ignore the rights of others to their voices and their visions.

Comments

What strikes me about this account is that in using participatory methods for research, we can easily start processes of participation that alienate the very people we are attempting to open spaces for. She is a highly educated woman, with plenty of capacity to make herself heard, even under adverse conditions. However, she describes the ongoing struggle in engaging with people about HIV/AIDS, the difficulties faced by those who live with HIV/AIDS, in ensuring that their rights are respected. This makes me reflect on the situation of those people, less articulate, less confident, who face almost insuperable obstacles to satisfy basic needs. These are the people with whom many of us work, and who we invite to participate in research processes. Welbourn forces me to reflect about the ethical implications of the processes I initiate. She makes me aware of my responsibility to carefully consider how my attempts to innovate about ways to find out by using participatory methods need to include safeguards for the rights of the participants and the wrongs I may be inflicting on them.

I believe that the risk of disempowering and alienating vulnerable people through the bad use of participatory approaches is high when these approaches are adapted for research that fulfils the information needs of external stakeholders.

We need to constantly ask ourselves whether we are using people rather than empowering them. When institutional support is permanent, such as in the case of PRADAN, or there is a strong grassroots organization such as in the case of Samata, the conditions exist for good participation. There are other cases where participatory tools are used for enquiry, in the absence of institutional support, with little opportunity for follow-up. This type of practice is justified on the basis of enabling people to express their voices, the work in Malawi described by Levy (Chapter 10 , this volume; Barahona and Levy, 2003). However, the risks are much higher here. Practitioners of participatory approaches and researchers need to think carefully about their actions and how they affect those who get involved with them.

Concluding thoughts

From a human perspective, the most important of the potential pitfalls described in this chapter is the ethical one, and we cannot afford to ignore it. From a technical perspective, the challenge is that of combining needs of the local and remote dimensions: the empowering, learning and acting at local level and the decision-makers' information needs. The process of adapting and navigating trade-offs could probably be summarized as follows.

A need to achieve the right level of standardization

Although standardization is often seen as something to be avoided in participatory work, these case studies have shown that it is an essential requirement for research. The solution to this conflict may be found when we look more carefully at what is meant by standardization in this context. The arguments against it describe it as a straitjacket that, if imposed on a participatory process, leads to a loss of richness and local ownership of the process. It could also be argued that the agenda can be easily hijacked by external actors and that the benefit of the analysis shifts towards the external actors. The argument in favour of it is that unless a suitable level of standardization is in place, information collected in different settings is not comparable, the quality of the evidence gathered is under threat and the credibility of the findings is jeopardized.

Both sides have a point and the search for an optimal trade-off requires a more detailed analysis. We need ask what is standardization is, what can and cannot be standardized, and when is it allowable to standardize. However, there are no quick answers to these questions. During each process there is a need to take a decision according to its specific conditions. What the two case studies show is that it is possible to achieve a balance that can generate benefits for the local participants and the external stakeholders. These show that a level of standardization can be found in such a way that the participatory process remains flexible and rich at the local level, while comparable information can be acquired for aggregation across sites. Standardization should not be a restriction, but the means to provide the structure required by the research objectives.

Expanding coverage

The challenge of expanding the coverage of a PM is sometimes referred to as scaling up, and implies trade-offs. First, can more individuals and groups become part of the process of information gathering, analysis and action, spreading the learning-and-action process at the local level more widely, to expand the impact? This is related to the needs of local stakeholders, and concerns the developmental and social change aspects of the process. Second, how many individuals and groups need to become involved in the information-gathering process so as to allow the results of any aggregated analysis to be reliable and representative? How should these individuals and groups be selected? This is related to the needs of remote stakeholders. This could be regarded as the external research side of the process.

Perhaps these two sides should be addressed separately. They have different functions, require different strategies and resources and can potentially run in parallel. In navigating the trade-off we seek to make efficient use of resources and the time that is demanded from individuals and groups at the local level. Scaling up and ensuring sufficient coverage for external research purposes require different technical skills too, in the first case from planners, managers and development workers, in the second from statisticians. Part of the challenge here is to bring together these skills into teams that are able to communicate effectively.

My conclusion is that there is an opportunity, supported by successful experiences, to take advantage of the synergies of participatory approaches and research methods to generate reliable information. The experiences so far demonstrate how the resulting process can be useful both at the local and the macro level for good information-based decision-making. However, more still needs to be learned and optimal trade-offs will have to be found. In doing so innovation, resistance to prefabricated solutions and ethical considerations should be central to our activity.

CHAPTER 13

Creating, evolving and supporting participatory methodologies: lessons for funders and innovators[64]

Robert Chambers

> Increasingly donors expect us to define clearly in advance what all our outputs and outcomes are going to be, and who the funding is or is not going to be spent on. So there is no investment in creativity, there is no faith in us as creative agents of change, nor in the people with whom we might work, as independent thinkers who might come up with new good ideas for themselves, based on their own experiences, along the way. The set agenda which allows no room for exploration or experimentation is stifling critical opportunities for learning. (Welbourn, Chapter 9 this volume)

Introduction

A recurrent theme and concern in the workshop which led to this book was relationships with funders, often referred to as donors – both the agencies themselves and those who work within them. This chapter sets out to review the roles of funders in supporting the creation, evolution and spread of participatory methodologies (PMs); and seeks to derive practical lessons for them and for those innovators and practitioners whom they sponsor and support. To do this I draw on two main sources: my own involvement with Rapid Rural Appraisal (RRA) and Participatory Rural Appraisal (PRA); and the experience and accounts of contributors to this book.

All the innovations and evolutions described in this book required resources. These took three forms.

First was funding by donor agencies for the creation, evolution and spread of PMs. In some cases this was over a period of years: *Reflect*, for example, was evolved and piloted through a three-year grant from the UK's Overseas Development Agency (ODA, now Department for International Development, DFID) to ActionAid (Archer); and the development and spread of Internal Learning Systems (ILS) were supported for years by the Ford Foundation (Noponen, Narendranath, Nagasundari). Other funding agencies for the methodologies described in this book included the Aga Khan Foundation, the

Asian Development Bank (ADB), Charity Projects, Diakonia, Humanistic Institute for Development Cooperation (Hivos), Marie Stopes Foundation, Netherlands Organization for International Development Cooperation (Novib), Oxfam, Redd Barna, Save the Children Federation (SCF), the Swedish International Development Agency (Sida), the Swiss Agency for Development Cooperation (SDC), the United Nations Development Programme (UNDP) and the World Health Organization (WHO). Several of the authors (Barahona, Jupp, Levy, Mayoux, Remenyi, Welbourn) have innovated when contracted as consultants.

A second source was partial or total funding by parent organizations. Partial support applied with *Reflect* within ActionAid in its early stages (Archer), and total support to the mapping of participatory practices within ActionAid (Newman). My own experience began with support from the Institute of Development Studies (IDS) at the University of Sussex.

Third, innovators of PMs funded or subsidized themselves, pervasively doing more than was commissioned or paid for. Every consultant and every committed development professional know this, and it applies to all the contributors. It is a corollary of creativity.

Those who fund have power. Funding agencies have had a big influence on the creation, evolution and spread of PMs. This chapter draws on the experiences of relations with funders in the evolution of RRA and PRA and on other chapters to explore how funding agencies, their staff and those whom they fund could adapt and change their practices and multiply pro-poor impacts.

RRA and PRA: a personal journey

In recounting some of the history of RRA and PRA I am relying on memory as well as written records. My personal involvement carries three dangers. First, I may attribute too much to my own role and my view may be over-coloured by my own ego and experiences: there were innumerable other actors, events, experiences and streams of innovation, evolution and spread that I do not describe or do not know about. Second, because I have myself worked in a funding agency and had contacts of long standing in funding agencies, obtaining support for those RRA and, more so, PRA activities in which I was involved may have been less difficult than it often is for others, and I may have been allowed more freedom than is usual. Third, while some sought to integrate RRA and PRA methods and approaches into organized and standardized systems, what actually spread could be, and usually were, ideas and methods which were versatile and could be adopted and adapted individually, for example semi-structured interviewing in RRA and participatory mapping in PRA. These three conditions may not be found, either separately or in combinations, with other methodologies, and so confront us with the familiar dangers of moving from the particular to the general. The cases of RRA and PRA raise issues shared with other accounts in this book and provide material for comparisons, adding some relevance and credibility to the conclusions.

RRA

RRA was, and remains, a quiet professional revolution, a loose coalescence of many small innovations underpinned by some common practical principles like triangulation (various forms of crosschecking) and optimal ignorance (not finding out more than is needed). While less participatory than most of the other methodologies described in this book, it was one major flow that led into PRA.

From today, in the middle of the first decade of the 21st century, it is difficult to imagine oneself back in the professional values and practices of the 1960s, 1970s and even 1980s. In those days, three modes of learning about rural life and conditions prevailed and were largely unchallenged: extended social anthropological immersions; large-scale and lengthy questionnaire surveys; and brief rural visits which came to be described as rural development tourism. For purposes of policy and practice, all three had serious drawbacks: social anthropological approaches were too slow, and their outcomes esoteric and inaccessible; large questionnaire surveys were laborious, expensive, insensitive to local knowledge, inaccurate, slow to process and often misleading or inconclusive; and rural development tourism was vulnerable to biases of place, project, person, season, politeness and professional interest. In response to these deficiencies, many practical fieldworkers, consultants and researchers created and evolved their own ways of finding out. But they did not parade these. Most of what they improvised, invented and used was not respectable among normal professionals, and was not written up or shared. Instead it was hidden to avoid ridicule or condemnation by colleagues.

A much cited and apt illustration comes from the agricultural economist, Michael Collinson, working in East Africa. In a week he could identify agricultural research priorities for a farming system or farming area. But he felt he then had to follow with a three-month questionnaire survey. In no case did this contradict his earlier insights or findings, but he was obliged to do this in order to convince the establishment. For this sort of survey, not only were funds available, but funders themselves as part of the establishment demanded it (Collinson, 1981).

My base, IDS, was privileged for funds. Founded in 1966, it received a core grant of some 80 per cent of its budget from the Ministry of Overseas Development. Providing they could convince their colleagues, the faculty of IDS could gain access to funds to convene workshops and conferences. We were a relatively small group of 20–30 fellows, and knew one another. To obtain funding for a workshop or conference all that was usually required was a two-page memo and a small meeting at which plausible enthusiasm was likely to carry the day. So it was that Richard Longhurst and I, together with Ian Carruthers at Wye College, were able to convene a workshop on RRA early in 1979. This generated enough evidence and excitement to put a proposal to the Ford Foundation, which then supported a conference later in the year to which were submitted over 30 papers. It was clear that this was a vital subject. There were new criteria of rigour, methods which were cost-effective, and the seeds of a revolution to provide methods and approaches which were alternatives or complements to those already professionally entrenched.

We invited an accomplished editor, Arnold Pacey, to come and to edit the papers of the conference. But we had no provision in the budget for editing, publishing or dissemination. This was one of the grossest errors of my life. In those days of the 1970s, difficult to conceive now, research budgets rarely included these.[65] Better late than never as I thought, I submitted a supplementary proposal for $10,000 to the Ford Foundation. This was turned down. The champion of the first grant was moving on, and when I worked for the Ford Foundation later I learnt a small grant could be as much work as a larger one. The error was not including the provision in the original proposal. I have since reflected on how much faster the evolution and spread of RRA would have been if we had had that $10,000 for the book. We sent copies of the papers to people who asked for them.[66] But a book on RRA had to await publication of papers from the University of Khon Kaen's international RRA conference (Khon Kaen University, 1987), some six or seven years after those earlier papers would have been published.

PRA: early days

The Khon Kaen conference owed much to agro-ecosystem analysis and its sketch mapping and diagramming (Conway, 1985) which Gordon Conway and his colleagues, supported again by the Ford Foundation, had evolved at the turn of the 1980s at Chiang Mai in Thailand and then disseminated in Southeast Asia. After Khon Kaen, combinations of methods were more widely recognized and used, such as focus groups, semi-structured interviewing, transects and observation, and especially sketch mapping and seasonal and other forms of diagramming, freed from the constraints of conventional scientific notions of precision. The potent brew of these mixtures spawned more and more improvisations and inventions. Many of these were evolved by the Sustainable Agriculture Group at the International Institute for Environment and Development (IIED), led by Conway, who with his colleagues and myself, conducted annual one-week trainings in RRA with the staff of SDC in rural Switzerland, and I gave a couple of development lectures in Berne.

In 1988 Conway, Jenny McCracken and I held a 10-day RRA training for the Ethiopian Red Cross, funded by the Swedish Red Cross, in Wollo in Ethiopia (Ethiopian Red Cross Society, ERCS, 1988). Learning by training was intense. We were on the edge of participatory approaches. There were big, dare I say, seminal, 'ah has!'. Conway was amazed at the detailed recall by two farmers of rainfall over the previous five years. I was startled, in a small hut, watching two Ethiopian professionals interviewing three farmers. On the basis of what the farmers said, the professionals drew a histogram of the labour demands of agriculture by month. When this was shown to the farmers to see if they could understand it, they looked and replied, 'Yes, you have drawn what we said.'

Another 'ah-ha!' was coming to realize the gross roadside bias, distortion and inaccuracy of the sketch map we drew.

Later, yet another revelation was with agricultural scientists in West Bengal. This time we asked tribal men and women to draw their own histograms on the ground of their agricultural labour by month. They did it, and then the women protested, and added a block across the base of theirs for all the other work they did. In parallel, other threads and evolutions – by the Aga Khan Rural Support Programme (AKRSP) in Gujarat, and with community action planning in Kenya – indicated that something was on the verge of happening.

Support from IDS, a welcome from the Administrative Staff College of India (ASCI) in Hyderabad and funding from the Ford Foundation, the Aga Khan Foundation and the ODA, then gave me two years based in Hyderabad. The funded proposal was 'for support for popular participation in the management of rainfed agriculture and enhancing professional contribution to rainfed agricultural research and watershed management'. Apart from these terms of reference, the only strings were that I would spend a minimum of 44 days with AKRSP (India) and the Sadguru Water Development Foundation, both in Gujarat. ASCI made few demands on my time, giving freedom to spend most of it with those in India who were innovating with PRA, participatory approaches in which local people were facilitated to do their own appraisal, analysis and planning.[67] There was a rapid sequence of shared 'ah-ha!s': a seasonal diagram on the ground with stones which showed how the timing of migration prevented children's education; a 3-D coloured model farmers made of a watershed; a social map showing all the houses in a village; matrix scoring of varieties of millet using seeds, and a veritable explosion of creativity and inventiveness released by the enthusiasm and sensitive facilitation by colleagues, some of it captured and presented in *RRA Notes* No. 13.

The freedom was extraordinary. I wrote short six-monthly reports to the three funders and they imposed no constraints. This meant that I could be a freely moving colleague and almost co-conspirator with those innovating in the field, as well as photographer and, as things rapidly evolved, disseminator. For quite soon, and unexpectedly, I found myself conducting familiarization workshops of one or two days, over 30 of them in 18 months, for NGOs, the government, academics and training institutes. Whether this was the right thing to do can be questioned. We warned from near the start about behaviour and attitudes, and the dangers of going to scale. But the bad effects of the subsequent massive adoption of PRA rhetoric by donor agencies, NGOs and governments led to much abuse. At the same time what happened because of the spread of PRA, though often bad, may have been less bad than it would have been, and may have sown seeds for later changes. The counterfactuals are not knowable. There were many inspiring examples of good practice and some of the bad practice was improved. But I do ask myself whether, had I had more foresight, less enthusiasm, more self-restraint and perhaps also less freedom, spread would have been slower and abuse less. The jury is out, and may always be.

PRA: training, networking, dissemination

When I returned to IDS in mid-1991 the overriding priorities were training, networking and dissemination. Since IDS was receiving less and less core funding, other support had to be raised. The Ford Foundation, ODA and Sida combined for two years, and other donors – the Paul Hamlyn Foundation, Danida (the Danish aid agency) and Novib (the largest) followed on. Their grants were used for South–South roving workshops, enabling Indian trainers to spread PRA to other countries, seeding and encouraging networks, and sharing materials and ideas. So I was in effect funded to be a funder. The grants gave independence within IDS, where few knew or understood what we – my secretary Helen McLaren, myself and occasional research assistants – were doing. My real colleagues were in the South and in IIED. The latter came to IDS for perhaps a dozen brainstorming workshops. IIED produced *RRA Notes*. PRA spread like wildfire. At the same time, bad practices in the name of PRA led to much criticism, not least by academics and by participatory practitioners in other traditions or schools. In early 1995 Novib funded a three months' breathing space during which I prepared a proposal for £760,000 for 'Activities in support of Participatory Appraisal, Learning and Action through capacity-building in the South, South–South sharing, networking, research, workshops and dissemination'.[68] Novib turned this down, requiring a year during which PRA would be evaluated. A PRA innovator and trainer to whom I mentioned this exclaimed incredulously, 'They must be joking!' To him the strengths and benefits were so much a part of his daily experience. But we were up against another rationality.

Devastated and depressed by Novib's rejection, I flew direct from Amsterdam to Berne. Three staff from SDC met me at the airport. I could scarcely believe what followed. Within a few hours, they had pledged support for the whole programme.

Lessons from the RRA and PRA experience

The conditions which allowed me to be involved in supporting the emergence, evolution and spread of RRA and PRA were unusually favourable. While, as Heraclitus said, we can never step into the same river twice, it is worth examining those conditions in order to see what lessons they hold. Four stand out.

- *Diverse experience*. When seeking funds I had the advantage of having been a nomad between organizations and roles – administrator, researcher, consultant and funder myself when working in the Ford Foundation in 1981–4. This helped me to be proactive, rather than reactive, in raising funds for what I thought needed to be done.
- *Long-term relationships with funding agencies*. Long-term relationships were important. I never thought of working in the Ford Foundation or training SDC staff as investments. The trainings in Switzerland were simply good experiences with lots of learning and much fun. But I see now how they must have helped, especially when SDC saved the day in 1995.

- *Flexibility.* I was astonished in 2005 to read in my original 1989 proposal that I went to India to work on rainfed agriculture, agricultural research and watershed management. I had forgotten that. The main focus rapidly became PRA and its dissemination. What happened in India took me and others by surprise. It was anyway unknowable in advance. These were the days before the virus of logframes had infected donor agencies and their relationships. Had I had one, my time would have been anxious, constrained and less productive.
- *Engagement in the field.* Again and again it was involvement in field situations that led to 'ah-ha!s', insights and innovations, especially uncontrollable social processes which forced adaptive improvisation and inventiveness. This was experiential learning, learning by doing and observing, with cycles of action and reflection, being provoked and stimulated to try to understand what was happening and to work through its practical implications.

Enabling conditions

These experiences with PRA and the creation, evolution and spread of other PMs, show that PM projects differ from most others. For a physical infrastructure project, detailed planning, time-schedules and targets can make sense. For process projects where the future is less controllable or predictable, they make less sense, and can distract and demoralize. For projects to generate, or which require, new PMs, the misfit is even sharper. What can be evolved, how long it will take, what obstacles will be encountered, where the process will lead, what unforeseen 'ah-ha!s' will open up new vistas and opportunities – these are among many unknowns. It is not like building a bridge. It is more like setting out on a voyage. Enabling conditions for creating, evolving and spreading PMs have their own character compared with conventions for most other projects. Four sets of issues stand out.

First, a key enabling condition for creating and evolving PMs is continuity of champions and institutional support. Again and again this has been critical. One example is the Ford Foundation's championing and support for ILS (Noponen, Chapter 4 this volume). Another is Nick Menzies of the Ford Foundation in China (Remenyi, Chapter 11 this volume) with the progressive introduction into China of questionnaires, then RRA, and then PRA.[69] In these cases the personal and institutional support was spread and sustained over close to or more than a decade. With SDC's support for PRA and its spread, and for the other participatory activities to which it led, the continuity has been even longer.

Second, organizational responsibility for dissemination and spread is largely overlooked. Donors who sponsor the creation and use of a PM often see it as a one-off exercise to achieve a particular programme objective. Many PMs like those for the Starter Pack Programme in Malawi (Levy, Chapter 10 this volume) do have a tailored fit: their principles, methods and how they were evolved may have wide value but their detail limits them to one context. Other PMs, like some pioneered by Jupp (Chapter 8 this volume) – for example, the visuals for participatory assessments of human rights abuses, and the Views of the Poor study in Tanzania – have wider applicability but have not been spread by the sponsoring organizations or anyone else.

In contrast, the use of positive deviance – identifying and learning from the feeding practices of poor families whose children were nevertheless well-nourished (Jupp) – was spread by Save the Children Fund to eventually cover 2.2 million people in 265 villages. The difference was the existence of and ownership by an organization and its partners and their wish and ability to use the innovation. The potential gains to poor people through the dissemination of what are still only one-off PMs must be one of the biggest missed opportunities in development.

Third, issues of time, resources and scale of impact are as vital as they are contradictory, varied and nuanced. Sometimes open-endedness, trust and patience, without strict timetables, are conditions for innovation. Evidence includes piloting *Reflect* over months, even years (Archer, Chapter 1 this volume), how Stepping Stones took much longer to produce than originally envisaged (Welbourn, Chapter 9 this volume) and also how the elaboration and simplifications of ILS painstakingly took place over years (Noponen, Narendranath, Nagasundari, Chapters 4, 5, 6 respectively this volume). But others' experiences (Jupp, Mayoux, Chapter 7 this volume) have been the opposite. Thus Jupp in her chapter:

> As a consultant I am often asked to work on short contracts with strict budgets. Whilst this has obvious constraints and can be frustrating, I would also claim that it has forced me to be extremely creative. I find the fact that I almost never have resources to write manuals or guidelines means that approaches used are always fluid and evolving ... I am free to invent and innovate for every new circumstance and this is very liberating. Of course, this also means that clients have to have trust in me.

The time and scale of impact involve intriguing trade-offs. When support is for years, as with ILS, a methodology may go to scale through organizations, but over-elaboration and time-consuming routinization can creep in (Noponen, Narendranath and Nagasundari). When support is for a short time, the gains from innovation may be brilliant but one-off, localized, temporary and without wider impact: the guidelines, the training workshops, the facilitators who would disseminate are missing, and with them is lost the chance of a far wider impact. The challenges for funders and consultants alike are to recognize the trade-offs and optimize outcomes. Where there is time-bound pressure for innovation it may need to be followed by sustained support for further evolution and dissemination.

Fourth, multiple sources of funding can similarly cut both ways. Some organizations prefer a single source of funds, to minimize distracting visitors and reporting requirements. When SDC was the sole agency supporting participatory work at IDS, less time had to be spent on donor relations than earlier or later when there were more funding sources. Others see benefits in having several funders. Welbourn, for example, writes of the development of Stepping Stones:

> I feel that the freedom to take the time needed, multiple funding sources and the wide range of skills and experiences of the advisors were all key contributory factors which facilitated the production of a package that is far more eclectic in its content and diverse in its appeal than might otherwise have been the case.

Single and multiple funders present different vulnerabilities: a single funder who withdraws support can be sounding a death knell, but such withdrawal may be less likely precisely because responsibility is so clear; multiple funders appear to provide more security, but the withdrawal of one can set off a chain reaction in which all end their support without any accepting responsibility.

Disabling conditions

Abrupt termination of funding

The unexpected end of Novib funding for PRA activities (see above) would have been devastating had not SDC stepped immediately into the breach. Other PMs are not so fortunate. A stark example is the withdrawal of support by one donor to Stepping Stones in Africa. Leaving aside the discordance of this decision with the acuteness of the HIV/AIDS crisis in southern Africa especially, and the official priority of aid to Africa, it also at a stroke left unemployed the Stepping Stones facilitators who had been trained through prior funding from that donor (Welbourn). As in this astonishing case, the ethical issues of cutting off funding can as be as vast and acute as they seem to be ignored.

Inappropriate indicators and evaluations

There is a paradigmatic tension between linear thinking and objectively verifiable numerical indicators, on the one hand, and evolutionary thinking and validation by adoption, on the other. This contributed to Novib's decision not to renew support for PRA at a time when it was spreading fast in perhaps 50 countries, and to the withdrawal of one donor's support for Stepping Stones despite its adoption and spread in over 100 countries. The request from the World Bank for literacy performance figures from *Reflect* so that these could be used internally for support in the bank was resisted because it was reasserting the traditional idea of literacy as narrowly focused on reading and writing.

Fracturing relationships and trust

All too often relationships and mutual understanding and trust carefully nurtured over years are fractured and destroyed by staff transfers in funding agencies, the new person having other priorities. Trust may be lost, and distrust inhibits through controls and the sense and reality of loss of freedom.

Practical advice for funders

For funders who wish to support the creation, evolution and spread of PMs, the list below presents practical advice. This draws on evidence, experience and ideas from the workshop, from contributions to this book, and from the funding of RRA and PRA networks and dissemination.[70]

- Be circumspect and sensitive in selecting PM innovators. Prefer those with good non-negotiable ethical principles and whom you are confident to trust.
- In a PM development phase, work with organizations that are enthusiastic and committed. Do not impose on unwilling organizations.
- Judge time scales carefully to optimize creativity and impact.
- Accept that achievements and setbacks in evolving and spreading PMs cannot be forecast.
- Avoid premature evaluation. Entrust evaluation only to persons who themselves have experience of and understand PMs.
- Recognize the importance of training and mentoring for facilitation, and provide budgets and time for this, especially early in a project's process.
- When sponsoring the development of a PM, do not treat it as a one-off or leave people in the lurch. Be prepared to provide resources and support for follow up, perhaps with other agencies, for recording, learning from, writing up, training, dissemination, and supporting NGOs and CBOs and further evolution of the methodology.
- When seeking to spread a PM avoid targets for disbursements. Provide for unspent budgets to roll over year on year.
- Encourage transparency and consistency in your organization, on websites and in hard copy. To help those seeking support for developing and spreading PMs, make it clear and public what you fund, your criteria, how you can be approached and what your accountability system is.
- Undertake 'immersions' and promote them among your colleagues to gain first-hand experience of PMs and an understanding of what they entail.
- Promote within your organization the use of non-written reporting systems, including photographs, audio and video diaries, especially those produced by community members.
- Fight and resist procedures and requirements when they conflict with the above.

Lessons for innovators

Those who seek and receive support – grantees, recipients, beneficiaries, consultants, innovators, pioneers, protagonists, activists, managers – whatever their roles and identities, are easily tempted or provoked into criticizing the organizations and the staff who finance them. And as we have seen, criticisms can be well founded. The other side of the coin, though, is that those who are supported often have much to learn and understand about the orientation, perceptions, incentives and constraints of funding agencies and their staff. From the RRA and PRA experience, and from the contributions to this book, these practical guidelines can be suggested.

- *Take pains to understand funders and their organizations.* They are often opaque and unpredictable. But try to find out who funds what, and what their requirements are. Donors suffer reorganizations, disruptions and changes of priority. Keeping up-to-date with these can save time and effort otherwise spent on wild goose chases that are doomed from the start.
- *Find and work with allies and champions.* In most funding agencies some staff are on a participatory wavelength, even when the organization itself is not. Search for the like-minded, and find ways of working with and supporting them.
- *Develop long-term relationships.* This was a lesson of the RRA/PRA experience, especially with SDC: the late 1980s training of SDC staff in RRA and lectures delivered in Berne seem to have prepared the seedbed for understanding and support later in the 1990s.
- *Negotiate and be prepared to say no.* Power relations are two-way. Those in funding agencies are not always as powerful or imperious as they appear. Sometimes they need help to spend budgets. Those who fund participation and PMs need support within their organizations. They may even need those who are funded to be critical so that they can use those criticisms internally. Those funded are often too deferential, too sensitive to real or imagined signals. A light suggestion is then interpreted as an imperious instruction. There are times for saying no for reasons of conditionality, co-option or reputational risk, as *Reflect* did to the World Bank (Archer).
- *Insist on flexibility.* Funders are often less controlling and more open to change than they appear. Logframes and proposals that have been accepted can be taken as more constraining than they should be. At one time, ActionAid Bangladesh was funded by DFID for *Reflect*, and wished to change direction, but felt it could not do this or modify its logframe before a mid-term review. However, donors may be open to change if they are informed and consulted. Their requirements can also sometimes be made less demanding, as with Noponen's Eureka moment when she realized that statistics from a sample of ILS users would be enough.
- *Provide funders with information and materials they can use.* They need to be able to show results. Conventional reports, which are often unread, can be complemented or replaced by visuals. The pictures taken by poor people in Tanzania became an exhibition in Berne which was seen by senior officials, civil society and political leaders (Jupp). The ILS diaries in south India gave information which could potentially be used not only for proposal writing, advocacy and lobbying, but also for reporting to donors (Nagasundari). Visuals, videos and stories can be more persuasive than long written reports.

- *Involve funders*. Understanding and trust are built on familiarity and shared experience. Part of the solution is for both sides to have common experiences in the field. Funders often welcome personal and professional involvement. Working for the Ford Foundation in Delhi, my best times were not making grants, which I did not enjoy or do well, but times in the field with grantees. Aid agency bureaucrats have become increasingly caught in a capital trap of meetings, negotiations, policy discussions and workshops, reducing or eliminating contact with other realities including those of poor and marginalized people.[71] They can be invited to take part in reviews and reflections like those of ActionAid (2000, 2001). In Tanzania, the emotional experiences and insights of the staff of SDC and its partners in their field research meant much to them. Even a year later, they were still repeatedly referring to them (Jupp).

Funders can, then, be invited to the field to take part in processes and activities. Seeking their participation and advice will often be personally and professionally rewarding for them, give them a break from their normal bureaucratic life, and equip them better to exercise influence in support within their organizations. Often such field visits will be the best and most memorable work experiences they will have. Creators and evolvers of PMs have something good to offer them.

Pro-poor symbiosis for creativity, innovation and spread

In these various ways, funders and funded need and can help one another. Too often, those funded do not understand the constraints or culture of the funding agency, and those in the funding agency do not understand the conditions for creativity, innovation and good spread. But with mutual understanding, the relationships can be symbiotic and win–win.

PMs are not, however, inherently pro-poor. Participation can take forms which further impoverish those who are poor or further marginalize those who are already excluded. Elites can gain at the cost of non-elites, men at the cost of women and so on. Participation ladders demonstrate how the P word can be used to cover anything from slave labour to spontaneous action, with many roles and relationships in between.[72] So the questions – who participates? who does not participate? who gains? and who loses? – have to be asked again and again. Honest answers are often uncomfortable. That said, as examples in this book so strikingly show, PMs can be created, evolved and facilitated which are pro-poor, benefiting and empowering many of those who are weaker and marginalized.

The challenge and opportunity now are to put to use the lessons of experience and to invent, multiply and spread more methodologies which are both participatory and pro-poor. Lessons will continue to be learnt, and will add to and qualify those postulated above. Contributions to this book show some of the potential of PMs to reveal unrecognized realities and to transform power relations. The scale of potential impact from spreading existing PMs wider and from others yet to be invented is hard to assess. It depends not least on the commitment, creativity and mutual understanding of those who sponsor and fund and those who innovate and spread. If all parties can combine well, many more PMs may be created. Although how funders, innovators and disseminators can combine is beginning to be better understood, much remains to be learnt. Nothing is certain. How big the potentials and impacts prove to be, only time will show. But the possibility that they may be vast makes the case for vigorous and sensitive exploration by funders, innovators and disseminators alike.

Endnotes

Introduction

1   The Institute of Development Studies at the University of Sussex, UK.
2   The main exception is Remenyi's account in Chapter 9 of the spread of the PPI through the Chinese local governance system.
3   For examples of the innovation and learning that is emerging from experiences of participatory citizenship and deepening democracy, see the Learning Initiative on Citizen Participation in Local Governance (LogoLink): http://www.ids.ac.uk/logolink/index.htm
4   Historically the terms 'participatory research' and 'participatory action research' have been used interchangeably in the PAR tradition, which has its origins in popular adult education and social movement experiences of the 1960s and 1970s (Freire, 1974; Fals-Borda, 2001). However, the term 'participatory research' is also used by social scientists to describe methods which involve participants in the processes of determining indicators or collecting data, and which may also have objectives of contributing to participant learning and action.
5   The spread of ILS was intentionally restrained by its donor, the Ford Foundation, out of concern that the approach be comprehensively tested and developed before being taken up on a wider scale. As we went to press, reports have arrived that other NGOs in India such as Seva Mandir in Rajasthan are now learning from and adapting aspects of ILS in their work.

Chapter 1

6   Set up in 2000, CIRAC is a democratic space for *Reflect* practitioners from different countries, organizations and networks to come together and learn from each other.
7   This logo was designed by Barry, a graphic artist with ActionAid at the time.
8   The Overseas Development Agency (ODA) of the UK was later renamed the Department for International Development (DFID).

Chapter 2

9   Stepping Stones is a training package in gender, HIV, communication and relationship skills. It is also a life-skills training package, covering many aspects of our lives, including why we behave in the ways we do, how

gender, generation and other issues influence this, and ways in which we can change our behaviour, if we want to. See Welbourn, this volume.

Chapter 3

10 For more information on ALPS is see the ActionAid International website: http://www.actionaid.org

11 'Rights to End Poverty' is available on the ActionAid International website: http://www.actionaid.org/425/strategy.html

11 See 'Transforming Power' at www.reflect-action.org, under 'Reflect Resources' for a full report of the workshop and activities to analyse power.

12 See: ActionAid in Practice: Understanding and Learning About Methods and Approaches of Rights and Empowerment

13 See Archer and Newman (2003). The nine principles are: Power and voice; a political process; a democratic space; an intensive and extensive process; grounded in existing knowledge; linking reflection and action; using participatory tools; power awareness; coherence and self organization.

14 Each theme is structured slightly differently, with a mixture of a core team with focal points spread across the organization at country programme level. As such, it was not possible for the themes to meet and discuss the mapping in the same way as people from the country programmes; however, some people (especially for the HIV/AIDS theme) did attempt to get a broad range of inputs into the mapping through email discussions.

15 These exercises drew on experiences from the *Reflect* ICTs pilot project. Information about the project and resource materials designed to support discussion on communication and information are available on the *Reflect* website: http://www.reflect-action.org. The exercises were adapted for an Asia regional network and documentation workshop, to explore why people were not currently documenting their work. This is also available on the web.

16 All the mapping tools are available from ActionAid through: kate.carroll@actionaid.org

17 In 'Taking Stock 2' one of the external consultants was asked to look at gender issues, both how ActionAid was working at community level and within the organization. She chided ActionAid for its patriarchal structure and way of working, and repeated these criticisms at an international staff conference in July 2004 (attended by about 70 people from across ActionAid, including all the international directors, AAI's highest level of management). At this staff conference her comments were discussed and analysed, and endorsed. This was followed by the decision to both mainstream women's rights, and create it as a separate theme, to invest heavily at exploring these issues at every level. The process is documented internally in the staff conference report (available to ActionAid staff on the intranet) and the analysis fed into the production of our strategy R2EP.

18 See Simanowitz (2001) for an excellent discussion of the multiple objectives for impact assessment. Available online at: http://www.imp-act.org

Chapter 4

19 Self-Employed Women's Association (SEWA), and Friends of Women's World Banking, India (FWWB (I)) and the DHAN Foundation

20 Activists for Social Action (ASA) , Professional Assistance for Development Action (PRADAN), New Entity for Social Action (NESA) and Bangladesh Rural Advancement Committee (BRAC)

21 The work on producing diaries for Banaskantha Dwarka Mahila SEWA Association (BDMSA), a SEWA rural association, was made possible by two-year funding from a PROWID grant from the International Center for Research on Women.

22 ILS Task # 1 – collect data.

23 ILS Tasks # 2 – assess data, and #3 troubleshoot outcomes.

24 ILS Task # 5 – reinforce programme values.

25 ILS task # 4 – plan.

26 ILS task # 5 – share information and learning.

27 One of my greatest fears was that the wife-beating picture indicator would result in a woman's death.

28 Self-Help Group (SHG), the most popular microfinance model in India, is an association of 10–20 rural poor women living in a neighbourhood, engaged in savings and credit to meet their needs for financial services. It is also a solidarity group as it provides the women a space of their own and initiates collective action on issues of concern.

Chapter 5

29 Cluster is an association of 10–15 SHGs of neighbourhood villages spreading over an area of 5 km radius. The forum provides support to groups in conflict resolution, peer learning, monitoring and so on.

30 Approximately equal to R12 a day per head on purchasing power parity (PPP) . The international poverty line of US$1.08 a day translates to approximately Rs16 a day.

31 Improving Impact of Microfinance on Poverty: an Action Research Programme (Imp-Act) was an action research project aimed at unpacking the impact of microfinance on poverty. It involved over 20 NGOs and microfinance institutions (MFIs) across the world, was coordinated by three UK universities and funded by the Ford Foundation.

32 In NESA's context, a *sangam* is a group of around 20 members who come together to take collective action. In contrast to SHGs (e.g. those described by Narendranath, Chapter 5), which are usually formed for savings and credit, for *sangams* the first priority is taking up issues that concern members and working for change.

Chapter 6

33 The decision-making body of the network, constituted by voting.

34 Five individual women come together and form one pressure group; four such pressure groups form one group; two or three groups form one centre; 10 centres come together and form one cluster; seven clusters come together and form one federation or branch.

35 Editor's note: 'Indicators' is the term used by NESA and by the author, although these might be understood by others as issues for which indicators and measurements are subsequently developed.

36 Ongoing updated versions of this chapter and all manuals and references for PALS can be found on the author's website: http://www.lindaswebs.org.uk/Page3_Orglearning/PALS/PALSIntro.htm and videos, interactive learning materials on the PALS website: http://www.palsnetwork.info

Chapter 7

37 For overviews of these debates in microfinance see: http://www.genfinance.info

38 For details of ANANDI and the participatory review see: http://www.anandiindia.org

39 See LEAP website: http://www.leap-pased.org

40 In ancient Greece, Archimedes exclaimed 'Eureka' when he discovered that his body displaced water in his bath, thus inventing the concept of specific gravity. Subsequently used in common speech to refer to any surprising discovery.

Chapter 8

41 The most frequently cited dissatisfaction being 'inordinate delays in processing applications', which was mostly perceived as a deliberate attempt to frustrate the customer into paying bribes to speed up the process.

42 Which were developed by PromPT from my earlier work in an SDC-funded grain storage and credit programme, Shogorip.

43 This experience was recorded in the BBC documentary 'Killers Don't Cry' first broadcast in April 2001.

44 All members of the household, young and old alike, were given an opportunity to use the cameras.

45 Such as the 'ABC' rhetoric, standing for 'Abstain, Be Faithful, Use Condoms', a message widely disseminated by the Bush regime and others. See Welbourn(2002) for a critique of this; see also: http://www.icw.org/publications

Chapter 9

46 Strategies for Hope Series, http://www.steppingstonesfeedback.org and http://www.stratshope.org
47 http://www.healthcomms.org/learn/learn01.html
48 See http://www.stratshope.org and http://www.talcuk.org and http://www.steppingstonesfeedback.org
49 See the Official Stepping Stones Adaptation guidelines, through http://www.steppingstonesfeedback.org
50 See http://www.steppingstonesfeedback.org for some examples of their comments, and reported changes which they say have taken place in communities, such as a reduction in gender violence, as a result of well-run workshops.

Chapter 10

51 The best known probability-based sampling method is simple random sampling, but it is often not the most efficient. In this case, we used a two-stage sampling process (Chinsinga et al., 2002).
52 Robert Chambers made this suggestion after hearing about the study at a meeting of the Parti Numbers group (personal communication, 2003).
53 The problem of surveys is that they often produce bad information. This led to a reaction against them by many people in the 1970s. Often, it was the use of questionnaires that was blamed for the problems. In fact, the culprit is not the questionnaire (unless badly designed – and all badly resigned research produces bad results); it is the idea that poorly motivated outsiders with little grasp of local reality can collect good information. If surveys are designed through consultation with the sort of people they are designed to collect information about, and preferably owned by them, they are likely to be much more effective. There is no reason why locally owned information systems should not use questionnaires for collecting information in circumstances where they are the best tool to collect the type of information that is required.
54 This idea was originally suggested by Roger Stern of the Statistical Services Centre, University of Reading (UK), who works with climate statistics in Africa.

Chapter 11

55 Dean of the College of Agricultural Development, China Agricultural University, Beijing.
56 For full details of how the PPI is constructed from raw data, see Li and Remenyi (2006).
57 The PPI is defined as follows.
     PPI = $[\Sigma I_i {}^* w_{it})^* W_t]^* 20$

where: $W_{t=1-3}$ = poverty weights by type of poverty, Livelihood (W_1), Infrastructure (W_2) and Human Resource (W_3) poverty; further, $\Sigma W_t = 1$.
$I_{i=1-8}$ = eight poverty indicators (i), the values of which are converted to a common base with a range of 5 (poorest) – 1 (least poor); and
w_{it} = poverty weights for each of the eight poverty indicators (i) grouped according to three types of poverty (t), where i = 1–8 and t = 1–3 and $\Sigma w_{it} = 1$.

Chapter 12

58 Deductive logic uses general rules to make inferences about the particular, individual observation. In contrast, inductive logic is the process of reasoning in which the premises of an argument support the conclusion, so the general statements are based on particular observations or facts.
59 Realism is the philosophy that proposes that the world has an existence independent of the human mind.
60 Discussed by the author with people involved in each of the experiences during the IDS writeshop of June 2005.
61 However, as discussed by Narendranath and Nagasundari (Chapters 5 and 6 this volume), different applications of ILS have relied exclusively on group-level data-gathering
62 How to use statistical sampling in this context and the basic reasons why statistical sampling is required are discussed in detail by Barahona and Levy (2003).
63 Namibian participant, Young Women's Dialogue, quoted in ICW Vision Paper No. 1 'HIV positive young women' (2004, p. 4), ICW, London.

Chapter 13

64 I am grateful to participants in the workshop for information, ideas and advice, and to Karen Brock, Dee Jupp, Jethro Pettit and Alice Welbourn for detailed comments. Responsibility for opinions, errors and omissions rests with me.
65 Later, in 1978–80, when sitting on ESCOR, the Economic and Social Committee for Overseas Research of the Ministry of Overseas Development, which advised on government grants for development-related research, I found myself repeatedly arguing that budgets submitted were too low because they did not provide for workshops, publications or other forms of dissemination.
66 The papers are still in boxes in my overfull office, vulnerable to recycling, waiting for a friendly archivist to save their lives and take them into care.
67 Those with whom I worked included Jimmy Mascarenhas, Vidhya Ramachandran and others from the NGO MYRADA, Anil Shah, Parmesh Shah and others of the AKRSP (India), Sam Joseph of ActionAid, Venkat Ramnayya of Youth for Action, John Devavaram and Sheelu Francis.

68 Subsequently I was happy to be able to hand over to John Gaventa the management of what became known as the Participation Group at IDS. This expanded and diversified into a much wider range of activities, as work on PRA became less needed. The Participation, Power and Social Change team, as it is now (2006) known, is managed by Rosalind Eyben and has some 20 members, and funding from sources including SDC, Sida, DFID and the Ford Foundation.

69 Over at least a decade, Menzies, through the Ford Foundation, sponsored training and the introduction of questionnaire surveys, RRA and then PRA, especially in Kunming.

70 While others have contributed to this advice, I accept responsibility for its content, and for errors or omissions.

71 See Chambers (2005), pp. 43–4.

72 For a review of some participation ladders see Chambers (2005), pp. 103–7.

References

ActionAid (1998) 'Gender and Reflect workshop report, Nicaragua', unpublished, ActionAid, London. Website: http://www.actionaid.org

ActionAid (2000) *ALPS: Accountability, Learning and Planning System*, ActionAid, London.

ActionAid (2001) *Notes to Accompany ALPS*, ActionAid, London.

Adong, R. (2004) 'The impact of Western management tools on Ugandan NGOs: some contextual notes', *CDRN Civil Society Review*, Community Development Resource Network, Kampala.

Archer, D. (2004) 'Participation, literacy and empowerment: the continuing evolution of Reflect in critical reflections, future directions', *Participatory Learning and Action* No. 50, International Institute for Environment and Development, London.

Archer, D. and Costello, P. (1990) *Literacy and Power: The Latin American battleground*, Earthscan, London.

Archer, D. and Newman, K. (2003) 'Communication and power', Circle for International Reflect Action and Communication (CIRAC), available online at: http://217.206.205.24/enghome.html (last accessed 14 November 2005).

Asian Development Bank (ADB) (2000) 'A study on ways to support poverty reduction projects', Final Report, TA3150 – PRC', ADB, Beijing.

ADB (2002) 'Preparing a methodology for development planning in poverty alleviation under the new poverty strategy of PRC', TA 3610 – PRC, Asian Development Bank, Beijing.

Barahona, C. and Levy, S. (2003) 'How to generate statistics and influence policy using participatory methods in research: reflections on work in Malawi, 1999–2002', Working Paper no. 212, IDS, Sussex.

Barahona, C. and Levy, S. (forthcoming) 'The best of both worlds: producing national statistics using participatory methods', *World Development*.

Boal, A. (1992) *Games for Actors and Non-Actors*, Routledge, London.

Buzan, T. with Buzan, B.(1996) *The Mind Map Book: How to use radiant thinking to maximise your brain's untapped potential*, Plume Books, New York.

Chambers, R. (1997) *Whose Reality Counts? Putting the first last*, Intermediate Technology Development Group, London.

Chambers, R. (2005) *Ideas for Development*, Earthscan, London and Sterling, VA.

Chandler, D., Gilbert, C. and Fuglesang, A. (1994) *Walking and Talking in the Village*, Redd Barna, Norway.

Chen, S. and Ravallion, M. (2004) 'Learning from success: understanding China's (uneven) progress against poverty', *Finance and Development*, **41**, 4 (December), pp. 16–19.

China State Council (2001) 'The development-oriented poverty reduction program for rural China', Poverty White Paper, Information Office, China State Council, Beijing.

Chinsinga, B. (2005) 'Practical and policy dilemmas of targeting free inputs', in S. Levy (ed.), *Starter Packs: A strategy to fight hunger in developing countries? Lessons from the Malawi experience, 1998–2003*, CABI Publishing, Wallingford.

Chinsinga, B., Dulani, B. and Kayuni, H. (2004) 'Malawi 2003 winter targeted inputs programme: a qualitative evaluation report', report for the Government of Malawi and DFID, UK.

Chinsinga, B., Dzimadzi, C., Chaweza, R., Kambewa, P., Kapondamgaga, P. and Mgemezulu, O. (2001) '2000–01 TIP evaluation module 4: consultations with the poor on safety nets', report for the Government of Malawi and DFID, UK.

Chinsinga, B., Dzimadzi, C., Magalasi, M. and Mpekansambo, L. (2002) '2001–02 TIP evaluation module 2, TIP Messages: beneficiary selection and community targeting, agricultural extension and health', report for the Government of Malawi and DFID, UK.

Collinson, M. (1981) 'A low-cost approach to understanding small farmers', *Agricultural Administration*, **8**, pp. 433–50.

Conway, G. (1985) 'Agro-ecosystem analysis', *Agricultural Administration*, **20**, pp. 31–55.

Cooperrider, D.L. (1996) 'The child as agent of inquiry', *Organisation Development Practitioner*, **28** (1, 2), pp. 5–11.

Cooperrider, D.L. and Srivastva, S. (1987) 'Appreciative inquiry in organisational life', *Research on Organisational Change and Development*, **1**, pp. 129–69.

Cornwall, A. (2001) 'Beneficiary, consumer, citizen: perspectives on participation for poverty reduction', SIDA Studies no. 2, SIDA, Stockholm.

Cornwall, A. and Brock, K. (2005) 'What do buzzwords do for development policy? A critical look at participation, empowerment and poverty reduction', *Third World Quarterly*, **26** (7), pp. 1043–60.

Cornwall, A., Guijt, I. and Welbourn, A. (1993) 'Acknowledging process: challenges for agricultural extension and research methodology', in I. Scoones and J. Thompson (eds), *Beyond Farmer First*, IT Publications, London.

Cromwell, E., Kambewa, P., Mwanza, R. and Chirwa, R. with KWERA Development Centre (2000) '1999–2000 Starter Pack evaluation module 4: The impact of Starter Pack on sustainable agriculture in Malawi', report for the Government of Malawi and DFID, UK.

Dixon, H. and Gordon, P. (1990) *Working with Uncertainty: A handbook for those involved in training on HIV and AIDS*, Family Planning Association, UK.

Dundon, E. (2002) *The Seeds of Innovation*, Amacom Books, Saranac Lake, New York.

Estrella, M., with Blauert, J., Campilan, D., Gaventa, J., Gonsalves, J., Guijt, I., Johnson, D. and Ricafort, R (eds) (2000) *Learning from Change: Issues and experiences in participatory monitoring and evaluation*, Intermediate Technology Development Group, London.

Ethiopian Red Cross Society (ERCS) (1988) *Rapid Rural Appraisal: A closer look at life in Wollo*, Ethiopian Red Cross Society, Addis Ababa and International Institute for Environment and Development (IIED), London.

Fals-Borda, O. (2001) 'Participatory (Action) Research in social theory: origins and challenges', in P. Reason and H. Bradbury (eds), *Handbook of Action Research: Participatory inquiry and practice*, Sage, London.

Fiedrich, M. and Jellema, A. (2003) *Literacy, Gender and Social Agency*, DFID, London.

Fine, N. and Macbeth, F. (1992a) *Fireworks*, Youth Work Press, Leicester.

Fine, N. and Macbeth, F. (1992b) *Playing with Fire*, Youth Work Press, Leicester.

Freire, P. (1970) *Pedagogy of the Oppressed*, Penguin, London.

Gautam, K. (1998) 'Encounter with a seventeenth-century manual', in *PLA Notes 32*, IIED, London.

Gender and Health Group, Liverpool School of Tropical Medicine, Liverpool Associates in Tropical Health, Liverpool VCT and Care (Nairobi, Kenya) and Reach Trust (Lilongwe, Malawi) (2005) 'Analysis of the gender dimension in the scale-up of antiretroviral therapy and the extent to which free treatment at point of delivery ensures equitable access for women', Liverpool School of Tropical Medicine, Liverpool. Available online at: http://www.liv.ac.uk/lstm/research/documents/report_gender_equity_art_scale_up.pdf

Guijt, I. (1995) *Questions of Difference: PRA, gender and the environment*, IIED, London.

Guijt, I. and Shah, M.K. (eds) (1998) *The Myth of Community: Gender, issues in participatory development*, Intermediate Technology Publications, London.

Hay, J. (1992) *Transactional Analysis for Trainers*, McGraw-Hill International, New York.

Heron, J. (1999) *The Complete Facilitators' Handbook*, Kogan Page, London.

Hulme, D. (2000) 'Impact assessment, methodologies for microfinance: theory, experience and better practice', *World Development*, **28**, pp. 79–88.

International HIV/AIDS Alliance (2006) *Tools Together Now! 100 Participatory tools to mobilise communities for HIV/AIDS*, International HIV/AIDS Alliance, Brighton, available online at: http://www.aidsalliance.org

Irvine, R., Chambers, R. and Eyben, R. (2004) 'Learning from poor people's lives: immersions', Lessons from Change no. 13, IDS, Sussex.

IT Transport (2002) *The Value of Time in Least Developed Countries, Final Report*, IT Transport, Ardington, available online at: http://www.ittransport.co.uk/documents/Final%20Report%20Value%20of%20Time%20Study%20(R%207785).pdf

IT Transport (2005) *The Value of Time in Least Developed Countries: The African studies, final report*, IT Transport, Ardington, available online at: http://www.ittransport.co.uk/VOTAMS.htm

Jamaica Social Investment Fund (2000) *Community Development Handbooks,* Jamaica Social Investment Fund, Kingston, Jamaica.

Jewkes, R., Nduna, M., Levin, J., Jama, N., Dunkle, K., Khuzwayo, N., Koss, M., Puren, A., Wood, K. and Duvvury, N. (2006) 'A cluster randomized-controlled trial to determine the effectiveness of Stepping Stones in preventing HIV infections and promoting safer sexual behaviour amongst youth in the rural Eastern Cape, South Africa: trial design, methods and baseline findings', *Tropical Medicine and International Health*, **11**, 1 (Jan.), pp. 3–16.

Johnson, H., and Mayoux, L. (1998) 'Investigation as empowerment: using participatory methods', in A. Thomas, J. Chataway and M. Wuyts (eds), *Finding Out Fast: Investigative skills for policy and development*, pp. 147–72, London, Thousand Oaks, New Delhi, Sage, Open University.

Jupp, D. (2002) '*Let us talk...' Peace and reconciliation in Puntland*, Diakonia, Aberdare, Kenya.

Jupp, D. (2003) *Views of the Poor: The perspectives of rural and urban poor in Tanzania as recounted through their stories and pictures*, Swiss Agency for Development and Cooperation, Tanzania.

Jupp, D. (2004) *Views of the poor: Some thoughts on how to involve your own staff to conduct quick, low cost but insightful research into poor people's perspectives*, Swiss Agency for Development and Cooperation, Berne.

Jupp, D. and PromPT (1996) *Financial Services for the Urban Poor; Users' perspectives* and *Financial Services for the Rural poor; Users' perspectives*, UNDP, Bangladesh.

Jupp, D. and PromPT (1997a) *The Poor Do not Lie Down Sick in a Bed: An analysis of the present situation and needs of project target groups*, Marie Stopes Clinic Society, Bangladesh.

Jupp, D. and PromPT (1997b) *Hard Cash; A listening study of stakeholders' perspectives on bank credit services for small entrepreneurs*, Swiss Agency for Development and Cooperation, Dhaka.

Kanbur, R. (2002) *Q-squared: Combining qualitative and quantitative methods in poverty appraisal*, Orient Longman, London.

Kelly, J.A., St Lawrence, J.S., Hood, H.V. and Brasfield, E.L. (1989) 'Behavioral intervention to reduce AIDS risk activities', *Journal of Consulting and Clinical Psychology*, **57**, pp. 60–7.

Khon Kaen University (1987) *Proceedings of the 1985 International Conference on Rapid Rural Appraisal*, University of Khon Kaen, Thailand.

Leading Group Office for Poverty (LGOP) (2000) 'Key poverty reduction documents of the Chinese Government, PRC', paper prepared for the International Conference on China's Poverty Reduction Strategy in the Early 21st Century, LGOP, Beijing.

LGOP, UNDP and World Bank (2000) 'China, overcoming rural poverty', Report No. 21105-CHA, Rural Development and Natural Resources Unit, East Asia and Pacific Region, World Bank, Washington, DC.

Learning for Empowerment Against Poverty (LEAP) 2005 'Annual Report', LEAP, Port Sudan.

Levy, S. (2003) 'Are we targeting the poor? Lessons from Malawi', *PLA Notes* 47, pp. 19–24, IIED, London.

Levy, S. (ed.) (2005) *Starter Packs: A strategy to fight hunger in developing countries? Lessons from the Malawi experience, 1998–2003*, CABI Publishing, Wallingford.

Lewin, K. (1951) *Field Theory in Social Science*, Harper and Row, New York.

LGOP, UNDP and World Bank (2000) 'China, overcoming rural poverty', Report no. 21105-CHA, Rural Development and Natural Resources Unit, East Asia and Pacific Region, World Bank, Washington.

Li, X. and Remenyi, J. (forthcoming 2007) 'Whose poverty? Making poverty mapping and poverty monitoring participatory', *Journal of Development Studies*.

Li, X., Wang, G., Remenyi, J. and Thomas, P. (2003a) *Training Manual for Poverty Analysis and Participatory Planning for Poverty Reduction*, China International Books, Beijing.

Li, X., Ye, J. and Zhang X. (2003) 'Survey report on participatory poverty alleviation', Japan International Cooperation Agency, Tokyo.

Lynch, E. and Gordon, G. (1991) 'Activities to explore: using drama in AIDS and family planning work', AIDS Prevention Unit, International Planned Parenthood Federation (IPPF), London.

Marshall, J. (2001) 'Self-reflective inquiry practices', in P. Reason and H. Bradbury (eds), *Handbook of Action Research: Participatory inquiry and practice*, Sage, London.

Mayoux, L. (1995) 'Beyond naivety: women, gender inequality and participatory development: some thorny issues', *Development and Change*, **26**, pp. 235–58.

Mayoux, L. (1998) 'Participatory programme learning for women's empowerment in micro-finance programmes: negotiating complexity, conflict and change', *IDS Bulletin*, **29**, pp. 39–50.

Mayoux, L. (2003a) 'Grassroots action learning: impact assessment for pro-poor accountability and civil society development', available online at: http://www.enterprise-impact.org.uk/informationresources/toolbox/grassrootsactionlearning.shtml

Mayoux, L. (2003b) 'Thinking it through: using diagrams in impact assessment', available online at: http://www.enterprise-impact.org.uk/informationresources/ toolbox/thinkingitthrough-usingdiagramsinIA.shtml

Mayoux, L. (2003c) 'Empowering enquiry: a new approach to investigation', available online at: http://www.enterprise-impact.org.uk/informationresources/toolbox/ empoweringenquiry.shtml

Mayoux, L. (ed.) (2003d) *Sustainable Learning for Women's Empowerment: Ways Forward in Micro-finance*, Samskriti, New Delhi.

Mayoux, L. (2003e) *PALS Manual: Draft August.* Kabarole Research and Resource Centre, Western Uganda.

Mayoux, L. (2004) Intra-household impact assessment: issues and participatory tools', available online at: http://www.enterprise-impact.org.uk/informationresources/ toolbox/intra-householdIA.shtml

Mayoux, L. and ANANDI (2005) 'Participatory action learning in practice: experience of Anandi, India', *Journal of International Development*, **17**, pp. 211–242.

Noponen, H. (2001) 'The Internal Learning System for participatory assessment of microfinance', *Small Enterprise Development*, **12** (4), pp. 45–53.

Noponen, H. (2005) 'Balancing qualitative and quantitative aspects of ILS', notes from IDS writeshop, 21–24 June, IDS, Sussex.

Professional Assistance for Development Action (PRADAN) (2005) Available online at: http://www.ids.ac.uk/impact/asia/pradan.html

PromPT and IDHRB(1996) 'Assessment of human rights situation: perspectives of rural poor and concerned service providers', Action Research Study on the Institutional Development of Human Rights in Bangladesh (IDHRB)) (Oct.–Nov.).

Quaker Peace Centre (1992) *South African Handbook of Education for Peace*, Quaker Peace Centre, Cape Town.

Pretty, J.N., Guijt, I., Thompson, J. and Scoones, I. (1995) *Participatory Learning and Action*, IIED, London.

Remenyi, J. (1991) *Where Credit is Due*, Intermediate Technology Publications, London.

Remenyi, J. and Li, X. (2004) 'Towards sustainable village poverty reduction? The development of the CPAP approach', in J. Taylor and J. Plummer (eds), *Capacity Building in China*, DFID, London.

RRA Notes 1–21 (1988–94), becoming *PRA Notes* 22–49 (1995–2004), and then *Participatory Learning and Action* from 50 (2004).

Sardar, F. and Mumtaz, N. (2004) 'Women's and men's views of empowerment', Kashf Foundation, Lahore, available online at: http://www.genfinance.info/ 1Empowerment.htm

Scoones, I. (1995) 'PRA and anthropology: challenges and dilemmas', *PLA Notes* 24 (Oct.), IIED, London.

Selener, D., Zapata, G. and Purdy, C (1997) *Manual de Sistematización: Documentando, evaluando y aprendiendo de nuestros proyectos de desarrollo*, 2nd edn, International Institute for Rural Reconstruction, Quito.

Simanowitz, Anton (2001) 'Virtual meeting on impact assessment methodologies', background paper for the ImpAct – Improving Impact of Microfinance on Poverty: an Action Research Programme, IDS, Sussex.

Simanowitz, A. (1999) 'Understanding impact: experiences and lessons from the Small Enterprise Foundation's poverty alleviation programme, Tshomisano', paper presented at the Third Virtual Meeting of the CGAP/Working Group on Impact

Assessment, Methodologies. http://www.ids.ac.uk/impact/resources/plan simanowitz_AIMS_paper.doc

Sternin, J. (2002) 'Positive deviance: A new paradigm for addressing today's problem today', *Journal of Corporate Citizenship*, **5**, pp. 57–62.

Taylor, J. and Plummer, J. (eds) (2004) *Capacity Building in China*, DFID, London.

Taylor, J. and Stewart, S. (1991) *Sexual and Domestic Violence: Help, recovery and action in Zimbabwe*, A. von Glehn and J. Taylor, Harare.

Van Donge, J., Chivwaile, M., Kasapila, W., Kapondamgaga, P., Mgemezulu, O., Sangore, N. and Thawani, E. (2001) 'A qualitative study of markets and livelihood security in rural Malawi (Module 2, Part 2 of the 2000–1 TIP Evaluation)', report for the Government of Malawi and DFID, UK.

Van Riet, M. (2004) 'Field report, Uganda', unpublished, Trickle-Up Program, New York.

Weisbord, M. and Janoff, S. (2000) *Future Search: An action guide to finding common ground in organisations and communities*, Berrett-Koehler, San Francisco, CA.

Welbourn, A. (1984) 'Endo knowledge, technology and power: the social construction of Endo material culture through age, gender and authority', PhD dissertation, Cambridge University.

Welbourn, A. (1991), 'RRA and the analysis of difference', *RRA Notes* 13, IIED, London.

Welbourn, A. (2002) 'Gender, sex and HIV: how to address issues that no one wants to hear about', in A. Cornwall and A. Welbourn (eds), *Realizing Rights*, pp. 99–112, Zed Press, London.

Williams, S., with Seed, J. and Mwau, A. (1994) *The OXFAM Gender Training Manual*, OXFAM, Oxford.

Willis, L. and Daisle, J. (1990) *Springboard*, Hawthorn Press, Stroud.

Index